MW00878002

With best wishes
Ugo Macciar

ACCIDENTAL
AFRICAN BLESSINGS

ACCIDENTAL
AFRICAN BLESSINGS

A Memoir

Ugo Nacciarone, SJ.

Copyright © 2012 by Ugo Nacciarone, SJ.

Library of Congress Control Number:		2012904524
ISBN:	Hardcover	978-1-4691-8239-1
	Softcover	978-1-4691-8238-4
	Ebook	978-1-4691-8240-7

All rights reserved. No part of this book may be reproduced or transmitted in any form or by any means, electronic or mechanical, including photocopying, recording, or by any information storage and retrieval system, without permission in writing from the copyright owner.

This book was printed in the United States of America.

To order additional copies of this book, contact:
Xlibris Corporation
1-888-795-4274
www.Xlibris.com
Orders@Xlibris.com
112686

CONTENTS

I dedicate this book to the people of Africa who have been such an inspiration to me.

FOREWORD

In his poem, "The Weaver Bird", Kofi Awoonor, arguably Ghana's most famous literary figure, compares the early European Christian missionaries to the Weaver Bird. The latter is portrayed as defiling the ancestral shrine by the metaphoric droppings of foreign religions. The semblance of the weaverbird, notorious for its colonizing habits, not to mention its destructive effects on the host tree, calls forth, at least in the minds of many educated Africans, the infamous role of the Church in the scramble for and the pillage of Africa's material and cultural wealth.

Against this backdrop of the Christian missionary being perceived as holding the cross in one hand and the gun in the other, and in spite of their message of "agape," the early Christian missionaries were seen as having failed to sympathize with African culture and African spiritual equality. As an American missionary working in Ghana, Fr. Nacciarone's task was even more daunting than the haunting experiences he had already gone through in war-torn Nigeria. He arrived in Ghana on the eve of a military coup d'état, led by Flt. Lt. Rawlings, that would spew one of the most vitriolic anti-American rhetoric anywhere on the continent. Yet Fr. Nacciarone not only survived West Africa but would go on to endear himself to more Africans in southern Africa, especially his beloved Zambia. Zambians on every level appreciated Fr. Nacciarone and brought out the best in him as a priest and as a human being. Zambians are amongst the most amiable people in Africa.

Born of second-generation Italian-American parents in Brooklyn, New York, Fr. Nacciarone always considers himself a Brooklynite. He grew up in a lower middle class residential area of a very mixed ethnic composition. Brooklyn could boast of some famous composers such as Aaron Copland, writers such as Walt Whitman, and religious founders such as William Taize Russell, founder of the Jehovah Witnesses but none would have such a profound influence on the young Nacciarone as another Brooklynite,

Dorothy Day, the founder of the Catholic Worker Movement, whose portrait sits on his writing desk.

Accidental African Blessings is a portrayal of a wondering soul, the musings of a true revolutionary who celebrated the African spirit in its essence. This memoir is also an indispensable contribution about the Catholic Church, the Jesuits and politics in Africa. Fr. Nacciarone came to Africa when most of the newly independent states had just shirked off the colonial yoke and were hardly coming to terms as new nations. In an already tense atmosphere, what was impressive about Fr. Nacciarone was the calm confidence he exhibited. Fr. Nacciarone's genius is largely genius of character—of empathy, loyalty and trust. These are products of self-searching and introspection. They seem common enough virtues, but they were extraordinary given the extremely turbulent times he lived especially in Nigeria and Ghana. At a time in Ghana when it was a crime just being American, Fr. Nacciarone was able to make friends with anyone, a quality that would have been the envy of even Sts. Ignatius and Francis Xavier. He has a long-standing army of friends who go back to his grade school days but it was as a Jesuit that he perfected the art of friendship from his life-long friend, Tony Mahowald, now a retired professor of genetics at the University of Chicago. In Africa Fr. Nacciarone not only adapted to the different cultures he lived in but he also showed deep respect and an understanding of them. Unlike Awoonor's *Weaver Bird*, Fr. Nacciarone did not come to Africa to defecate on what is most sacred to Africans. In return, Africans trust him and revere him. He is our Prometheus who not only unveiled to us the hidden knowledge but taught us how to stand up for ourselves when bullies, visible and invisible, demand of us to turn the other cheek. No, Fr. Nacciarone demanded of us the very best; that we could be whomever we wanted to be despite what we have been brainwashed to see ourselves as a people. And for that we will forever be grateful to him.

The publication of *Accidental African Blessings* coincides with the 60th anniversary of Fr. Nacciarone as a Jesuit. Forty of these precious years were given to Africa. Forty years, for some Africans, is a life time. So, as you read these pages, I invite you all to join in this celebration of life, of a man who put character above wealth, who is larger than his vocation, and never hesitated to take the chance of going to Africa so that some of us might have a dream.

Cheers!

Kofi Addo-Nkum

White Plains

June 3, 2010

ACKNOWLEDGEMENTS

This book could never have been written except for the countless African friends who entered my life. It is their part in shaping my life and values that is recounted here. I owe them more than I could ever express. In a particular way I want to thank two particular Africans now living here in the United States whose encouragement motivated me to complete this project. They are Kofi Addo-Nkum and John Yaw Ofori. They not only encouraged me but also read through the manuscript and made valuable suggestions. Others who read the manuscript and whose comments were very helpful are Eneya Maseko, Inacio Jussa, S.J., James McGloin, S.J. and Leonard Chisala. It would take too long to list all the individual African friends who have in various ways contributed to this memoir. One other African I want to explicitly acknowledge is my Nigerian friend, Francis Otuonye, who contributed to the publication of this book. I also want to express a great debt of gratitude to my sister, Mrs. Claudette Hickey, who not only read the manuscript and made valuable comments, but also has encouraged me in so many ways since my return to the United States. I am also very grateful to my Jesuit superiors for giving me the time to adjust to life here and offered me the opportunity to write this memoir. A special word of thanks to Jack Wise whose friendship and generous financial support made this publication possible.

INTRODUCTION

When I first left the shores of the United States to live and work in Africa in 1967, I never had any idea how long I would last there. I would never have anticipated spending 40 years on that continent. At the end of the first two years, when I was allowed to return to the United States for my first home leave, I was tempted to remain there. I had suffered several severe cases of malaria in those first two years. I was also finding it difficult to adjust to the hot humid climate that seemed hardly to change. I questioned just what I was doing there. Just about everything was shouting that I was in the wrong place. The only thing that kept me there was a sense of duty to the 5 other Jesuits there. I felt that if I had decided to remain in the USA, it would have been demoralising. There were only 6 of us there, and so, even the loss of one would seem substantial. Furthermore, the province had only taken on this mission in 1962 with one Jesuit, followed a year later with two more. The mission was very young in 1969 when I went on my first leave. The enterprise needed encouragement. And so I returned. It was one of the best decisions I ever made.

As I pondered on a title for this book, I thought about situations like this that brought many turns to my life in Africa, bringing me from Nigeria to Zambia to Ghana and back to Zambia again. These events were like accidents. Accidents are unexpected, unplanned and often painful. It was just an accident of history that the mission was just getting started and that it had so few people on it. It might have been another accident of history that the Biafran War began just as I made my way to Nigeria that made it more difficult to recruit new members to the mission. These accidents of history brought me to a painful decision to return to Nigeria when I didn't feel attracted to the prospect. Yet, this painful experience turned out to be a great blessing for me. I came to love the people and the continent more than I could ever have imagined, and found myself greatly enriched by the experience. It is this development in personal growth that I want to share with the reader. I owe a great debt of gratitude to Africa and her people for making me the person I am today. And so the book is primarily written for the African people as an expression of appreciation. But I also hope others will read it. As they follow me in my journey through good times and bad, I hope they will find encouragement through the ups and downs of their own lives.

I managed to find blessings resulting from the painful moments of my life.

One of the most painful revelations for me over the years of my life in Africa has been the ignorant and often negative image of the continent that I have found in the media of my own country and among the majority of people. This is a second reason for my writing this. I want to shout to all who are willing to listen that there is more to Africa than the rather superficial treatment it is given in the press and mass media. After all, I not only survived 40 years there, but managed to come back to the United States in robust health.

I would hope that one fruit of this book would be the revelation of the richness of African culture. I think we all have much to learn from other cultures. The openness to other people is not only the way to personal growth, but is a formula for world peace. I hope that reading this book will open the eyes of the reader. The exercise of writing it has been a very rewarding one as I relived many of the wonderful moments in my life in Africa, and even renewed friendships that distance and time had diminished. As I recalled many people, I made an effort to find out where they are now and opened up communication with them. I am now back in touch with people I hadn't heard from in years.

I am now back in touch with my own family. I left them when I was a teenager, and never had much opportunity to come close to them. I realise now how much they contributed to my life and work.

As I mention in the book, my parents were very encouraging, and always gave me the freedom to develop in ways they might not always understand. I appreciate the loving support I have received since my return from many members of my family, as they help me to adjust to a new way of life.

Chapter One

WELCOME TO NIGERIA!

Imagine what it must be like to be sent alone to a strange country torn apart by a Civil War in which you know no one. The people of this country are of a different race and culture, and you cannot even speak their language. If you can do that you have some idea of how I felt when I was being sent to Nigeria in 1967. True, I had volunteered to go to this mission territory. However, I knew almost nothing about Nigeria since the American papers had little or nothing to say about the continent of Africa. And if they had something to write it was almost entirely negative. Although I had spent about six weeks trying to study the Igbo language, I could barely do more than utter a few greetings and ask some few trivial questions. The so-called Biafran war had just begun. Fighting had broken out in July and I would be going in September. I knew no one there. Even my fellow Jesuits there were people whom I had not met. And so my journey from the United States to Europe to Africa was an adventure into the totally un-known. Obviously, there were anxieties.

There was the added concern that my motives in volunteering to go to Africa were very mixed. I had been asked by superiors to complete a doctoral program in chemistry at MIT, but failed to complete the course. I had asked them to allow me to drop out of studies as I felt I could not succeed. In volunteering to go to Africa, was I simply running away from my sense of failure? I honestly don't know the answer to that question. After I had volunteered, my superiors first accepted my offer and then, politely turned it down. I had to repeat my request with additional reasons for desiring to go. After some time, I received a letter from my superiors appointing me to Nigeria.

Was I trying to manipulate my superior's mind? Was I sincerely convinced that this was truly God's will for me? And so, I was not only filled with anxiety about such an assignment but even questioned my motives.

As the plane left Europe and flew over the Sahara I wondered just what I was going to meet there. I cannot even remember my feelings at that time, but I doubt if I were completely at peace as the plane approached the borders of Nigeria.

My first encounter with the continent of Africa occurred on the early morning of 11 September 1967. My flight was on Lufthansa that began in Frankfurt. It landed first in Kano in northern Nigeria, and we were asked to disembark while the plane took on fuel. When I descended the stairs and put my first step on African soil I wondered why I had even asked to come here. The air was very hot. I found myself stung by small sand flies, and was made to sit for an hour in a rundown transit lounge. This was not an encouraging welcome. The plane then took off toward its final destination into Lagos. Once again I was hit by the hot humid air and the rundown airport. I was too dazed to notice much about people at immigration who processed my passport or the people who passed me through customs. My Jesuit superior, Joe McKenna, welcomed me warmly as I exited from the airport. He drove me from the airport in Ikeja to our residence in Surulere. We passed through terrible slums lined with open sewers that reeked of rotting garbage.

What had I gotten myself into?

My anxieties were not eased by the fact that I had no particular work to do. The fact of the matter was the superior had not encouraged my coming at this particular time. To understand this, I have to back up a bit in time. On May 30 of that same year 1967, the southeastern part of Nigeria declared itself an independent state and seceded from the Federation of Nigeria. It called itself the Republic of Biafra.

The background to this would probably take me astray from the purpose of this reflection. Needless to say, there were solid reasons for this move, though to most observers it was a rash solution to a serious problem besetting the young state of Nigeria that achieved its independence from Great Britain just 7 years before on October 1, 1960. A war broke out to preserve the Union and hostilities began in early July. The Jesuit superior decided it would be unwise for me to come out at this particular time. He, like many others, reasoned that the war would not last long. No country rushed to recognize the new state of Biafra, and its resources were limited.

It did not even have the full support of the minority ethnic groups of the region which was dominated by the Igbo people. In the light of these developments I had enrolled at the London school of Oriental and African studies. Just days before I was to set off on my journey to London I received a phone call from the provincial inviting me to a meeting.

"Wouldn't you be better off pursuing African studies in Nigeria than in London?" "Of course, I would."

"Then sell your ticket for London and buy a ticket for Lagos.

I will inform the superior there. When you have made travel arrangements, tell me when you expect to arrive."

Being an obedient Jesuit, I did as he asked. I must admit that I was quite excited at the prospect of finally going to Africa which had been my strong desire for about three years.

When the provincial sent a telegram to Lagos that I will be arriving on September 11, he received a reply telling him not to send me as there was no specific work to do. In 1967 telephone links were difficult and unreliable. By the time these exchanges took place, I had already left so that I could spend a few days in Europe to visit friends. And so the provincial sent his final cable telling the superior in Lagos to welcome me.

We are back to my arrival and my anxiety about this strange new world in which I didn't even have a job to do. Lew Cox, one of the Jesuits there, kindly agreed to spend a few days giving me an orientation to the city of Lagos, at that time, a city with a population of about one million. Presently, the population of Lagos is estimated to be about 10 million.

After my tours of the city, Lew and I started to look for a possible job. I was by training and inclination a science teacher having completed a master's degree in chemistry before setting out for Africa.

The search was a humbling experience. The schools I visited had no idea who I was. Having an American master's degree but with no experience or even knowledge of the British educational system did not make me an attractive prospect. This was another lesson learned in my first week. The Third World wasn't ready to reach out in appreciation for just anyone who appeared on the scene no matter how eager or qualified that person might be. They were not beggars ready to accept just anything that was on offer. This lesson was the beginning of a new understanding of just what I was doing in Africa. It was not a dramatic conversion but a slowly changing understanding of the people of Africa.

I was not a rich man coming to give to the poor. Although it took many years before the full understanding took root in my mind, I would eventually come to realize that, in fact, I was a poor man who came to Africa not so much to give but to receive. It is that transition and the sharing of all I received that is at the heart of this reflection.

My first job was a very short term assignment to assist a young Nigerian, Vincent Achimu, who was the national coordinator of the Young Christian Students in Nigeria. He was drawing up a program of discussion outlines to aid in many individual YCS sections in the various schools around the country. I had never heard of the YCS, although it is an international movement with sections in the US. Here I was, only a week or so in Africa already a learner at the feet of a young African.

The next opportunity for work was again a temporary assignment.

An American woman was teaching science at a Catholic girls secondary school, Holy Child College. She was returning to the United States on maternity leave. The Holy Child sisters, hearing that I was trained in science, asked if I would be willing to teach chemistry and physics to the two final years at the school, preparing them for their O level exams.

Again, I was first a learner. I had to learn what "O-level" chemistry and physics meant. With the help of the girls themselves and using their text books I managed to begin classes with them. The girls were very bright and I was now learning and teaching at the same time. I found the students eager to learn and easy to relate to. I quickly made friends with them and began to feel a bit at home in Nigeria.

Within a month of my teaching a full-time schedule, I was offered another job. One of my fellow Jesuits, who was a lecturer in sociology at the University of Lagos told me that the College of Education at the University was looking for a lecturer in physical chemistry. I went for the interview and was offered the position. From being in a position of having no work I suddenly found myself with two jobs. The two institutions are separated by several miles or so. Since I never drove a car in my life, my superiors had to arrange for a car and driver to shuttle me back and forth. The driver, Solomon Alagbe, was a former taxi driver from Lagos and certainly knew how to move our little VW beetle through the most incredible traffic I have ever experienced.

He also had the task of trying to teach me how to drive so that I could one day look after myself.

In December, I informed the sisters that I would be leaving my position with them, even though they had recently learned that the woman who went on maternity leave in September would not be returning. By January,

I was a full-time lecturer in chemistry at the College of Education, training future science teachers. I was beginning to feel more and more useful. I had not yet realized how much more I would learn and not just about the British education system.

One early experience at the College of Education stands out in my mind even after 40 years. I was giving a lecture on Raoult's law concerning the properties of ideal solutions. It was somewhat mathematical, though not intensively so. I had not advanced very far when a young man raised his hand.

"Sir, perhaps in your country, students can comprehend this. It is too advanced for us."

"If I had said that," I replied, "you would have rightly called me a racist. Why are you saying this? Perhaps, I went too fast, or presumed some concepts; but you will learn this and you will be better than you think you are."

This encounter revealed something I found all too often in my years in Africa, namely, the low opinion too many young people had of themselves. One of my motives in writing these reflections is to express the great qualities I found in most young people in Africa and perhaps reveal to them things they have not seen. Some of the brightest students I have ever encountered were found in the classrooms of Nigeria, Ghana and Zambia.

I began to enjoy my lectures at the college. The students were very appreciative of what I tried to do for them, and I began to make friends both with students and staff. One of the most impressive men I met was my head of Department, Mr. Theo Fayiga, who sadly passed away at a very early age. He was a devout Anglican in practice, and a genuinely Christian gentleman. One incident that made a very deep impression on me revealed his extraordinary sensitivity to the feelings of others.

I was in the chemistry lecture preparation room. It was a long room with the head of department's desk at one end. At the other end were a worktable and the chemicals and equipment needed for the preparation of a lecture demonstration. I was preparing a demonstration and Mr. Fayiga was working quietly at his desk. A laboratory attendant knocked and entered and went to Mr. Fayiga's desk. He said something in the Yoruba language. He was probably only asking what he should do when he finished sweeping the floor. He would not have been a highly educated person, having only a primary school certificate. Mr. Fayiga stopped him mid-sentence and said:

> "Don't you see that Father Nacciarone is in this room? When he is here, you speak English."

I have never forgotten this; for many times in my long years in Africa, people would converse with others in my presence, and use a language I did not understand. I always felt as if my presence wasn't even noticed. This would not be done with any ill will, it was simply a lack of sensitivity. I treasured this lesson from Mr. Fayiga and shared it with many others.

Away from the college, I had an early pastoral experience that remains with me all these years. An Irish missionary priest of the Society of African Missions invited me assist in one of the many out stations of his main parish about 50 miles north of Lagos. He drove me there early on a Sunday morning, and left me there while he celebrated Mass at another station. The occasion was the harvest festival. This is a common feature in most of the African cultures in which I have been. It is a very big celebration especially in rural areas. It is an expression of appreciation to God for a good harvest.

In 1967 Mass was still celebrated in Latin and so my inability to speak Yoruba was not a problem. One of the parishioners would preach the homily. I met my first challenge when I was asked to hear confessions before the Mass. First, I wouldn't understand the language for those who knew no English, and secondly there were about a hundred Catholics in this small rural village, and I couldn't possibly hear that many confessions before Mass.

The first problem did not bother me too much as I would presume all those good simple people were truly sorry for what they had done or they wouldn't be coming to confessions seeking reconciliation. I would give them a simple penance spoken in simple English which I am sure they would understand, such as "Say three Hail Mary's" holding up three fingers of my hand. In my many years I have listened to confessions in many languages which I did not understand. As for the second problem, their number, I simply addressed them as a group and through the interpreter led them through an examination of conscience, asked them to say an act of contrition, and then gave them general absolution. I wasn't quite sure what the church authorities would have said about this. But I was in this situation where I had to make some decision for the good of the people. The people who make the rules do not always have first-hand experience of situations that missionaries face in the third world.

The Mass was a very enthusiastic celebration. Everything was sung, and I sang all the parts of the priest. The fact that the Mass was still in Latin did not diminish the joy of the occasion, for in fact, though largely illiterate, the congregation sang from memory all the parts of the Mass in Latin.

At the end of the Mass, the harvest celebration began in earnest.

People began dancing up to the altar in small groups or individually, carrying an offering of their first fruits, and as they reached the altar, I would bless them and sprinkle them with holy water. At the end, they invited me to move to the back of the church and dance with a group bringing the final offering, which was specifically for the priest. The celebration went on for several hours. It was a wonderful introduction to the joy with which most Africans celebrate Mass. Religion means a great deal to them, and going to church is always a celebration and never just an obligation. This was a lesson I learned over and over again through-out my 40 years. I cannot remember a Mass celebrated that was not full of joy.

As I settled into my work as a lecturer in chemistry at the College of Education I began to realize that there was more to my life in Nigeria than giving lectures. After one year of commuting between the Jesuit residence in Surulere and the campus, I asked for accommodation on the campus. I was given a staff flat, and I found myself living with six neighbors all of whom were lecturers at college. I now began to relate to lecturers as friends as well as colleagues. In this way I began to draw closer to Nigerians than I ever had before. I was beginning to feel a part of the college community.

There was another advantage to living on the campus. Students would now come by to visit. Here I learned another important human lesson. Students would come by and greet me politely. I would invite them to sit down and we would begin conversation. After a while, they might take a magazine from the table and begin to read. I would feel somewhat embarrassed and tried to continue the conversation. It took me some time to realize that the main purpose of their visit was not to engage in conversation but simply to be present. More important than speaking with one is simply being present to one another. There was more to relationship than polite conversation. After a while, I learned to let them get on with the reading while I continued with my own work. Eventually they would say, "We would like to go now."

Again we would exchange greetings of farewell and they would depart.

I slowly began to appreciate the deeper meaning of this visit. Friendship is seen more in presence than empty conversation. Friendship might begin with a polite greeting. The greeting was important to establish the beginning of the relationship. Further conversation in these early stages of friendship was not important. The silent presence, becoming used to one another, and feeling comfortable with each other were more important than anything we might have to share at this early stage of friendship. After some time, more meaningful conversation and sharing would flow more naturally.

There is a beautiful passage in St. Exupery's "The Little Prince" that expresses this well. It is a passage when the little prince meets the fox. The fox is explaining to the prince how to tame him.

> *"You must be very patient," replied the fox. "First you will sit down at a little distance from me—like that—in the grass. I shall look at you out of the corner of my eye, and you will say nothing. Words are the source of misunderstandings. But you will sit a little closer to me, every day.*

Silence can be beautiful and enrich a relationship. I also learned that from the African people.

One of the great joys of Africa is discovering the hidden talents among many students and others. I might have had a very poor image of the students at the beginning. But it did not take me long to realize that there was an incredible talent hidden in these students. I can still remember an examination I gave not expecting the students to do very well. One of the papers I marked stands out in my mind. The chemistry problem I gave them could have been approached in many ways. This student had tackled the problem in exactly the same way in which I would have done it myself. It was like looking at a paper I had myself written. This student had not only learned how to solve a particular problem but seem to be thinking in the same way that I was. This only confirmed what I already suspected:—that the learning ability of these students was no less than that of any Americans. Throughout the years of my teaching I have encountered students with very high IQs. In their future studies they achieved heights I could not have reached myself.

It pains me to hear people say that the Africans are somehow slower than students in the developed world.

It was not only in lecture halls that I discovered gifted people.

There was a young man, Abiodun Adebisi Ajuwon, who used to sweep the classrooms at the college. He was a very friendly, cheerful person, and greeted me each time I passed him on campus. One time, I engaged him in conversation as his English was quite good. I discovered he was 16 years old, an orphan, who had dropped out of school after grade seven because of financial difficulties.

One day I asked him if he would like to go to school. His face lit up. I explained to him that this would depend on my ability to find a place for him in form one (grade 8). Most schools were hesitant to accept older boys in this basic grade because they might be obstructive.

The average age of pupils in this grade would have been 12 or 13.

I finally found a place for him in a Catholic mission school, and, with the help of generous benefactors, was able to pay fees for tuition and boarding. His performance was above average. When he completed secondary school I sponsored him through teacher training college.

Eventually he went on to earn a bachelor's degree in education and became a dedicated teacher. I believe he is still such. He married and raised a family, and, as I write this, is probably now retired. How many young men and women in Africa are wasting away in menial jobs who could be more valued members of society and contributors to the development of their countries? This experience of discovering great hidden talents will appear many times in this writing.

One of the places where I found remarkable hidden talents was the Pacelli School for the Blind. Shortly after I arrived in Lagos, my superior Father Joe McKenna, asked me to be chaplain at the Pacelli School for the Blind. This was a primary school run by the Irish Sisters of Charity. I was most impressed by the training that these sisters gave to the young children. Most of them learned how to read Braille at a very early age, and it was wonderful to listen to them do the readings of Mass from the Braille text of the Bible. They read more clearly than many sighted children who were older than they. I began to make very good friends among those young pupils, some of whom went on to university and became professors and lawyers. One of the young pupils who impressed me so much was a very brilliant musician. His name was John Yekinni. He had a remarkable ability to play the trumpet. He also became proficient at the keyboard and the guitar. When he completed his primary school, the sisters did not consider him sufficiently academically capable to go into the ordinary secondary school. However, they kept him at the school as a teacher of music. After one year of this experience, they sent him to the United Kingdom to study Braille music at The Royal School for the Blind in Craigmillar Park, Edinburgh, Scotland. He successfully completed his course and then returned to the Pacelli School and remained a teacher there for many years. He is presently teaching at a government primary school.

Now back to my work as a college lecturer. My growing involvement with the college community brought invitations to participate in extracurriculars and one that stands out in my mind was assisting in the staging of two plays. The moderator of the drama society was a very devout woman, Carina Robins. She had come to Nigeria some years before me with the mission of using drama to spread the good news of Christian revelation. She was very gifted in her work. She put on two plays I was involved in. One was T.S. Eliot's *Murder in the Cathedral,* and the other was Robert Bolt's *Man For All Seasons.* My part in the work was organizing musical background. I was impressed by the dedication and acting ability of the students who participated in these performances. There were very talented actors and the entire production would have made any college in the United States proud.

It was at the scheduled performance of one of these plays that I was introduced to the African concept of time. I was invited to the play, and was told that it would begin at 8:00 p.m. I had a prior engagement, and arrived about 8:10, rushing out of my car and apologizing profusely to the students who were awaiting my arrival. When they brought me to the auditorium, I found I was the first one to arrive. After that I never interpreted a given time as meaning that precise hour and minute. The late archbishop of Cape Coast once said to me: "You Europeans are slaves to time; we Africans are the masters of time." He was absolutely right. I suppose you couldn't run a highly efficient factory on that concept, but not everyone is running a factory. The African concept of time is more human and less mechanical.

My friendship with Carina Robins enriched me a great deal because she helped me to discover gifts I never knew I had. This discovery began with her asking me to assist with the musical background for two plays. But a far more interesting challenge occurred when she invited me to be the chaplain for an ecumenical workshop she was organizing on the theme of liturgy and the arts. It was to be a five-day workshop involving drama, painting and music. She would take responsibility for the drama group. She invited a well-known Nigerian artist to guide budding artists, and another lecturer in music from the University to guide those interested in music.

Each group was to explore how they could use their medium to express their faith. My task as chaplain was to create an ecumenical Morning Prayer service to start each day's work. Before breakfast, I would also celebrate a Mass for the Catholic participants. After the first day, I discovered that almost all participants were attending the Mass and many would come for communion. I never refused them as they were all baptized and approached the altar in good faith. On the last morning of the workshop, an Anglican priest came to conduct a communion service for the non-Catholics. For the first time we were separated for our celebration of the Lord's Supper. At the Morning Prayer after breakfast, I felt the un-ease in the group. I reflected with them on this as I too felt uneasy. But it reminded us that despite the way we had worked so happily together all week, we were not yet one Christian family as we so longed to be.

As the workshop grew to its climax, it was my task to take the fruits of the various sections, and, with the help of the moderators of the groups fashion a liturgical celebration that would incorporate elements of drama, painting and music. This was to be a public function to which many outsiders would be invited. The closing liturgy was a beautiful expression of the faith of the group and how this faith helped them to make sense of the most significant event in the country—the Biafran war—which had torn the newly independent country apart. The war had ended just two months before this workshop, and the liturgy reflected the pain of the war and the hope of reconciliation. Attending the liturgy were the Catholic Archbishop of Lagos, the Anglican and Methodist bishops and a large number of friends and well-wishers. I owe Carina Robins a great deal, first for inviting me to be the chaplain, then by uncovering a hidden talent in myself. As for the war, that will be the next chapter in my reflections.

Chapter Two

THE BIAFRAN WAR

There is one great event that colored all my experiences in those first years in Africa, and that was the civil war that erupted shortly before I arrived in September 1967. It is more frequently referred to as the "Biafran War". I am not a political analyst, and I do not feel qualified to comment on the causes of the war, nor of the rights and wrongs of each side. I mentioned in the beginning how this affected the beginning of my mission in Africa. I would like to share my own experiences that were directly related to that war.

One of the experiences that might help in understanding my position was an interview I read about during the war between a journalist and the Anglican Archbishop of Lagos. The Archbishop was asked whether God was on the side of the federal government. His reply was simple and profound. "The question is not whether God is on our side, but rather whether we are on God's side." I was a newcomer to Africa and did not pretend to know all the complex issues that brought about the war.

This ambiguity in my own thinking made it impossible for me to make a simple moral judgment about the war. One evening a young man approached me and asked me if it was right to join the Army.

I could not give him a simple answer. I asked him to reflect on the reasons for the war, and whether he felt the war was just. If he were convinced it was a just cause, then he could in clear conscience join the Army. Personally, I am a pacifist by conviction and would be opposed to all war. But here was a young man un-employed, looking to support his family. He did not enjoy the luxury of simple clear choices between right and wrong. Perhaps the best he could do was to choose between two options, neither of which was particularly attractive to him.

This was the beginning of my education concerning what one author called "bourgeois morality". Moral judgments seem to be easier if you have a job and know where your next meal is coming from. For the very poor, those with no security in their lives, things do not seem so clear.

Another experience, outside the context of the war, confirmed this growing understanding of the challenge of making moral judgments in the context of poverty. I had a good friend in Lagos who had completed his schooling and was looking for a job. He was told there was an opening at the government's security printers. He went for the interview.

After the interview he was told to go for a medical checkup. He had to go to an approved doctor. When he went to the recommended doctor he was told that he had a hernia. He knew that he did not have a hernia.

To be sure of this he went to another doctor. This doctor told him he did not have a hernia. However, he had to get the recommendation from the approved doctor. And it was obvious that this doctor wanted a bribe before he would give him the necessary medical clearance. Being a devout Catholic he refused to give the bribe. He came to consult me about this matter. I told him I was willing even to get a lawyer to fight his case. This would not have been easy. The judicial system might be just as corrupt as so many other areas of the civil service. He wanted time to think about it. His problem was resolved when some of his friends knowing his sensitive conscience paid a bribe for him. And so he had his job. I assured him he had done nothing wrong. It is easy to feel righteous when you come from a comfortable surrounding and nothing is at stake.

Let me now return to the situation of the war. I too found myself with difficult moral decisions to make. What does one preach about at Mass when the country is in the midst of a civil war. There was a point in the war when the federal government issued a decree that all planes violating federal airspace would be shot down. Being marked with a red cross would not protect them. At this point in the war it was impossible to get into Biafra without overflying federal airspace. Shortly after this decree was issued I was preaching in a large church in Lagos. I forget the exact readings of the day from Scripture; but somehow I applied the Scriptures to the current situation. With some emotion in my voice I said I did not think a Christian could agree with the policy of shooting down Red Cross planes. Since these planes were carrying food and medical supplies, it would be unkind, to say the least, to interfere with these flights as they were bringing life to their fellow Nigerians.

After the Mass, one of the parishioners asked if he could come see me at my house. I agreed and we arranged the time.

"Father, you should be very careful what you say in your sermons.

We are at war and the government must take difficult decisions."

"I thought I was only preaching the gospel that taught us to love our enemies and to do good to those who persecute us."

"But father, we cannot take these sayings too literally during a time of war."

"I didn't know that the Lord put conditions on his teachings.

If we can choose when to take his teachings literally and when not to, then I am not sure how to understand the Gospels. Perhaps there is some way to show love for our neighbor even as we destroy a means of keeping them alive. I wish there were some other way to interpret this text in this situation. But we simply must apply the gospel teaching to the concrete situations in which we live."

It was impossible for me not to speak about the war in my preaching. After all, it was the most significant thing happening at that moment in Nigeria. How could one pretend that all was well, and preach about more routine matters. I thank God that the man who came to me tried to understand that I was a stranger and did not fully comprehend all the intricacies of the Biafran war. I suppose he could have reported me to the government and I would have been expelled. That would have been a very painful decision as I was beginning to come to love the people of Africa. If I had been expelled from the country I would have been able to find some other work in another country. An indigenous priest would not have such a choice. If I had been such a priest would I have spoken as boldly? I hope I would; but it is easy to say that from my position of safety.

All during the war I listened each day to radio Biafra on the shortwave radio. I must admit that I had a great deal of sympathy for the people of Biafra. Perhaps this was simply because they were the underdog. It is hard to explain the emotion I felt each time I heard their national anthem, which was taken from Sibelius' Finlandia. From my position in Lagos, where I suffered very little as a result of the war, I felt the pain of the little enclave that Biafra was becoming as more and more of their territory was taken over by the federal forces. Biafra received very little recognition from the international community, and whatever supplies they received in terms of arms were being sent clandestinely and had to be bought with hard-earned money. Within the first few months of the war, they would be reduced to a very small area which was completely land-locked and could only be reached by flights originating from the small island of Sao Tome.

Within the first year of the war, the town of Calabar in the eastern province fell to the federal forces. In the battle most of the men and grown boys were killed. This left only women who were now widows and their children. They were brought to Lagos by the federal forces. They were housed in an incomplete housing development that had not been occupied.

A temporary fence was placed around the compound, and they were fed by the government. This makeshift refugee camp was very close to where I was living. I got permission to go and visit there, and became a sort of chaplain to the people. Since they were mostly Igbo women and children I thought I might be able to use my limited knowledge of the language.

I was very impressed by the courage and the spirit of these women. Within a few months if not weeks, they were organizing catechism classes for their children and even rudimentary education classes.

A very moving experience occurred during my second Christmas in Nigeria when I celebrated Mass at this refugee camp. It was a time of harmattan, and the air was filled with dust. We had a table set up in the middle of the field just outside the buildings. The women and children either stood around, or sat on the ground, or brought small stools. In this very austere setting we tried to celebrate the joy of Christmas day.

Despite the pain of loss and the very real poverty of the people they sang with great enthusiasm and something of the heaviness of the situation was transformed into a lightness. I've never forgotten this experience because it reminded me of the original Christmas. As a Christian I believe that God came down to this earth and was born in a cave in Bethlehem. The situation in Palestine was also a very depressing one for the Jewish people. They were an occupied country ruled by a cruel Roman governor. And yet in the midst of this dark scene a light shone in the world. What I experienced on a dusty field in a refugee camp, celebrating Mass for a group of people who have suffered loss, was a re-living of the original Christmas mystery. On that rough table God was once again physically present to suffering people.

There were two other incidents during the war that could have caused a great deal of trouble for our Jesuit mission. The first one occurred when I was the acting superior of the mission, because the superior Fr. Joe McKenna was back in the United States on sick leave.

He sent me a letter, handwritten, whose contents had to be deciphered.

During the war, all our mail was being opened before being delivered to our boxes. So we had to be careful about what we wrote.

I cannot find the letter I received at that time, but I do remember very well the extraordinary language of the message. It went something like this: "John McLaughlin a journalist would like to do some writing about the Biafran war. He would first want to study the angelic doctor in preparation for this article and is particularly interested in his commentary on Matthew two. What do you think?" It took a little while to figure out what was going on. But then my mind began to click. The angelic doctor is St. Thomas, and São Tomé was the island from which flights into Biafra began. The gospel of Matthew chapter 2 tells the story of the Magi who returned by another route. I presumed Joe McKenna was asking me whether it was prudent to allow John McLaughlin to fly into Biafra and then to return to the United States via Lagos. It could've been risky but I felt it was worth the risk if some good journalism would come out of it.

Sometime in early January 1969 John arrived in Lagos. He got through customs and immigration without difficulty because he had not received a Biafran stamp in his passport. However after dinner, when he brought down his luggage, and showed us a spent artillery shell with Russian markings, I was a bit disturbed. He had brought this back with him to show that Biafra was being bombed by the federal government using weapons from the communist Soviet Union.

If this had been discovered in his bags, he would've been in serious trouble for it would have been obvious that he had visited Biafra. Since he was a Jesuit he could be creating difficulties for the small Jesuit community in Nigeria. When he returned to the United States, he wrote three articles for America magazine. The first two were fairly factual accounts about the relief work of charitable agencies in Biafra, and about his Christmas in Biafra. The third one was an attempt to analyze the causes of the war. In this he was way off the mark. Father Joe McKenna wrote a follow-up article for the same magazine using a pen name to correct the false impressions that the McLaughlin article would have given.

Another difficulty arose when another Jesuit, an American in the United States, was part of a panel to discuss the Biafran war with the Nigerian ambassador to the United Nations. The Jesuit implied that the war was a religious one which aimed at diminishing the work of the Catholic Church. He implied that schools and hospitals were being closed. When the ambassador asked him where he got his information, the Jesuit said that all his information came from the Vatican. The ambassador suggested that he consult people nearer to the source and communicate with the Catholic Secretariat in Lagos. They would have informed him of the true situation. The Jesuit then replied that he presumed the Vatican received all its information from the Catholic Secretariats throughout the world. He seemed to imply that the Catholic Secretariat was a listening post or even a spying agency for the Vatican. A tape copy of this interview was sent to Lagos to General Gowon, the military head of state. He summoned the Catholic bishops and asked for an explanation. The fact of the matter was that there was no persecution at all. The church was functioning quite normally and there were no signs of any government antagonism. Of course there were Catholics on both sides of the war, and the church had made no statement concerning the rights or wrongs of either side.

The secretary-general of the Catholic Secretariat came to see me as the acting superior of the Jesuits, and asked me to write to Rome to ask that the superior General reprimand the Jesuit who gave this interview.

I could neither report him to Rome nor reprimand him myself since I had not seen the film. I wrote to Fr. Joe McKenna, and explained the problem. He tried to get the Jesuit to rescind his statement and apologize to the ambassador. He would not. Fr. McKenna did write another article explaining that the Civil War was not a religious one. The whole affair blew over, and I was once again grateful for the understanding of the government which could've taken strong action and did not. These two incidents showed me how patient the government was in the face of uninformed statements that were critical of her actions. This was a sign of the desire of the government that when the war ended there should be general reconciliation all around. At least that is how I saw it. I think I was not mistaken as I will go on to show from the experiences that I had immediately after the war.

The war ended in January 1970. Within a few months many of the students at the College of Education who had abandoned their places at the beginning of the war returned to Lagos wanting to return to the college. The academic year was already in full swing, and the hostel facilities were full. In addition to this, the syllabus had changed. Despite this, the college tried to accommodate the returning students. Those of us on the faculty tried to assist them to catch up in their studies. Students in the hostels tried to make room for their returning brothers and sisters. Those who were in their final year were even given the option of having the final exam set on the old syllabus. Considering that there had been a very serious war in which a million people died I thought it was quite extraordinary that the federal government should have taken so much trouble to accommodate those who only a few months before were considered rebels. I did not observe any tension in the relations of the students. I was very impressed by this behavior, and often preached about this as an example of a true desire for reconciliation. There was no sign of any desire to punish those who had once been rebels.

This was also true on the level of the army. The leader of the rebellion, Chukwuemeka Ojukwu, had fled from Biafra just before it collapsed. He had turned over authority to Philip Effiong, a member of the Efik Tribe, one of the minority groups in the former Biafra. He was not imprisoned nor put on trial for war crimes. As far as I remember, the only punishment he suffered was to be dismissed from the Army. Only twelve years later, the leader of the rebellion, Chukwuemeka Ojukwu, returned to Nigeria and was a candidate for the Senate in a civilian government. Again, as far as I can remember, he suffered no punishment for the rebellion which brought the country into a very bloody civil war. I was most impressed by this further example of reconciliation.

There was another impressive sign in the abandoned properties commission that was set up by General Gowan at the beginning of the fighting. They would look after the properties abandoned by the Igbos who had fled to the east at the beginning of the war. These properties could be rented but not sold. At the end of hostilities, the original owners could apply to the abandoned properties commission for the return of their property. This was generally done without difficulty provided they had the documents to show ownership of the property. The one region of the country where this did not work so effectively was the Rivers State. The bitterness against the Igbos here was stronger than anywhere else in the country. Perhaps this had been because the minority ethnic groups of that region felt that they had been very oppressed by the Igbos in the past. I will speak more of the difficulties in the Rivers State in my later reflections, when I experienced them first-hand when I went to Port Harcourt at the end of the war on a new assignment.

Before I move on to my transfer to Port Harcourt, I would like to make one last comment about the spirit of reconciliation after the war. Only a few months after the war ended, General Yakubu Gowon made a trip to the Eastern Province, the former Biafra. He was received enthusiastically by the people. I commented to one of my Igbo friends that perhaps this was because they were looking for help in the reconstruction of their land.

I suppose I was being rather cynical. He replied that the welcome was sincere, because the outcome of the war could have brought them far more suffering than they had anticipated.

General Gowon was a Christian gentleman, and he did his best to minimize the bitterness that could have been the fruit of more than 2 1/2 years of conflict, and the loss of so many lives. Even to this day, I hold General Gowon in great esteem.

Chapter Three

A NEW ASSIGNMENT

Around the same time that the war ended, I was becoming very comfortable at the College of Education. I enjoyed my lectures, as well as those students who were now becoming my friends, and also my fellow staff members with whom I felt a common bond. My problem was that the university would only give me one year contracts. This did not entitle me to leave pay, nor to any other benefits that would come with a proper contract such as had my fellow Jesuit, Fr. Joe Schuyler, with the university. It also meant that I could never plan more than one year in advance. I spoke to my head of department, Mr. Theo Fayiga, who was very much in favor of my having a long-term contract. This would allow him to plan more effectively for the needs of the department. I knew he was happy with my work and with my relations with the other members of staff. However when he applied for a full contract for me, he was turned down. He came to me and told me what happened. He had the impression that it was my being a priest that worked against me, since there was already a Catholic priest on the staff. I thanked him for his efforts and assured him that I had no hard feelings toward him. I told him I would not continue working on this one year contract. He would have to find a replacement for me. In the meantime I was offered a position as a teacher at St. Gregory's College, a Catholic secondary school which was considered one of the best in Nigeria. It was run by the Society of African Missions, more commonly known as the SMA fathers. They were looking for someone who could handle the advanced level chemistry course. Since the material in this course was similar to what I was teaching at the College of Education I thought I could handle the job. The students were very bright, in fact, they were than those at the College of Education. These students were intending to go on to do degrees in science at one of the universities in the country. Students at the College of Education were often those who did not qualify for degree courses at the University.

During the week I would live with the SMA Fathers since the school was a boarding school and I could be more available to assist the students both in personal counseling as well as in their chemistry work. I was very happy with this new position. After I started, the head of the Chemistry Department from the College of Education came to visit me at St. Gregory's. He said he could not find a replacement for me in the chemistry department. He asked if I would come back as a part-time lecturer for the sake of the final year students. I told him I would continue the lectures to the final year students on a part-time basis, as long as it did not interfere with my work at St. Gregory's.

I also told him I would accept no pay for this work, as I was doing it as a personal favor to him and was not doing it for the University who had rejected my application for a regular contract. And so, though most of my time was taken up by the students at St. Gregory's, I did find three hours a week to go to the College of Education to finish up the syllabus for the final year students. Many of the students were amazed that I would do this for no pay. I hoped I'd given them an example that there is more to life than money.

There is one incident that occurred during my time at St. Gregory's that also shaped my thinking about my work as a priest. One day, I was asked to celebrate a class Mass for the sixth formers, that is, the boys in the advanced level chemistry class. It happened that before the afternoon Mass, there was some unpleasant experience when the boys had acted in a way not in keeping with the discipline of the school.

When it was time for Mass, I told them I did not feel I could celebrate Mass with them since I was not feeling very kindly toward them after their unruly behavior. I told them that the Mass was a celebration of love and unity, neither of which was evident after the unfortunate incident.

I suggested we simply go our separate ways and reflect on what had occurred. About an hour later, a student representative came to me and apologized for their behavior, and asked if we could not have Mass.

I told him to gather the students into the chapel and I would come and celebrate with them.

Before the Mass began I also apologized to them for my rash decision to cancel the Mass. I was also at fault, and that I judged them harshly, perhaps more harshly than they deserved. We then celebrated a wonderful

Mass together, which now was an expression of the love and unity we felt. I recalled this incident many times even when teaching seminarians many years later in Ghana. The Mass must never be simply a ritual exercise, but must truly express the faith of the people. I have never forgotten it, even if I have not always had the courage to practice what I taught. After one year at St. Gregory's, my superiors thought it was time for me to move on, as that assignment had only been a stopgap measure when I could not get the contract I had first sought.

Before I move on, I would like to share an experience of visiting the family of one of our Jesuit candidates. Obi Obiekwe, a young Igbo man had been in touch with us Jesuits all during the Biafran war.

Since all the schools in Biafra were closed during the war, he could not complete his secondary education although he was in his final year when the war began. Instead of wasting the 2 1/2 years of the duration of the war, he studied philosophy with the Holy Spirit Fathers, making it clear to them that it was his intention to join the Jesuits as soon as that was possible. When the war ended he came over to Lagos having completed philosophy but not having completed his secondary school education. He was then told to register in a secondary school in Lagos where he would be able to complete his final year and do the examinations. He was at a school very close to the College of Education where I was teaching. And so for about six months I was tutoring him in the various subjects to make sure that he did well in the standardized O-level examinations. It also gave me a chance to get to know him in order to assess the sincerity of his vocation. So I became his spiritual director as well as his tutor.

During one of the school holidays, he invited me to go to Enugu in the Eastern Province, the former Biafra. We traveled together and went to the house of his family. I was given the usual warm African welcome, and then experienced a very traditional ritual for welcoming visitors. A cola nut was brought out on a plate and given to the father of the family. We were all sitting in a circle in the living room at this time. He said a traditional prayer over the cola nut, and it was passed reverently around the group of people until it was returned to the father, who then cut it up in small pieces and passed it around again. This time we each took one of the small pieces, and together, consumed it. This experience once again confirmed in my mind the importance of ritual in almost all African cultures. I believe that was one of the attractions of the Catholic Church. Many of the Igbo people were attracted to the Catholic Church when the missionaries first arrived and became very staunch members.

When I was first assigned to Nigeria it was the intention of my superiors that I should work in Port Harcourt. The war made that impossible when I first arrived. Now that the war was over, I could make a change and move from Lagos to Port Harcourt. An opportunity presented itself when an advert appeared looking for lecturers for a new teacher training college that would open in Port Harcourt. This was in the spring of 1971. I applied for a position as a lecturer in chemistry, and then went on leave to prepare myself for this new position.

In June 1971 I went on leave to the United States for three months holiday which was a common practice at the end of each two years. During the holiday I was asked by my superior in Nigeria to represent him at the Vow Mass of our first two Nigerian Jesuit novices. They were Joe Ajakaiye and Edwin Emaikwu who later changed their first names to Jad and Adem. Jad would be taking his vows in Lusaka, while Adem would be taking his vows in Kinshasa.

This was an exciting assignment for me since it would allow me to see two very different parts of Africa. I also felt very privileged to be asked to preach at both of these Masses. At the end of my leave in the United States, I flew via London to Tel Aviv, as I wanted to take advantage of this trip to East Africa to see the Holy Land. I had five days in Israel.

I stayed at the Jesuit residence in Jerusalem, and, with the help of my fellow Jesuits, I visited most of the places that were most precious to me. I visited and prayed at Calvary, Bethlehem, Nazareth, Qumran and felt awed to walk through the streets of Jerusalem and just to be in the places where Jesus once walked. However, I was also saddened by the tension that obviously existed between the Palestinians and the Israelis.

When I visited there it was shortly after one of the many wars that broke out between the Arabs and the Jews. This made it impossible for me to visit the site of the baptism since the Jordan River was the ceasefire line after the Six Day war. I was even more saddened by the obvious divisions in the Christian churches. On Calvary itself where Jesus died to gather together the scattered children of God, there were three altars, each belonging to a different Christian Church. I did celebrate Mass on Calvary and also at the shrine of the Nativity, which again was divided by altars belonging to different churches. All this division and tension between Arabs and Jews, and between Orthodox and Catholic Christians took away much of the joy that I might have expected. Still, it was a privilege to be in this holy place.

From Israel I flew to Nairobi in Kenya. There I stayed with friends I had come to know in the United States. They were gracious hosts and took me around the city, where we also visited a small game park. For the first time in my life I saw the animals of Africa in their natural habitat. During my first four years in Nigeria I never saw any of the typical animals of Africa, because Lagos was so densely populated. In fact there are very few game parks in Nigeria for the same reason. I also found that Nairobi was a very different city from Lagos. It was a modern city with all the infrastructure that you would have expected to find in Europe. I was only there for about two days when I took off for Lusaka.

I was met at the airport by some of the Jesuits working in Zambia. They took me to the Jesuit novitiate which would be the venue for the vow day. I was very happy to see Jad Ajakaiye, whom I had met several times in Lagos and Ibadan during my first years in Nigeria. The vow Mass was celebrated on the eighth of September, and I preached for this joyful occasion. I remained in Lusaka for several more days, and on one day I had permission to take the novices from Ghana and Nigeria on an outing. We had a most enjoyable day, and I was quite surprised at how different Zambia was from Nigeria. Physically it was far more developed. There were none of the open drains that marred Lagos. Lusaka was a modern city with beautiful shops. I was also struck by the number of white people. In Nigeria I would not have noticed them very much, and you would never have found them running the shops in town. Here in Lusaka almost all the shops on the main shopping street were run by Asians. I also found the climate to be quite different. It was cooler and drier than anything I experienced in Nigeria. In fact, it was quite pleasant. As I left Lusaka to move on to Kinshasa I never thought I would ever see Lusaka again. I did not realize that in three years time I would be living in this country of Zambia.

So I went to Kinshasa in what was then called Zaire, now called the Democratic Republic of the Congo. I found the formalities of the airport very difficult as my French was not very fluent and the officials were quite corrupt. I was very grateful that there were some Zairois Jesuit scholastics who rescued me from all the difficulties and drove me the 30 some odd kilometers to the Jesuit house of studies. There I met Adem Emaikwu, whom I also got to know in my years in Nigeria when he expressed his interest in becoming a Jesuit. Once again I was privileged to be at his vow Mass and to preach the homily at the Mass.

Unfortunately I had to preach in English even though the language of the house was French. I was assured that most people would understand English. I did manage, with my limited French, to make myself at home in this community. As in Lusaka, I got permission to take the Anglophone scholastics on a picnic. We went to a beautiful resort area known as Nsele. It was right on the Zaire River and we had a beautiful day. Once again I saw an Africa that was different from both Zambia and Nigeria. I appreciated this excursion both because I wanted to be at the vow Mass of these men whom I had known and because it expanded my understanding and experience of Africa. In addition, celebrating the vows of these two men had a special significance. They were our first two Nigerian vocations, and marked the launch of a new presence of the Jesuits in Nigeria. Now we would not just be foreign missionaries, but would be a family that included indigenous Nigerians. Sadly, both of these men left the Society of Jesus in time, but they did mark the beginning of a movement that would eventually grow so that today we have in Nigeria and Ghana an independent province of the worldwide family of Jesuits—the Northwest Africa Province. I felt like I was present at its birth with the entry of these two men.

In September 1971, I returned from my leave in the United States and moved myself to Port Harcourt. The city, which today is a thriving metropolis, was then a small town still bearing the scars of the terrible war. I still remember the large Kingsway store which was burned to the ground by the Biafran people at the beginning of the war because it was a British owned company and Britain was backing the federal Nigerian government. The roads were full of potholes due to the mining of the roads to prevent the advance of the federal army. The signs of the war were everywhere.

The new college was to be housed in an abandoned primary school which had been somewhat rehabilitated to become the new Rivers State College of Education. The small faculty were accommodated in abandoned houses which were a short walk from the school. I was given a house with three bedrooms. It had a front veranda, had been completely renovated, and was a very comfortable home. I would be living alone, far away from my nearest Jesuit brother. Shortly after I arrived there, another Jesuit did come to lecture in English literature at the University of Nsukka. However this University was several hundred kilometers from Port Harcourt. We only met perhaps once a month when Father Joe Landy came with his driver to visit me on the weekend. This was all I had for a Jesuit community. In order to find religious community life I became very friendly with a group of Vincentian fathers who were working in Port Harcourt.

The diocese of Port Harcourt was without a bishop. Bishop Okoye, who had been the Bishop of Port Harcourt before the war, could not return to that diocese. He had been a loyal supporter of Biafra during the war and would have been unacceptable to the people of Port Harcourt. Providentially, the Bishop of Enugu had died during the war. Enugu was at the heart of the Igbo rebellion. It was considered a capital of the Igbo people. Bishop Okoye was named to be the Bishop of Enugu. This left Port Harcourt without a bishop.

The position of the Church in Port Harcourt immediately after the war was rather precarious. Not only did we not have a bishop, but there were only about seven priests in the entire diocese. The size of the diocese was equal to that of the archdiocese of New York. It was not only large but difficult to travel through because much of it was in the delta of the Niger River. The roads were also severely damaged by the war, adding to the difficulties. In addition to these physical problems there was also the hostility toward the church on the part of many people who associated the Catholic Church with the Biafran cause. There was no solid grounding for this belief. The Igbo people, who made up the majority of the Biafrans, were only about 40% Catholic. However, the work of foreign missionaries back in their home countries raising money for the Biafrans gave the impression that the church was solidly behind the Biafran cause. The papers did not distinguish between the sympathy of the missionaries for the suffering people and the political cause of Biafra. As a result the hostility against the church in the Rivers State Government was very real.

I remember going to the post office one day in my white cassock and one of the clerks shared with me why many of the people of the Rivers State felt so negative about the Catholic Church. He claimed that when the Biafrans were running the city of Port Harcourt the non-Igbo people of the city felt very oppressed, in fact, even persecuted if they showed any antagonism toward the Biafran cause. I could only sympathize with him without understanding the background to all that he was saying. I tried to be sensitive to the feelings of the people.

The life of the Church was extremely difficult, especially when members of the congregation were Igbos. Since Igbo people did not feel very safe in Port Harcourt after dark, they would come into the city to find work and then at sunset retire to the town of Aba, some 15 or 20 km distant from Port Harcourt. In addition to our disappearing congregations in the evening, there was also a great shortage of priests. Before the war many of the priests were Irish missionaries of the Congregation of the Holy Spirit. All these Irish missionaries were expelled immediately after the war.

There was only one exception. Father Jim was allowed to return because in his work he had always labored among the Ogoni people and not among the Igbo people. In addition to Father Jim, a priest of the Congregation of the Holy Spirit, there was myself, a Jesuit, one local diocesan priest, one diocesan priest from another diocese, and three Vincentian fathers, who were all missionaries from Ireland. The seven of us made up the entire clerical population of the diocese. Bishop Dominic Ekandem, the bishop of Ikot Epene, a neighboring diocese, was the administrator for the diocese of Port Harcourt. He would spend two weeks with us and two weeks in his own diocese. He had the difficult job of rebuilding the church in Port Harcourt and winning the good will of the people. I felt privileged to work with him, and I found a real community among the few priests working in the diocese. Bishop Ekandem was made a cardinal in 1976, and died in 1995.

I had gone to Port Harcourt having signed a contract with a new college of education, and had a full-time position with them as head of the chemistry department in the new college. However in addition to this work, I was expected to take on one of the parishes of Port Harcourt. In addition to these two responsibilities I had two further responsibilities.

I was chaplain at a technical college in the new city. I was also responsible for seven villages on the outskirts of the city. This meant that every Sunday I would say Mass in my parish, go to the technical college and celebrate Mass for the students, and then finally make my way out to one of the villages for a third Mass. This became my routine every Sunday. I would leave the house at about 6:30 in the morning and not return until about three o'clock in the afternoon. And this was done without so much as a glass of water during the whole of that period.

I must admit that I did not mind this at all because I was very keen on all the work that I was doing. I had never been a parish priest before in my life. It was an experience that I would not have again, and I appreciated it very much. This experience would be invaluable when I was teaching the seminarians in Ghana and in Zambia. The experience taught me how to run a parish when I could not be there all the time and when I had many other responsibilities. Many young African diocesan priests would find themselves in a similar position when they were ordained. It was another learning experience for me. Again, I am grateful for what I learned from the wonderful people of Nigeria.

I could hardly do more than celebrate Sunday Mass for the people in the parish. I had to put most of my trust in the chief catechist of the parish. I still remember his name, which was Charlie King, and I think I would recognize him even now 35 years after the events, if indeed he is still alive.

He would come any time in the week if one of the parishioners was sick or wanted to see me. I would then go to visit that parishioner, and they would feel that I was there for them. I would ask Charlie to form committees to help with the day-to-day work of the parish. They would organize all the ceremonies for the Sunday Mass. I would simply go and carry out a plan they had made. I trusted them with the finances of the parish, leaving it in their hands to count the Sunday collection and to deposit it into the bank. I never had any difficulty with them. I would follow a similar routine at the college.

This gave me the freedom to be a lecturer in chemistry and to head that department while at the same time trying to be available in the rebuilding of the Catholic community in Port Harcourt.

Perhaps the most interesting part of this weekend parish work was going out to the bush to celebrate Mass for the largely uneducated congregations in these villages. I had a most remarkable catechist, Christopher Wede, in one of the villages, who became almost my administrator for the work of the church in all the villages. He was an educated person, very good in English, and was totally reliable.

On the first Friday of every month, I would meet with the catechists from the various villages. I would invite them to my house in Port Harcourt and would prepare a meal for them. We would all be together and eat from the same dish using our fingers. It was a wonderful sign of our union together, dipping into the same dish, enjoying the same meal.

After the meal, we would sit down together and I would go around the group asking them to share the problems they had with their particular community. We would then discuss these problems in common and I would give a final word of advice. It was an opportunity for me to learn what was going on in the church in the rural areas. Once we completed that part of the meeting, I would then share with them an understanding of the Scriptures for the next four Sundays, so that when I could not be there for a Mass they would know what to preach about.

When our meeting was over, those who could went back to their villages. If any could not, they were invited to stay at my house. In this way, as a parish priest, I could keep in touch with all my communities, no matter how scattered. Every community felt that I was somehow present to them, though I could not be with them each Sunday. This was an important lesson for me to learn: how to delegate authority and trust that those working with me would be responsible in the tasks assigned them.

It did not take long for me to be aware that the people in the villages could not understand my English, or for that matter, anybody's English. They were mostly illiterate people, who could only speak and understand their own vernacular language. I decided that this was not very good. I asked Christopher Wede to translate the ordinary parts of the Mass into the Ikwere language. Since I could not read this language, I had to check the accuracy of the translation. I asked one of my chemistry students, who was not a Catholic and was not familiar with the text of the Mass, to join me and my chief catechist one afternoon.

I asked the catechist to read his translation aloud, and then after every few sentences would ask my student friend to tell me what he said in English. I discovered that he had written a very good and accurate translation. I typed out the translation, and asked the chief catechist to read this into a tape recorder. I then followed the text and listened to the tape many times, until I was able to pronounce the words very accurately and somewhat fluently.

The next Sunday, I was able to celebrate Mass in the Ikwere language. I was probably the first priest in the world to celebrate Mass in that language. I recall one of the priests asking me if the translation was approved. I asked him who was going to approve it since no one in Rome knew this language, and the people needed to participate more intelligently in the Mass. Even to this day, as I write these memories I can still recite the opening lines of the Mass in Ikwere from memory. Once again, as I found a few years before during the harvest ceremony that I described above, that I had to make decisions for the good of the people and trust the spirit to guide me. There were no church authorities I could consult, and I had the confidence of the Bishop, though, I must admit, I never asked him about this explicitly.

I also had my first experience in enculturation. One time the catechist approached me and told me that there was a woman in his village that had lost her husband during the war. She had been mourning him for over a year, and wanted to end the mourning. She said she would like to do this in the church. So I asked the catechist what is the tradition among his people when someone wants to end a mourning period.

When a woman is in mourning, she neglects her personal care. She does not brush her hair, she does not wash, and she does not change her clothing. When she decides to end the mourning period, she informs the elders of the village. The catechist told me that the women would first shave the head of the woman who wanted to end her mourning, then take her to the stream to give her a bath, dress her with new clothes, cover her bald head with a head tie, and then bring her back to her home. I told the catechist that I did not see why this could not be done within the context of a Mass.

When the word went out to the village, some relatives of the woman came to me and said they did not want her to end her mourning period in the church. They claimed they had their own traditional way of doing this. I explained that we intended to respect their traditional practice but that the woman wanted this done in the church. They said they would not agree to this. I consulted the catechist. He said the woman definitely wanted this done and that the relatives were prolonging the mourning period, because they were punishing her for having been the cause of her husband's death. There seemed to be no basis for this belief and I asked the catechist what would happen if we went ahead with the ceremony. He said once that was done there would be no further consequences. And so we planned to go ahead.

On the Sunday morning I went to that village for Mass. A good number of people had gathered in the church. The woman who was ending the mourning period was led into the church and was given a seat in the front. I introduced the Mass and explained to the people what we were about to do. After the readings and the homily, some of the women gathered around the woman who was ending the mourning period and began to shave her head. While this was going on the rest of the congregation sang hymns, recited prayers, and waited for the women to complete their task. They then led the woman down to the stream to bathe her and change her clothes. She was led back to the church radiant in her new appearance. She then brought the offerings of the Mass to the altar, and resumed her seat in the front of the church. The Mass continued as usual. At the end of Mass, we formed a procession and led the woman with singing and dancing back to her home. I took part in this procession, and blessed the home when we arrived there. I then led the woman into her house with great rejoicing. Her mourning had ended.

I was always looking for ways in which to bring the church closer to the traditions of the people. I would always first consult the catechists and use my own sense of what was proper in the church to guide me in making the final decision. I don't recall ever having complaints from the people or any reprimands from the bishop. If what I was doing was somehow offensive I am sure the bishop would have heard, and I would have been cautioned. Once again I am grateful to the African people for encouraging me to find new ways to use my priesthood in their service, and so bring Christ to them. He would then find his own way to console and comfort them. My task was only to create the environment in which they could come to God.

Another beautiful experience of enculturation took place on a Christmas morning when we conducted the wedding of a young man and woman in a small village. The women led the bride from her home with singing and dancing to the front of the church. Similarly the men did the same for the groom. I met them at the front of the church, welcomed them, said a blessing over them, and led them into the church. The nuptial Mass went on as usual. At the end of Mass we all danced and sang to the newlyweds' home. We then ate the prepared food and drank the local brew. It was a very happy occasion and a wonderfully happy Christmas for me.

Since there were no other Jesuits around, I would often come home on a Sunday afternoon, having celebrated three Masses, only to find an empty home. On that particular Christmas, I came back to an empty house, prepared myself a scrambled egg and got some rest. I did not feel lonely because I had just taken part in a wonderful family celebration.

Chapter Four

DARK CLOUDS

Let me now return to some less pleasant aspects of my experiences in Port Harcourt after the Biafran war. As I've already mentioned there was great tension between the government and the church because of our alleged involvement in prolonging the Biafran war. Immediately after the war the Rivers State Government took over the control of the schools from the church. Since the schools were often built very close to churches, there could have been a problem as to exactly where the church property ended and the school property began. Fortunately, Bishop Okoye, while he was bishop of Port Harcourt before the war, had legal deeds drawn up to demarcate the property of the school and the property of the church.

The Vincentian fathers were taking care of a parish which was next door to a secondary school for girls. The headmistress of the school had approached the fathers to ask if she could use the church for weekly assemblies. Since these were always on school days, there would be no conflict with the Sunday Mass. This went on for some time, and the headmistress was given a key to the church so that she could use it for this purpose. When the exam time came one of the priests came to me to seek my advice. He told me that the headmistress had set up an examination hall within the church. The church was full of desks and chairs, and it was now Saturday and there would be Mass there on Sunday. The exams would begin on Monday, and so she had set up the church in advance to be used as an examination hall. The parish priest approached the headmistress and explained that this had gone beyond the permission she had been given. She refused to take any action and now the parish priest was seeking my advice. I suggested we go back to the church, remove the school furniture, and fit new locks on the door. I said I would assist them in this since I had some practical skills in replacing locks.

The bishop administrator of the diocese was informed of what we were doing, and he gave us his full backing. And so we went to the church, asked politely that the girls take the desks out of the church.

They refused, and we proceeded to literally throw the desks out of the church. We didn't know how the girls would react, but, in fact, they just stood around curious and puzzled. I then replaced the locks on the doors, but before leaving, we checked every room, nook and corner to be sure there were no Trojan horses. In fact we discovered a few girls hiding in lockers, ready to reopen the church when we had left. They were so frightened when we discovered them that they just ran.

On Sunday morning there was a Mass. Later in the morning an official from the Ministry of Education approached the parish priest and told him that the church was government property. The priest disagreed, and there seemed to be no resolution to the problem. I am not sure what they did about the examinations. All I know is that during the week the parish priest discovered that the new locks had been filled with solder so that even we with our keys could no longer enter the church. This was a challenge from the Ministry of Education. The bishop administrator was informed, and he said he would himself celebrate Mass in that church with all the priests of the diocese. And he also requested that all the parish Masses be canceled that morning so that all the people could attend his one Mass in the disputed church.

I arrived early the morning of the Mass with a bunch of tools so that I could break open the locks. I did so fully aware that I was in a sense on both sides of the fence. I was an employee of the Ministry of Education and therefore risked losing my position by going against their decree that the church belong to them. I was also a priest of the diocese of Port Harcourt, and felt an obligation to my bishop. There was a large gathering of people for the Mass. They came on lorries and buses, singing hymns, and ready to take on the battle with the Ministry officials. The bishop and his priests risked being sent to prison for violating government property.

During the Mass police vehicles patrolled back and forth along the road, but never interfered with the Mass nor with any of us taking part in the Mass. Everything passed quietly, and there was no further problem concerning the use of the church as a church and not as a school hall. I believe the government was nervous about taking on the church.

Most of the people were churchgoing people, and even if they were non-Catholics, they would not take kindly to the government interfering with church services. If they could claim our church, they could claim any church. But this was not to be the end of the issue.

Some weeks later I received a letter from the Ministry of Education. It claimed that a piece of Jesuit property in the rural area about 15 km from Port Harcourt belonged to the Ministry of Education. I immediately wrote to my superior in Lagos who sent me the title deeds of the property. I sent a copy of these to the Ministry. They complained about the readability of my copy, but eventually communications ceased, and the issues seemed to be resolved.

These incidents show the tension between the church and the government. It was not a pleasant time and I always felt a bit uncomfortable. You could never be sure when another crisis would arise. It would take some time before the Church could feel at ease in its relationship with the local government. I have to emphasize that this problem was largely restricted to the Rivers State, for the reasons I spoke of above. And yet the faith of the ordinary people remained strong and their commitment to the church was truly impressive. Sunday after Sunday, they were there in their numbers and participated fully in each Mass.

While all this was happening in my work as priest in the church I was at the same time a full-time lecturer in chemistry at the newly established Rivers State College of Education. I found the students very eager to learn as many of them had not been able to attend college during the whole course of the civil war. It was a pleasure lecturing to them, and the morale of the student body and the staff was very high. Our first principal was an African-American by the name of Bill Maxwell. He was a highly qualified person with a doctorate in education from Stanford University and a postdoc at Oxford. He had come to Nigeria at the end of the civil war as part of a team of USAID working in a large comprehensive school just outside of Port Harcourt. He was seconded by the Ministry of Education to help establish the new College of Education. He did a remarkable job making our new college one of the finest teacher training colleges in the land. He had a remarkable ability of relating with the staff and students alike, as well as with the ordinary workers on the college campus. Since our institute was housed in an abandoned primary school, its facilities were extremely limited, but we all worked very hard to make this simple physical structure into a first-class academic institution. The first year of its existence was a very happy one. There were some problems, chief among which was the lack of accommodation for the students.

Although most of the students could rent rooms in the town, there were two students who found this impossible. They were both Igbo students, and Igbos were not welcome in Port Harcourt. They found accommodation at a Salvation Army hall. The room they shared had no furniture, no windows, no electricity or running water. They slept on mats on the floor, and did all their studying at the college. When one of the young British volunteer lecturers became aware of their plight, he came to speak to me. Since there was no hope of the hostels being completed in the near future, he suggested that each of us accommodate one of them. I agreed to this arrangement since I was occupying a house with three bedrooms and was living alone. The same was true of the young British volunteer. And so we invited them to stay with us.

Francis Otuonye stayed with me, while David Okoye stayed with the young British volunteer. This was for me the beginning of a friendship that has lasted even to this day. I will say more about this later. Both of these young men went on to the University in Nigeria, successfully completed their first degrees, won scholarships to the United States for further studies, and are presently doctors of engineering. Francis is a professor at a university in Tennessee, and David is a managing director of a consultancy firm for the petroleum industry in Nigeria.

Having a student sharing a house with me brought another benefit. Students would feel free to come to my house, either to meet the student who was staying there, or to ask for assistance in their studies, or to consult me as the chaplain, or just to have a chat. During free time, there were often students in my house. I came to know them better and better. The Catholic students would come every morning to attend my Mass which I celebrated in my house. I was feeling more and more at home with them. I would often have one of them accompany me on my Sunday trips out to the villages for the celebration of Mass. I was genuinely very content with my situation both as a lecturer and as a priest. I had the ability to relate very easily with the students and the staff, and I could see a very pleasant future for myself in the college.

One experience that always helped me to understand the country in which I was living was to travel around the country and try to meet as many people as I could. So after my first year in Port Harcourt, having Francis Otuonye living in a house with me and he, having little or no family nearby, I decided to make a tour of Nigeria with Francis. He had seen very little of his own country and though I had made a tour some years ago with a fellow Jesuit I decided it would be nice for Francis and I to do a tour together.

We set out from Port Harcourt early Monday morning and drove east to the town of Aba, about an hour's drive from Port Harcourt. We then moved north through Owerri to Enugu. We stayed there for the night at a Catholic mission. Along the road we saw many signs of the recently ended Biafran war. The road from Port Harcourt to Aba was full of very large potholes the results of the mining of the road during the war to prevent the advance of the federal troops. From Enugu we continued north and climbed the plateau to the city of Jos. Since we were now at an altitude of several thousand feet the air was cooler and drier. After an overnight at the seminary in Jos, we moved on to Kaduna, where we were once again accommodated by the Catholic mission.

I could detect that Francis was a bit nervous as we drove north, for we were now deep into Hausa country. It was in this part of the country that the Igbos were cruelly massacred in the pogroms of 1967 just before the coup that brought Gowon to power. Since Francis was an Igbo he was understandably nervous although things had become very quiet since the end of the war. The other problem that made Francis a bit nervous was the fact that for the first time, as a Nigerian, he was moving into a part of the country where he could not understand the language and they could not understand him. There is very little relationship between the languages of Igbo and Hausa. Of course I understood neither language, and always had to make do in English. But I was a foreigner, and Francis was a Nigerian.

The next morning we moved on to Kano, a very old walled city which was at the heart of the Hausa territory. We took an interesting tour of the city, especially its marketplace. We were now at the edges of the Sahara Desert, and the scenery was mostly dry and sandy. We drove to the town of Malumfashi where the Dominican fathers and brothers ran a catechetical training center. We stayed there for the night and had an interesting conversation with the Dominican missionaries and heard of the difficulties they experienced in bringing the Gospel to a part of the country that was largely Muslim. From Malumfashi, we moved to Sokoto, Kainji, Minna and then back to Enugu, to Aba, and finally back to Port Harcourt. It was a very interesting journey to pass through so many parts of the country with varying landscapes, and with peoples of very different cultures, which gave me a new understanding of Nigeria. I'm sure the same was true for

Francis, as he moved into a part of the country in which he had never been before.

On the way back we drove through the town of Ihyala, made famous during the Biafran war. The road from Ihyala to Uli turned out to be a very wide highway for a distance of about 2 miles. This was the improvised airport for the Biafran people doing the civil war when they had lost all of their civil airports. There was a cemetery on the side of the road where some of the pilots were buried. These men lost their lives trying to fly in arms and supplies to a beleaguered people. It was a very moving experience to pass through this world which I had heard so much about. Back in Port Harcourt, Francis and I had much to reflect on and share with one another.

Francis soon after moved on to Lagos where I obtained a place for him at the College of Education of the University of Lagos, where I had once lectured. Being a more a established institution, I felt he had a better chance of higher education.

I returned refreshed, ready to begin a new academic year at the college. However, I came back only to hear the news that the Ministry of Education sent Dr. Maxwell back to his original assignment in the comprehensive school. A local man was appointed as the new principal.

Unfortunately, he was not very well qualified, having only a bachelor's degree in education. He was the least educated man on the staff, and must have felt very insecure. This insecurity began to reveal itself within the first few months of his arrival. He began to undo much of what Dr. Maxwell had done. I found myself in the awkward position of constantly questioning what he was doing at every staff meeting. This did not exactly endear me to him. I soon found myself being considered as a disruptive force in his administration.

One day during a lecture, I noticed a young woman sitting in the class who was a stranger to that class. After the lecture I asked her privately how she came to be in the class. She told me the principal had invited her to become part of the class. I asked to see her qualifications, and discovered that she was not qualified to attend the college. I was also the chairperson of the admissions committee at the time. I knew that I had not admitted her.

I sent a note to the principal inquiring about the matter. The only response I received was a simple note saying that she was to remain in the class and that there was to be no further questioning on the matter.

I then resigned from the admissions committee, since my work was being overtaken by seemingly arbitrary decisions of the principal. The principal refused to accept my resignation. And so the tension between us was beginning to grow. It was eventually revealed that the young woman was a friend of the military governor of the state, and that he had used his influence to find a place for her in the college.

This incident only intensified the tension between myself and the principal. But there was another problem in our relationship, and that was the incredible corruption that I witnessed in the giving out of contracts at the college. One of our many needs at the college was accommodation for students who lived outside of Port Harcourt.

There was an abandoned building that had been started before the war. A substantial amount of money was paid to a group of contractors to turn it into a hostel. We were promised that the building would be completed by March or April of the first year of college. It was still incomplete when Dr. Maxwell was transferred. The principal seemed incapable of getting any further work done. I recall visiting the contractors at the site more than a year after the project was due for completion, and asked them why nothing seemed to be happening. I told them that they had been paid a great deal of money and didn't understand how they could justify idleness on the job and the seeming indifference on their part as to whether the job was ever completed or not. I challenged the foreman and said to him: "What kind of a man are you?" His quick reply was: "Obviously not the same kind as you are." That was the end of our discussion. The hostel was never completed even after I had completed my two-year contract. The students were forced to find accommodation anywhere in the town.

With the appointment of a new principal, the morale at the college was in continual decline. There was no progress on the construction of the hostels; the structure of the academic program was no longer as clear as it was under the Dr. Maxwell, and much of the enthusiasm at the birth of the college was rapidly disappearing. A crisis erupted when the students of the Rivers State were not paid their monthly subsistence allowance. The students went on strike and demonstrated against the administration. Personally, I had little sympathy for the students because I felt they were already privileged people, having the chance to train for a profession, and paying no fees. I am sure that I made my thinking clear to the students. Eventually they were paid their money, and this crisis came to an end.

At a staff meeting shortly after the crisis was resolved, the principal announced that he had found the cause of the unrest among the students. "That cause", he announced very solemnly, "was one person who called himself a reverend father". Since I was the only one who was a priest on the faculty, he could only be referring to me. He then went on with a litany of problems at the college. After each of these he would announce that again the cause of the problem was one who called himself a reverend father. Everyone sat in silence. At the end one of the staff members attempted to say something in my defense. The principal would have none of it. I asked the secretary of the staff meeting to make a complete record of what was said at this meeting.

The next day I wrote a letter to the Ministry of Education, enclosing a copy of the minutes of the meeting. I suggested that they terminate my contract since I was such a cause of disruption in the college. Or, if they found the charges were without grounding, they should ask that these charges be removed from the record. The ministry did nothing. I simply continued with my work, trying as much as possible to avoid any further friction with the principal. I determined that I would not renew my contract at the end of the year. A new College of Technology was going to open at the beginning of the next academic year. I applied for a contract at this new College. The principal was aware that I would be leaving the College of Education at the end of the year. My course of action was to do my work to the best of my ability, and simply wait to the end.

As the year drew to an end a celebration was planned to mark the second anniversary of the opening of the school. And I would discuss this coming celebration with the students who frequented my house. I told them that I thought there was not much to celebrate since in my opinion the college seemed to have lost its way. I shared with them that I wanted to write an open letter to the students expressing my views on this matter. I made a draft of such a letter and showed it to many students who came to my house and were now my friends. In the letter I expressed my disappointment at some of the developments in the college. I did not express any criticism of the principal, nor did I imply that our problems were in any way due to him. Having considered the letter, my student friends urged me not to print it. They further advised me to be very careful in what I said concerning either the college or the government when a particular student was present. They informed me that he was going to the principal to tell him anything that might be used against me.

This particular student was a more mature person in age, married with a family, and not finding the studies easy. I felt sorry for him since he had serious responsibilities and qualifying as a teacher would make his future secure. So I spent time trying to assist him in his studies. I did not want to treat him as anything less than a friend. I wanted him to feel as much at home in my house as any of the students. Unfortunately, I did not follow the advice of the students who had my best interests at heart. I printed the open letter that I had shown them.

I gave a copy to each student in the college. I did not give it to any of the staff members since it was addressed to the students. In it I wondered what there was to celebrate, and listed the signs that our college was not in good health. Among the things I listed were: the unfinished hostels after two years of construction, the inadequate facilities of the college itself, the inability to recruit new staff, and the insufficient financing from the Ministry. I suggested that instead of celebrating we set aside a day of prayer and fasting to ask God's assistance for the future of the college. I also mentioned that the students seemed uninterested in what was happening, and that the only time they demonstrated or protested was when their finances were touched. Their concerns seemed to be completely self-centered. I had hoped that the letter would give them something to think about and even to pray about. However, the planned celebration went ahead, and I participated in the activities.

Perhaps two weeks later, a student from Lagos was staying with me, and another Igbo student was living with me. It was during a break in the academic calendar, and I was relaxing one afternoon with them. A vehicle pulled up to my house, and an official came out, and passed the usual greetings. Then he asked to see my alien registration and my passport. I showed them to him, and politely asked what was the reason for wishing to see these documents. I had been living in Nigeria for almost 6 years and no one ever asked for these. He suggested that perhaps they had not always been doing their duty. He then asked me to accompany him to his office. The students who were with me seemed a bit concerned. I told them not to be worried and that I would be back shortly.

I was brought down to the headquarters of the Central Intelligence Organization where I was questioned for several hours. At first they asked questions about my family, my work, and then, specifically, about a letter they had. They showed the letter and asked if I had written it.

It was a copy of the letter that I circulated among the students and it had my signature on the bottom. I told them that obviously I had written the letter since my name was on it. And they began to ask detailed questions about the contents of the letter. They took certain phrases as implying that I was stirring up the students to take actions that would disturb the peace of the college. They even seemed to imply that I was stirring up the students against the government. It seemed incredible to me that they could find these things in my letter. I tried to reason with them, but made no progress at all.

They were finally finished and said they would take me back to my house. However, they had taken my passport and would not return it to me. When I got back to the house I consulted one of the Nigerian staff members, Dr. Godwin Tasie, who was the vice principal of the college and also a good friend. He told me the matter was serious, and that I should consult someone in authority.

He suggested I go and see the Chief Justice of the Rivers State, Justice Ambrose Allagoa, whom I had met on other occasions and who was a very good Catholic. I saw him at his home and told him what had happened. I also gave him a copy of the letter. He read through it and remarked that there was nothing that could remotely be considered subversive. He told me not to worry about it, that he would consult others and let me know what I should do.

The next day was a Sunday and I was busy with my usual three Masses. When I returned home I found a note on my door from the Chief Justice suggesting that I see the Inspector General of Police of the Rivers State on Monday morning. I went to meet the man the next morning, and once again, told the story of what happened to me. He had a copy of the letter and had already read it. He made the same remark as the Chief Justice, that there was nothing subversive in this letter and I had nothing to worry about it. He added that if the intelligence service insisted on writing a letter to the federal government in Lagos it would have to go through him, and he would make his own comments. Eventually I returned to the office of the Central Intelligence Organization and reclaimed my passport.

When I went to the office to reclaim the passport, the officer in charge was quite annoyed and asked why I had gone to the Chief Justice and the Inspector General of Police. I told him that the matter was a serious one and I had to consult someone who could advise me. I did not question their right to bring me to their office and interrogate me. I respected their position, but I did need advice. He returned the passport to me and I went back to my house. A few days later I went to the immigration office to apply for a reentry visa as I would soon be going on leave. I had no difficulty getting the reentry visa, and wondered if perhaps the whole matter had been resolved.

The night before I was flying out of Port Harcourt, the young man, who worked in the library and would come to me as a friend from time to time, came with his wife and two sons to wish me farewell.

They brought some very simple gift, some sugar cane. I asked him if he wished to come to the airport the next day to see me off. He said: "No. If I go I will cry because I will never see you again." I replied: "I will be back in three months to take up my new position at the College of Technology." He simply repeated that he would not see me again. I could not have guessed the accuracy of this prediction.

The next day I flew off to Lagos where I then caught a plane to London and then onto New York. I looked forward to my leave, as I was tired after all the tension of the past two years, both in the Church and in the college. I looked forward to returning to take up a new position as a lecturer in chemistry in the new College of Technology. I also agreed to allow one of the Igbo students to continue living in my house. During that leave, I made my annual retreat. It was a very consoling retreat and I felt very close to the Lord. Little did I know that I was being prepared for one of the great moments of sadness in my life.

On September 17, my family saw me off at JFK and I began my return journey to Lagos. I spent the day in London and left on the night of the 18th for Lagos. I arrived in Lagos on the morning of September 19, 1973. My superior was waiting to welcome me back to Nigeria. I passed through the immigration control, and was welcomed by the officer there whom I had known. I then went to the customs desk and another friend welcomed me, chalked the bag, and I was about to leave the transit area. Unfortunately the strap on my bag broke, and I had to take a bit of time to tie things together. As I was doing this, the immigration officer came up to me and said that I would not be allowed to enter the country,—that my name was on a list of prohibited immigrants. I was told I would have to leave the country immediately and return to London on the same flight on which I had come in.

It would be almost impossible to describe my emotions at that moment. I was so confused, and was caught up in the practical details of what was to happen next. My superior got permission to come into the transit area, and tried to get the officials at immigration to contact their chief in Lagos. We never succeeded in contacting the chief immigration officer. The authorities at the airport insisted that I buy a flight to London. I told them I did not have the money as I had just come in from London and had no return ticket. There was much argument over this matter. Eventually, the Nigerian government had to buy me a ticket to London. They then said they would confiscate my bags to pay for the ticket. I could never agree to this since all my belongings were already in Nigeria and all my possessions were in those bags I carried.

They finally agreed to allow me to have my bags. The plane was by now very late taking off, and I was escorted to the plane by policemen as if I were a common criminal. I took my seat on the plane and was overwhelmed by a very deep depression. I had no idea what I would be doing when I landed in London.

When we landed in London I contacted Dr. Derrick Knight who was the British volunteer teaching with me at the college and who had convinced me to give boarding to one of those students. He and his fiancée had seen me off at the airport the previous day. They were surprised to learn that I was back in London. They offered me accommodation for the night and tried to console me. The next day they took me to a Jesuit residence where I could find a temporary home. It was the residence suggested by my superior in Lagos. He would be in touch with me there in the hope that the decision taken by the government could be reversed. After two weeks, I received a letter from him saying that my life and work in Nigeria was now finished. There was nothing he could do to reverse the decision of the immigration office because my case was considered a matter of security and not just immigration. I felt completely lost. I had really come to love Africa and I looked forward to continuing my work in Port Harcourt. I had become very attached to the people there and knew I would miss them very much.

It was about this time that I received one of the most moving letters I've ever received. It was sent by the wife of my friend who worked in the library. She was illiterate and she must've got a scribe to compose a letter expressing her feelings and thoughts. I would like to quote the letter in full at this point, as I have kept it for 35 years now and I hope it will be buried with me as it expresses so much of what I have learned in my time in Africa.

Mrs. Monica E. Bema
c/o Mr. Emmanuel D. Bema,
P. M.B. 5047,
Port Harcourt,
Nigeria, West Africa.
29th September 1973.

Father,

I came to Port Harcourt on the 19th instant from the instruction
of my husband when he sent me the news that he would arrive in
Port Harcourt on the 20th. He does not even tell me anything
when he sees me crying and it was only yesterday that he told me
that you had arrived on the appointed day in Lagos but you were
turned back the same day.

Oh my father that gives me food. My father that made me listen
to radio, the thing that I had never dreamt up since my life.

Father where are you! And how are you? To whom when my
two children, Seaboy and Samuel, cry, I will ask them that their
father from America when returned will buy them shirts for
their Christmas.

To whom when we are in trouble my husband will run to and we
all in the household laughed when he returned.

MAN IS GOD TO MAN but my only visible God is now
nowhere to see in person. My mother-in-law is crying with me
for she was happy seen us talking all the time of our father from
America. Please father, no matter how sinful I am, please let me
hear from you. Moreover, my husband is now sick and I'm sure
it is because of this thoughts. He now tell me that we may go
back to Bodo our hometown if the situation does not change.

Finally father, what do I tell Seaboy and Samuel when next they
cry. Please father, I pray you to send me your humble reply. May
God be with you and bless you in all your undertakings.

I am, yours in Christ,
Mrs. Monica E. Dele Bema.

(The emphasized words were all in capital letters in the original text and were also written with a red pen, whereas the rest of the letter was in blue.)

I am sure her sentiments were quite sincere, and somehow she experienced the presence of God in me. What the letter reminded me of was that I had certainly found God in the people of Africa. The letter expressed a profound theological truth, solidly founded in the mystery of the incarnation. I never ceased to be amazed at the profound wisdom that was often found in the so-called simple people. It was also the love expressed in the letter that made my departure so painful. If her husband would have cried when I was leaving Port Harcourt, I was certainly crying now because I could not return, and, in fact, I would never see him again. But I will never forget him or his family, and the letter is one of my greatest treasures.

Chapter Five

TRANSITION

For several weeks in London I felt just numb. As I reflected on why this had happened, what came to my mind was my vow of chastity.

Although my departure from Nigeria seemed to have nothing to do with any sexual misbehavior, I felt that the deeper meaning of this painful experience was wrapped up in the vow that I took many years before.

I always thought that the vow of chastity opened up the possibility of a wider human love than could've been found in a nuclear family. I really did experience this in my years in Nigeria. I had experienced great love and affection from many people, and I honestly felt they were as close to me as my own family. I thought that perhaps I had become too attached to them, and was no longer open to the possibility of an even larger family. Perhaps I had to be separated from them so that I could now reach out and form another family. I could not become so attached to any person or persons as to hinder my freedom to move in response to the call of the Lord. I will always hold the people in Nigeria with deep affection in my heart. But I've also discovered many others who have shown me equal affection and for whom I feel equal love.

Before I leave my reflections on my experience in the country of Nigeria I would like to put down a few thoughts about two people who made a difference in my life in adjusting to the strange culture. The first was Fr. Joe McKenna, who was my superior for the six years I spent in Nigeria. I don't think I have ever met a superior who was as concerned about my happiness there or as affirming of every small accomplishment I may have achieved.

It was he who offered me the job of chaplain at the Pacelli School for the Blind even though he had been doing that for some time. It was his way of helping me to get involved in the life of the people so that I could feel more useful when I had no specific assignment when I first arrived. He never missed an opportunity to pass on an encouraging remark by anyone who had heard a sermon that I preached or participated in a retreat that I'd given. He was a kind and gentle person. His simple lifestyle and genuine humility were a genuine inspiration to me. He was a man with a doctorate in political science from Yale University, who had once been head of the political science department at Fordham University. Now he was doing routine office work at the Catholic Secretariat at the education desk. I never once heard him even imply that he was not using his professional qualifications. He was available for whatever had to be done, and he did it cheerfully and generously. When the war ended, he spent a great deal of time writing up projects and proposals for the various international aid agencies that would help with the reconstruction. He would often have to go out to the airport to pick up various representatives of these agencies. He once joked that he was the most qualified taxi driver in Lagos. For other men, this might seem like a total waste of time and talent. But what he accomplished was recognized by all, and he was certainly respected by the Church authorities in Nigeria. He also assisted many congregations of sisters in writing their constitutions in the light of the second Vatican Council. He was constantly consulted by religious superiors, both men and women, because of his wisdom and understanding. After he left Nigeria to return to the United States, I never missed a chance to meet with him when I was on home leave. If I survived my first tour of duty, and decided to return to Nigeria, it could be largely attributed to the influence of this man. Unfortunately, I was not around when he died and so could not be present at his funeral.

A second person who made a profound influence on me was a woman by the name of Evelyn Pugh. She was a member of the Grail movement, an association of women with private vows, living in community and working for the betterment of women everywhere. At that time she was working with another member of the Grail. Evelyn was an American, and her companion was Canadian. I got to know her well during various workshops and retreats, and was always impressed by her cheerfulness. Many times when I was feeling a bit depressed, I just had to go and share a cup of tea or coffee, and she would soon have me laughing with her great sense of humor and genuine optimistic outlook.

When I returned to Nigeria in 1971 from my home leave, I found her at the airport ready to take off for the United States. She had been diagnosed with cancer and was returning for treatment. She never returned to Nigeria, but died on the 22nd of January 1972 at the age of 51. Her death was a great loss to me, and even to this day I keep a memorial card posted on my wall. I was very touched by the inscription on that card as well as by her smiling face. The inscription read: "Evelyn Pugh, whose light dawned on 27th of July 1920, achieved her fulfillment on 22nd January 1972." The deep faith expressed in that inscription was evident in her whole life.

When I realized I could not go back to Nigeria, I had to find something to do for the year. I had no desire to return to the United States. My heart was still in Africa, and it was my firm intention to return to that continent. I made my superiors aware of this desire and they had begun to make inquiries as to where else on the continent I might work. Letters were sent to the regional superiors of East Africa, Zambia, and Zimbabwe, informing them that there was a Jesuit who had worked in Nigeria for six years and wished to continue working in Africa. My superiors explained that my departure from Nigeria was no reflection on any inability or inappropriate action on my part. While awaiting some response, I enrolled at Roehampton College, run by the sisters of the Sacred Heart. It was affiliated to the University of London, and I would be able to do a nine-month course in education leading to the postgraduate certificate of education. From being a teacher in a college of education I now became a student. The year spent in a British university gave me an opportunity to prepare myself professionally as a lecturer at a college of education, but also gave me the opportunity to reflect further on my call to Africa.

I also learned a lot more about myself. I found that I could be at ease with British students, and I was a bit challenged learning something about the theories of education. During the course, I had to do several weeks of practical teaching. I asked to be posted to a school in the East End of London. I wanted the challenge of being at a difficult school, as I had heard that schools in the East End were notoriously difficult to teach in. I felt quite sure of myself as a teacher and was confident that I could handle any situation. I was quickly disillusioned. I found that I was not the gifted teacher that I thought I was. I had to struggle with discipline in the class, and found I was with a group of students who had little interest in academic work. The school leaving age in Britain had just been raised from 15 to 16 and the final year students I was teaching resented this because, if it were not for the new law they would have been out on the streets finding work and earning a living.

Although on a personal level, the students were friendly enough outside the classroom, in the classroom they made it very clear that they were not interested in anything I had to say. I learned that I should be a bit more modest in estimating my abilities. However, I did manage to pass the exercise.

During this year, I first found accommodation at a Jesuit residence in the center of London. I felt very welcome there, but I felt the cost of living was too high and having just come from a poor country I felt uncomfortable. After one month I transferred to a smaller Jesuit community near Heathrow Airport. There were just seven of us in the community, three priests and four scholastics. We took turns doing the cooking and each had his assignments in cleaning the house. This meant that the cost of living per day was much lower than in the community in the heart of London. Small as it was, I still wanted to live where I would not have to depend on anyone for finances. So I asked one of the priests in the community if he could find me a parish where I would be given accommodation in return for helping out with the Sunday Masses and occasional small assignments during the week. So after one month I moved to the parish of St. Thomas Beckett in the Fulham section of London.

This was a new and interesting experience for me since I'd never been involved in parish work in Europe. It was very different from parish work in Africa. It was more difficult to get to know the people and just as difficult to get any sense of how they were responding to your preaching. The priests I was living with were friendly enough, but always seem to have something to do in the evenings, and so I found it a bit lonely. There was one old retired priest there who became my good friend.

The year passed rather quickly, as I tried to decide with the help of superiors what I would be doing the following year. Once it was known that there was a young Jesuit eager to return to work in Africa, I received invitations from the Jesuits in Zimbabwe, Kenya, and Zambia. In all places I was offered a position as a teacher or lecturer in science. The offer from Zambia was for the position of a lecturer in science in a new teacher training college that was just about to open. It was a government college known as the Copperbelt Secondary Teachers College, more commonly known as COSETCO. I was called for an interview by representatives of the Ministry of Education in Zambia who were in London to recruit new staff. One of the interviewers was Mr. John Milimo, a graduate of one of our Jesuit high schools in Zambia, and a great admirer of the Jesuits. Within a few days I was offered the position of a lecturer in mathematics at this new college. My provincial in New York suggested I accept this position and when I finished my work in London, I moved to Zambia. This would be the beginning of a very different experience of Africa than I had had in Nigeria.

By the end of June I had completed all my requirements for the course I was doing, and I was awarded the Postgraduate Certificate of Education, more commonly known as PGCE, from the University of London. This now gave me the professional qualification in education that would allow me to be a lecturer in a teacher training college. Although I had already done this work in Nigeria for six years, in Zambia they wanted a paper qualification to prove that I could do the job. Having arranged to have my belongings shipped from Nigeria to Zambia, I made arrangements for my own personal flight to Lusaka. I arrived in Lusaka in the middle of July. I was warmly welcomed by the Jesuits there, and so began my efforts to find a new home and a new family in a new country. My reflections on the vow of chastity that occurred with my deportation from Nigeria would be put to the test. Would my heart be able to expand enough to reach out in genuine affection and love for a people very different from the Nigerians?

Chapter Six

STARTING AGAIN

A few days after arriving in Lusaka, I reported to the Ministry of Education, where I was informed that a vehicle would be leaving for the Copperbelt in a few days. And so about a week after I arrived I was traveling in a government vehicle to Kitwe, the hub of the Copperbelt.

The first thing that struck me as we drove the 400 km was how different Zambia was from Nigeria. In Nigeria driving along the road from one major city to another you would've passed countless numbers of people moving along the road. You would've seen many marketplaces set up on the roadside. I just couldn't get over the fact that there seemed to be so few people, and the landscape was a wide-open space, little of which was under cultivation.

The other thing that struck me so much was how cool the weather was. I arrived in July which is the middle of the winter for the Southern Hemisphere. The temperatures at night could go as low as 6 or 7°C (42⁰-44⁰F). The temperatures in Nigeria rarely went below 20°C (68⁰). Looking at a map of Zambia, I realized that most of the country was about 4000 feet above sea level, which accounted for the rapid cooling of the air at night even if the daytime temperatures could become quite warm.

I was a bit challenged moving up there since I didn't know anyone in the Copperbelt, and there was only one Jesuit in Kitwe, who lived by himself in the house of an expatriate who was out of the country. There was no Jesuit community in the Copperbelt at that time. It was in the plan of the province to start a Jesuit community in Kitwe, and the house had been purchased but was not yet furnished. I was offered a staff house at the college, and it was there that I moved. The other Jesuit working in Kitwe came to visit me a few days after I arrived. I had no vehicle and so could not move freely, and the college was about 16 km from the center of Kitwe.

Fortunately, a Dominican sister, Sr. Illumina Roth, a German by birth, was on the staff, teaching English and being librarian. She was also living on the campus in her own staff house. She gave me a warm welcome and was happy to have a fellow religious on the staff. She had a small Volkswagen and was generous in allowing me to use the car whenever I needed to do shopping. Of course, I had no Zambian license and so one of the first orders of business was to do a driving test and get a Zambian license. Although I was told that it was very difficult to pass the test on the first attempt, I did manage that feat and was now a licensed driver. The next thing that had to be done to give me the independence I needed was to purchase a car. When I look back on those days and compare them to the situation in much of Africa today, I am amazed at how wonderfully well everything seemed to work.

My salary as a lecturer in mathematics was the equivalent of about 700 US dollars a month. That seems like a very small amount, but in those days it was an enormous sum. After three months I was able to go to Lusaka and buy a small vehicle on the spot in cash. I purchased a Fiat 127 which was about the cheapest car on the market. I bought it for about $1500. The vehicle was assembled in Zambia in the town of Livingstone. Sadly no vehicles are any longer assembled in Zambia and no ordinary lecturer could afford to buy a new car at the beginning of the 21st century in Zambia. Living in a brand-new staff house, with a brand-new vehicle, and a generous salary, I was able to take up my work with a certain amount of comfort. My fellow Jesuit in Kitwe would come to see me every Sunday and we would go out to have lunch together. By January of the following year we had furnished the house that the Jesuits bought in Kitwe, and our first Jesuit community in the Copperbelt was born. I continued living at the college, coming into the Jesuit community on week-ends. The advantage of maintaining my residence at the college was to allow me to come closer to the students, all of whom were boarders.

It was a very interesting time to be at the college, since it was a brand-new institution with no traditions and had just received its first intake of students. Not having taught mathematics at a first-year university level, I needed time to prepare my classes. The head of the department was an English volunteer by the name of John Suffolk.

He was a very friendly and outgoing person and was delighted to have me as a colleague since we were the only two members of the mathematics department. He lent me some books to get me started, and I spent the whole of August and half of September preparing my subject matter. I would begin my lecturers at the beginning of the third term which started in mid-September. I was a bit anxious teaching a subject for which I felt I was not adequately prepared. However John Suffolk gave me every encouragement.

I was impressed by the sincerity of the students and also by their ability, despite the fact that in those days the only requirements for the college were incredibly low. All a young man or woman had to have was a GCE, which simply meant they had completed secondary school and had sat for all the subjects, and had passed at least English language and ordinary mathematics. Despite the low qualifications, many students had a bit more than this, and I personally found them quite intelligent. There was never a problem with discipline in the class, and the students seemed very eager to learn.

On October the 24th 1974 Zambia was celebrating the 10th anniversary of its independence. I had been at the college about three months at that time. It was the will of the government that all educational institutions should celebrate the 10th anniversary with appropriate programs to instill in the students a deeper love for the newly independent country. Preparations were made for weeks in advance.

One of the items on the program was to be a play put on by the Dramatic Society of the college. The moderator of this society was Sister Illumina. She prepared an African version of a medieval morality play, Everyman, written by a Nigerian author. In addition to the drama there would also be an oratorical contest on the theme, "What Independence Means to Me". The student who was the head of the Dramatic Society was a very arrogant young man who felt he was the best in just about everything he put his mind to. Not only did he take the lead part in the play, but he also entered the oratorical contest. It happened that Sister Illumina was also one of the judges of the oratorical contest.

A few days before the Independence Day, this young man came to me to ask my advice in preparing his speech for the oratorical contest. I suggested he reflect on just what it means to take full responsibility for your nation, no longer depending on some colonial power. Independence Day dawned. We began by gathering around the flagpole at sunrise to sing the national anthem and hoist the flag. We then had a prayer service to pray for the nation. After breakfast, there were various sports activities for the students. After lunch was the speech contest. After the speech contest Sr. Illumina had called the members of the cast together in the auditorium to prepare the stage for the play. Our young friend, who, by the way, happened to win the oratorical contest, did not show up for this exercise even though he was the head of the dramatic society. Sister Illumina, a bit annoyed and perhaps tired at the end of a long day, sent him a short note reprimanding him for his lack of responsibility. She even quoted the theme of the oratorical contest which he had won.

She wrote in the note: "If the future of this nation lies in your hands, then God help Zambia." Nothing more seemed to have come from this incident. The play went on after dinner, and it was a great success. It brought the celebrations of our 10th anniversary of independence to a very happy end.

About two weeks later, the British Council sent about five invitations to the college to attend a performance of "A Man for All Seasons" performed by a group of professional actors from the UK. The principal gave the tickets to Sister Illumina to use as a reward for those who took part in the drama. Unfortunately there were more than fi ve actors in the drama. So she called a meeting of the dramatic society and asked them to decide who should get the five tickets. The head of the society, perhaps still annoyed at the note he received from Sister, said she could choose whomever she wished, he had no interest in being at this meeting. Sister told him that if he had no interest in the meeting he could leave. At that, he left. The remaining members, aware of his absence during stage preparations before the play, decided he would not receive one of the tickets. The choice of who should go to the drama was made, and the meeting came to an end.

The next day, the student head of the dramatic society went to the librarian's office. He was clearly angry, and demanded to know why he did not receive a ticket to the British Council drama. Sister reminded him that he had the possibility of picking himself at the meeting the previous day, but said he had no interest in making a choice. He then threatened her. She became frightened and tried to go out of the room. As she passed by him, he slapped her, knocking off her religious veil. She was a very traditional religious Sister and had never been seen without her veil. She was in tears and went immediately to her house. She then went to see the vice principal, the principal being away, and made a report. The student was called in and told to write his report. When the principal came back he called a meeting of the staff to decide what should be done.

Many on the staff wanted the student expelled. But Sister Illumina, a true Christian, said this would destroy his future. He was a young man and she did not want to take away the possibility of his having a profession when he left here. She suggested that he just be suspended for a time. The staff decided that he should be suspended for one year, and return the following year to begin his course again.

When word of this decision became known to the students, they began a boycott of classes. They demanded that their friend be reinstated, and that Sister be fired. The situation on the campus became very tense.

The Ministry of Education was informed, and they sent an official out to speak to the students. They refused to meet him. The students in turn informed the ward chairman of the ruling party, the United National Independence Party, or UNIP, as it was commonly called. Students had informed this chairman that Sister had shown disrespect for the Zambian people, the nation, and its leaders. At this time, Zambia was a one-party state, and the party and the government were one. Of course the charges against her were nonsense, and she asked me to accompany her to a meeting with the party officials. At this time she was no longer living on the campus for fear of the students and was commuting each day from a Dominican convent in a nearby town. I went with her to the meeting and it was obvious that they had no evidence against her.

The next day in the national newspaper, there was a letter from the student body demanding the expulsion of all religious from the faculty of this government college. Since I was the only other religious, it was clear this was referring to me. They also said they would boycott all religious services conducted by me. The first night after this boycott was announced, I walked up to the chapel as usual. I had to put up with a lot of heckling as I walked from my house to the chapel. I didn't know whether any students would even be there. I was surprised to find that there were three students there. I admired their courage in going against the boycott of their fellow students. What impressed me even more was the fact that of the students one was a non-Catholic, one was a catechumen preparing for baptism, and one was a Catholic. I thanked them for their courage and their loyalty, and went on to celebrate Mass with them. I don't think I will ever forget those three people.

The sad thing for me was the fact that there were two religious sisters who were students at the college, and who normally attended daily Mass. But even they observed the boycott. For the next week or so, I celebrated Mass each evening in my house, and a few students came down to attend.

The coming weeks were quite tense. The students finally resumed classes and sister continued her work in the library. The suspended student remained outside the college. I no longer felt very comfortable in the college, and was not sure of my relationship with the students. It was as if there were an argument in the family, and it was unresolved. However I did continue my lectures and my work as a chaplain. The students began coming to Mass again, and the tension very slowly subsided. I do recall occasionally making comments in the class about the students' behavior during the boycott. Apparently this was reported to the principal, and he interpreted it as my unwillingness to let the matter go. This seemed to have its own consequences, as subsequent events would prove.

One evening after Mass, probably in late December, the assistant to the bursar at the college was waiting for me. He was not a Catholic and had not attended the Mass. He said he had something important he wanted to share with me. So I invited him down to my house and invited him to sit down. He then told me that during that day some men had come up from Lusaka from the Office of the President to ask questions about me. I tried to make light of it by saying of what interest would I be to the president. But he told me this was quite serious. He said they wanted to know how well I related to the Zambians, did I respect them, was I helpful to them. They also wanted to know why I had left Nigeria and what brought me to Zambia. I personally was not around when they came, and so they could not question me directly. They had to be content with talking to the workers in the office, and perhaps to some of the students. Fortunately, the workers all considered me to be their friend. I related very well to all of them. And the students appreciated my lectures in mathematics and the help I had given them outside of class. They were always welcome at my house, and by now the tension of the Independence Day episode had diminished considerably. The only person who knew that I had been deported from Nigeria was the principal himself. I wondered why he should bring this up as an issue with the men from the Office of the President. I began to be a little anxious that perhaps, I might once again experience a rejection by the government. However nothing more came of this incident.

During the semester break in December, Sr. Illumina was told by superiors to resign from the college. I felt very bad about this as it seemed to imply that she was somehow at fault. Before she left her house, she asked me to be gentle with the student who had caused all this trouble. In January, the students would be on their practical teaching experiment. I would be moving around the Copperbelt visiting the various high schools supervising our student teachers. I went to one school in Luanshya, and found the troublesome student in the staff room since he was one of the student teachers. Apparently he had been readmitted to the college full-time and his suspension had been barely more than two months. Remembering sister's advice to me, I went up to him and greeted him politely. I had to accept that even though a great injustice had been done—he was back in the college and sister was not—I had to carry on with my work in order to somehow affect the way the future teachers would carry on with their profession. I felt I had the power to influence the way they formed their values, and the way they valued the teaching profession.

When I look back on this experience, I once again admire the ability of the African people to let go of any resentment that might arise from an unpleasant incident. I have to recognize that there are long-term negative feelings of one tribe for another, and this sometimes results in violence too horrible to speak of. But these antagonisms go back over a very long period of time and not the result of an individual conflict between two people. In the case that I just related, there was a personal conflict between myself and the students. When this was resolved, all the resentment and hard feeling seemed to disappear. For the remainder of the year I never felt that the students had any hard feelings toward me over that incident and, learning from them, I was also able to forget the past. It did not interfere with the growing close friendship that I found with many of the students. I was once again confronted with the ability of the African people to forgive, just as I found it after the Biafran war in Nigeria.

Now that all the drama of the 10th anniversary of independence was over and the college returned to its normal pace, I began to enjoy my work very much. We had a very good staff of teachers who got along very well together and this helped form us into a real community. The fact that we had only one class of students in the opening year also helped us to be a true community since we all knew one another.

The teaching practice was the most interesting exercise for me. I don't recall ever doing this in my years in Nigeria. It meant moving from one school to another and sitting in on the classes where our students were teaching. I think in the course of three months I visited almost every secondary school in the Copperbelt. I was very proud of most of our students in mathematics; they proved to be very adequate teachers, and often much more than adequate. It also gave me the opportunity to come to know them much better since I had to work with them on a one-to-one basis as we went over a review of the class that they had taught. I would also be involved with them on a one-to-one basis when they came to ask for assistance in preparing their class. It was a wonderful period in my work at the college.

Chapter Seven

SETTLING IN

Throughout my three years at the college, my work as a chaplain began to grow. I would organize retreats and find a very enthusiastic response from the students. I was also the chaplain for the Young Christian Student Movement. In fact the bishop asked me to be the diocesan chaplain for this movement. This enabled me to move from one institution of learning to another to meet with the various sections of the movement. I can honestly say that I met some extraordinary young men and women who would one day turn out to be true leaders in their communities.

When I look back on my experiences in Zambia there are two things that I particularly want to reflect on. One of these was the socialist system that prevailed in Zambia when I first arrived in 1974. This was combined with a one-party state. When Kenneth Kaunda became the first president in 1964 at independence, he realized that most of his people suffered economically during the period of colonialism. He thought that the only way forward was to nationalize the copper mines and use the assets of the mines to lift up the economic standard of his people.

At the time the copper mines were nationalized the world market price of copper was very high. This meant that the government would have large funds available to assist its people. Being a one-party state meant that the government would not have to waste a lot of time on debate in parliament. The party and its government were in full control.

There were two very constructive ways in which this socialism was used to benefit the people. All education and health care were completely free and available to all, rich and poor alike. In the field of education, this meant that children could have education to secondary school level free of charge. Even the uniforms were given out freely.

The textbooks that were used in the class were distributed to the children without any cost. They were collected at the end of each term so they could be used again and again. Even the notebooks, pens and pencils were given to the students. I can still remember students coming up to me asking me to sign the last page of their notebooks. I would check to see that all the pages were properly used and then would sign the last page. With this in hand they could go to the bookstore of the school and collect a new note-book. It seemed to me extraordinarily wasteful, but then I was coming from a capitalist system in the United States where everything was bought. I appreciated the fact that no child would be left behind because the parents did not have the money to send them to school.

There was another advantage in the socialist system of education.

Since everything was free, including transport, children could be sent to schools in various parts of the country, because their room and board would be paid. This enabled Kaunda to allow young students to intermingle with their peers from different parts of the country who spoke different languages and had a different cultural background. When a youngster finished primary school, he simply expressed his wish to go on to secondary school. Provided he had successfully completed all the requirements for a primary school certificate, he would move on to secondary school. However, the school would be chosen by the Ministry of Education. In this way the students were scattered all over the country, learning new languages and mixing with youngsters they might never have met otherwise. This helped to build a sense of unity in the country.

Whenever Kaunda spoke at a rally of the people, he would usually begin by singing a song about unity since he was a reasonably able guitar player. Then would follow a little dialogue between him and the people.

"One Zambia"

"One nation"

"One nation"

"One people"

"One people"

"One leader"

By repeating this over and over, it was brought home to the people that they were one nation and one people. This did a great deal to bring down the spirit of tribalism that existed in so many African countries.

I was quite impressed by the results of these efforts, and it was quite a contrast to what I had experienced in Nigeria.

Regarding health care, anyone could go to the hospital for attention, knowing that they would not be asked to pay any fees, and would be given any prescribed medicines free of charge. This was quite a contrast to my later experience in Zambia when I returned in 1990. By then the socialist system had been dismantled, and as a result healthcare had also declined. I think those early days of independence were kind of utopia. I am sure there were many things that were far from perfect, but the contrast with the colonial days was so great that the people could not see the flaws in the government.

I should mention here that even higher education was free. Students at the training college, where I was lecturing paid nothing for their training. In fact, they were even given a monthly allowance for their personal needs.

Another extraordinary thing about Kenneth Kaunda was his ability to introduce into the country an official philosophy. He called it "The Philosophy of Zambian Humanism". He even wrote two small books about it: Zambian Humanism Parts One and Two. To be confirmed in any civil service job you had to pass an exam on these two books. I was very impressed by this as I've never lived in a country where there was an official philosophy that was expressed in writing. I would even boast of this when visiting others. I felt Zambia could be rightly proud of such a philosophy. Zambian humanism was based on the gospel, though there was no explicit reference to any religion, since there were many non-Christians in the country. Kenneth Kaunda was the son of a Presbyterian minister and a very devout Christian. There was no doubt that his Christian beliefs influenced his thinking. I'm sure it was this that brought him to recognize the state of Biafra during the Nigerian Civil War.

He did not wish to see people suffer unnecessarily. He was also open to being a peacemaker where ever possible. He would not hesitate to travel to South Africa, which was under the apartheid regime, to meet with Prime Minister Vorster, when any other African leader would have considered this completely repugnant. I think Kaunda genuinely respected every human being, even when he radically disagreed with that person's thinking.

In those early years of independence I believed Kaunda was one of the outstanding statesmen in the world. Sadly, in later years he tended to be dictatorial. He returned the country to multiparty democracy and was voted out of office in 1991, after 27 years in power. He accepted defeat graciously.

When I first settled into the college routine, I was occupying a staff house and living alone. I had to do all the routine housework myself. I had to go shopping for my food, do the cooking, wash my clothes and iron them, and sweep and clean my house. I found it difficult fitting in all of this while at the same time carrying on a fairly heavy schedule of lectures. I asked one of the clerks in the office if he knew anyone in his family who was looking for a job. He told me that he had a cousin who would be happy to work for me. However, this cousin lived in Chipata, 400 hundred miles away. He said he would contact him and that I could expect them by the end of the month, about two weeks from then. So, I would have to continue being both housekeeper and lecturer.

One day during this two week period I was in my house preparing lunch, when there was a knock on my back door. I opened the door to find a young man there dressed rather shabbily and looking for work. He was able to speak and understand English and I felt rather sorry for him. I gave him some small tasks to do during the lunch break. He did rather well and I tried to pay him generously. In the afternoon, I was back at my lectures. The next day he arrived again and asked if there was some other work he could do. So I asked him to do some washing of the bed linens. While he was at this task there was a knock on the front door. It was an American Jesuit brother and an American Marianist brother. They were inviting me out to lunch.

At first I readily agreed since at this time I had no vehicle and rarely left the campus. It would have an opportunity to go into town and have a decent meal instead of my rather poorly cooked lunch. But then I remembered my young friend who had come to work. I didn't even know his name and I wasn't comfortable leaving him alone in the house while I was away. At the same time, feeling sorry for him, I didn't want to ask them to leave before he had done much work. I explained my dilemma to the two brothers. But they insisted that I come. I decided to go, and trust that the young man would be honest. I was away for about an hour and a half. When the brothers brought me back to the college, I found my friend was still there and still working. He not only completed the task I had asked him to do, but had found other things that needed to be done and had gone on with it. I was quite impressed. Nothing was missing. He could have walked off with anything, and I would have had no way of tracing him. I invited him to come back the next day during lunch. He even worked on the weekend.

I told him I would not be able to hire him full-time since I was expecting another worker to come. However, he could come each day until the end of the month, and if the other worker did not show up by then, I would give him a full-time job. By now I learned his name, which was Lewis Mutale. I think it was one of the greatest blessings of my first mission in Zambia to have encountered Lewis Mutale. At the end of the month, the worker I had been expecting did not show up and so I was able to offer Lewis a full-time job.

As I came to know Lewis I realized that he had a great deal of natural talent. Unfortunately he never advanced beyond the second grade of primary school. He was too old now to go back to school. He was married with two children both of them already more advanced in their education than he was. Lewis had never learned to read or write, and when I offered to teach him he accepted the offer and was very quick to learn. Just through my engaging in conversation with him I realized he was a remarkably mature man with a very good head for learning. Had his circumstances been different I used to think he could easily have gone on to the University.

He was also an incredibly honest person, and I never had to fear the loss of anything in the house. I never even locked any of the doors to cabinets and nothing was ever missing. I felt so confident with him that when I had to leave for a week or more to give a retreat I would invite him to move into my house with his family so that it would not be empty during my absence. Theft on the campus was not uncommon and, in fact, my own house had been broken into one night and a few things were stolen. Unfortunately, the items that were stolen belonged to the college and not to me. It was an experience that led me to invite Lewis and his family to live in my house whenever I was away. A small example of his honesty can be seen in the fact that certain foodstuffs in the refrigerator were allowed to spoil because I had not explicitly told him that he could have those particular items. He was a very cheerful person, very hard-working, and always reliable. He never failed to show up for work, and if he was sick, he would always send someone with a message to me.

He was living in a shanty compound about a 40 minute walk from the campus. I did go to visit him at his house from time to time so that I could come to know the circumstances in which he lived. Obviously he was living in poverty and I did all I could to raise the salary and to give him anything I did not need in order to improve his standard of living. In fact, I was paying him much more than most of the other staff members were paying their domestic workers. He quickly learned to prepare a very decent meal, was a very capable gardener, and a very thorough housekeeper. He did just about everything for me and saved me a lot of money by planting a very good vegetable garden. He also planted fruit trees so that in years to come whoever lived in this house would enjoy fresh fruit every day. He became my friend and coworker more than a servant. He made my three years of teaching a lot easier.

At the end of my first year in Zambia I received a surprising letter from my mother. She informed me that she and my father would like to come and visit me in Africa. I was surprised because I always thought of my mother as being very timid when it comes to visiting strange countries. However I encouraged them to make the arrangements and I suggested that they come around August when we would be having an academic break in the year. And so, in August of 1975, my mother and father flew from New York via London to Lusaka. I had arranged for one of our Jesuits in Lusaka to meet them at the airport, entertain them at the Jesuit novitiate, and then put them on the flight to Kitwe.

I was very nervous that day and kept checking on the flight to see exactly when it would arrive in Kitwe. About an hour and a half before the flight was due to arrive I received a message that the flight would be detoured to Ndola, a city about 45 miles from Kitwe. I was able to get in my car and travel to Ndola before their flight arrived. The passengers were assured that a bus would take them to Kitwe, but my mother was very nervous that I would somehow miss them and they would be stranded in a very strange country. When she deplaned, and saw me in the waiting area, she was overjoyed. I drove my mother and father to Kitwe and made them comfortable in my staff house at the college. I also arranged for one of the students, Francis Chaswe, to be a guest at my house that night and accompany my parents and myself during the whole time of their visit. In this way they would have the opportunity to meet a Zambian to point out and explain many of the sites we would pass during our touring of the country.

I was very happy to have my mother and father visiting with me in Africa. I had left for Africa some eight years before and although we had corresponded every week my parents had no idea of what it was to live in Africa. It meant a lot to me to have them come and share at least a little of my life in Africa. I knew it would have relieved a lot of the anxieties of my mother.

I remember taking them to a large parish in Kitwe to attend the Sunday Mass. They were delighted with the joy and enthusiasm with which the people celebrated Mass. It was such a contrast to the rather subdued participation at an American Mass. After Mass, the people gave my parents a very warm welcome. It has always impressed me how much it means to an African to meet relatives of one of their friends especially a missionary. We stayed in Kitwe about two or three days so they could meet my friends there and get to know something of the Copperbelt. We then drove down to Lusaka where they were able to stay in the home of an expatriate who was on leave. It was a beautiful home with a swimming pool and my parents were very comfortable. I stayed at the Jesuit novitiate.

I took them around the city of Lusaka, and also drove them out to Kasisi which is the origin of the diocese of Lusaka. In 1905 Father Torrend a Jesuit missionary first evangelized that part of Zambia. The old mission is there and also a very beautiful orphanage run by a group of Polish sisters. My parents were very impressed by the incredibly beautiful work of the sisters with these orphans. This was before the age of AIDS. Today the number of orphans is probably twice what it was when my parents visited and many of the orphans who are there come to them as a result of the deaths of parents to the terrible plague of AIDS.

From Lusaka we drove south, and stopped at Canisius High School, a Jesuit school that opened in 1949. It was one of the first high schools to accept blacks into the student body. The Jesuit community there was very welcoming, and once again my parents experienced the warmth of the African people. One of the Jesuit priests there took us on a tour of his parish which covered a rather large rural area. They had a chance to see a typical African village and to meet some of the simple but good people who work the land there. From Canisius High School we moved on to the town of Livingstone. We stayed at a moderate motel, and from there we were able to make several trips to Victoria Falls, only 5 or 6 miles away. They were, like most visitors to that extraordinary place, overwhelmed by the awesome site of this magnificent gift of nature.

We spent about three days in Livingstone and then started moving north again stopping in the town of Monze. When we arrived we stayed at a mission house near the Catholic hospital. The next day when we took a tour of the hospital the nurses gathered around to meet my parents and spontaneously sang them a song of welcome. Here was another example of the incredible humanity of the African people who so spontaneously reach out to people who would otherwise be total strangers to them.

The next day we drove to a bird sanctuary, about 40 miles into the bush. We stayed at a rest house there and spent two nights. I was amazed at how well my mother took to the rather primitive living conditions there. The only electricity was from a generator and that was turned off at nine o'clock. We had a chance to drive around the bird sanctuary to see herds of lechwes, a unique species of deer that is found only in this part of Zambia. Of course there were also many beautiful birds. It was a chance to experience the circumstances in which most Africans live, far away from the built-up cities with all the modern conveniences. From there we went back to Lusaka to celebrate my father's 70th birthday. We found a lovely Italian restaurant in Lusaka, and this celebration marked the end of my parents visit. They flew back to New York very happy to have experienced the sincere welcome of the African people and with a better knowledge of the world in which their son was working. I'm sure that it put to rest many of the anxieties that my parents would have had. They could begin to understand why I so much desired to remain in this part of the world.

After my parents left, Francis Chaswe, who accompanied my parents and myself during their visit, invited me to visit his village and his family during the next break between terms. And so, in December I arranged to drive to Mansa in Luapula province together with another student classmate of Francis by the name of Dennis Chengo. Francis would have gone on before us so that he would have time to give notice to his family and make the necessary arrangements for my accommodation. So, about a week after the term closed Denis and I began our journey by car to Mansa.

In the strange geography of Zambia, one has to pass through a section of the Democratic Republic of the Congo in order to get from the Copperbelt to Mansa. There is a small section of the Congo which juts into Zambia like a finger pushing through a balloon. This goes back to the days of the conference at Berlin at the end of the 19th century when the colonial powers carved up Africa among themselves. Since Belgium wanted a share in the copper mines that were largely situated in Zambia, at that time known as Northern Rhodesia, a small finger of Zambia became part of the Congo. Today, that section is known as the pedicle

We arrived at the borders of Zambia and Zaire, now known as the Democratic Republic of the Congo or DRC, and went through the immigration and customs formalities. Then we drove across a narrow strip of land about 40 miles wide. We were now in the Congo and had to drive on the right side of the road since in Zambia, a former British colony, we were driving on the left. When we reached the end of this short strip, we arrived at the Luapula River. This further divided Zambia from Zaire. The only way across is by means of a rather primitive ferry.

We managed to get our vehicle onboard and move to the other side of the river. We were now back in Zambia. We continued the short drive to the city of Mansa where Francis had agreed to meet us at the Catholic mission. He then introduced me to the priest at the mission and arranged for me to stay there during my short visit. We then moved off into the bush to the village of Francis's family. By now it was late afternoon and we had been traveling for quite awhile. I was very warmly welcomed as if I were now a member of the family for they knew the way I had accepted Francis into the life of my family.

One of the first gestures of hospitality was to prepare a warm bath for me. This was an entirely new experience. The house was simply a mud block building with no running water or electricity. They got a very large metal basin, such as you would see in movies of the old time west. They also had heated water on a wood fire, and so prepared the bath. The only privacy I had was that the tub was placed behind a sheet hanging from a clothesline. After the bath I felt refreshed and then sat around with the family while the meal was prepared. While waiting for the meal, Francis took me around the village to greet the various people living there. It was another lesson I had to learn. You do not invite someone to your house without introducing them to all around since the village is like an extended family.

When the meal was prepared we all sat around the low table and shared the meal in common, but only after a washbasin was passed around so that we could all wash our hands. Here was another ritual that is always observed in an African household, and it reminded me of the incident when Jesus sat down at the table without washing his hands. Now I understand why the people were so disturbed by this behavior. It went against the whole culture of the people. In all my time in Africa, especially in Zambia, I would try to remember not to begin a meal without having first washed my hands.

After dark, we would sit outside around the fire and share stories. Since I could not speak the vernacular language, I had to communicate through an interpreter. However the people were very patient with me and never gave the impression that they were disturbed by this. On the contrary they felt honored to have a college lecturer, a teacher of their son, come to visit them. Each night I was brought to the mission in Mansa where I was accommodated. During the two or three days that I stayed there, I visited a secondary school to meet a young woman, a student there, who was the fiancée of Francis. I was also asked to celebrate Mass for the people in his village using the vernacular language. There was no difficulty in learning to read the language without necessarily understanding it. Francis would be there to practice the pronunciation of the Mass with me, and also interpret my homily.

I was delighted with this opportunity to meet the family of one of my students and experience the environment in which he was brought up. We had now become integrated into each other's family. The visit of my family was the opportunity to visit his family, and it opened up a tradition for me which I treasured very much.

Chapter Eight

A DEATH AND AN ENDING

On looking back over the visit of my parents, I thank God that he sent them at that particular time. Two years later, my mother would have passed away. The story of her passing was a very sad moment in my life. I received a letter from my sister in January of 1977 informing me that my mother was diagnosed with ovarian cancer. They would be operating on her in mid-February. Another letter followed after the operation informing me that they discovered that the cancer was far more advanced than they had thought. In fact, the doctor said she had only four to six months to live. My sister advised me not to come home too quickly since my mother did not know the seriousness of her condition, and if I suddenly appeared she would know that something was very wrong. My three year contract would come to an end in June of that year. I should then come home as quickly as possible after the end of the contract.

Sometime in March, my sister wrote to tell me that my mother's condition was deteriorating more quickly than the doctors expected and that perhaps I should try to come home immediately if I wanted to see my mother alive. I applied for compassionate leave from the Ministry of Education, and quickly made arrangements for a flight to the United States.

When I arrived in the United States, I was picked up by my father and taken immediately to the hospital to see my mother. I was quite shocked at her condition. She had lost a great deal of weight and seem to have tubes inserted in various parts of her body. She was surprised but very happy to see me and I was very happy to see her, even in a weakened condition. I discovered from the family that they had not yet told her that she was dying. From the time I first heard that my mother was dying, I read several books on the subject, especially Elizabeth Kuebler Ross's "On Death and Dying".

I was convinced that my mother should be told the true condition she was in. I first consulted the chaplain of the hospital, a Lutheran woman minister who was very understanding. She also advised me to let my mother know her true condition. However, she advised that no one in the family do this, but that it be done by a close friend whom the family and my mother trusted. I discussed this with my father, sister and brother. My father and my brother readily agreed, but my sister did so only reluctantly. We decided to ask an elderly doctor on the staff of the hospital who was well known to both my family and myself. He had been the one who first diagnosed the cancer in my mother. We agreed on a time when I, my father, my sister, and my brother could be there, and the doctor was invited to come down and speak to my mother in our presence. He had a most gentle way of telling her that medically there was nothing more that could be done, and that the prognosis was not very good. She obviously understood the implications of what he was saying. By this time we were all in tears, and we all went up and embraced our mother.

The chaplain had advised that we only stay a short time after breaking the news to my mother. She would need time to digest this. I asked the chaplain of the hospital to check on my mother from time to time during the evening and if she seemed to be too disturbed that I should be called immediately and I would go down and keep her company.

The next day I asked the chaplain how the evening went. She said my mother wept for awhile, and then became calm and had a restful night. Once the news was broken, my mother could talk about her funeral, and she seemed to be at peace. Easter was approaching, and on Holy Saturday morning she seemed well enough to be allowed to go home. So we took her home, and on Easter Sunday morning I was able to celebrate Mass with the family at home in the presence of my mother. This was a very consoling moment, and it was appropriate that it occurred on Easter Sunday morning when we celebrate the hope of life after death. She seemed to be doing well, and my month of compassionate leave was coming to an end.

The doctors said they had no idea how long this remission would last. I spoke honestly with my mother about my concern, but she said she would be all right and that I should return to my work. This was very typical of my mother and my father who never made me feel as if I was somehow neglecting them and they made no demands on me.

I valued this kind of love very much. I gave my mother the sacrament of anointing and gave her Holy Communion on the day before I would return to Africa. I left her at peace.

Just two weeks after I left my mother, my fellow Jesuit who lived in our community in Kitwe drove out to the college to my house. He called me aside, and told me that he received a phone call from my sister saying that my mother had just passed away. I told them I would be coming to their house in a short time to make a telephone call to New York, as I had no telephone at the college. I then informed my friend and worker, Lewis Mutale, and one of my students, John Sensele, who was staying with me for a few days during our term break. They sat with me in silence for a while and then I told them I wanted to be alone in my room while I celebrated Mass for my mother.

I did this, and then I told them I would drive down to the Jesuit residence to make a phone call to my father. John Sensele insisted on accompanying me, as he did not want me to be alone at this time. We said nothing on the short twenty minute drive to town. I did phone my father and also spoke to my sister and brother. It was a very difficult moment in my life. When I returned to my house on the college campus, John and Lewis continued to sit with me in silence. I told Lewis that he could go home after he had prepared a simple meal. The next day I noticed that the picture of my mother and father that I kept in my sitting room seemed to have disappeared.

I asked Lewis about this, and he told me he had put it away so that I would not be sad. When I look back over these days, I am deeply touched by the extraordinary human sympathy and affection shown me by these two men. I wonder if any family members could have done any more. I could not return for the funeral. However, my provincial Father Eamon Taylor celebrated the funeral Mass in my place and was accompanied by about 14 other Jesuits. I was told he preached a very moving sermon and I was very grateful to be a Jesuit where my brothers would always be available when I needed them most. The family was very grateful to the Jesuits for the consolation they offered at this very difficult time.

My contract came to an end at the beginning of July and I returned to the United States where I could spend the summer months with my father to help him to overcome the terrible grief he experienced at the loss of my mother. My parents were always very close and never did anything separated from one another. I've often used the following story in my homilies as an example of their love that I discovered at this time. One day when I was visiting my mother in the hospital, she only spoke about her concern for my father. "His health is not the best and he is not used to house cleaning or shopping. I worry about how he is going to manage." At the same time, whenever I was with my father his only concern was for my mother. "What can I do to make your mother a bit happier to-day?" Neither of them showed any concern for their own situation, but was only concerned about the other. I think that is what love is all about. As I was leaving my father at the end of the summer, he saw me off at the airport. As he said goodbye, he hugged me and said: "If anything happens to me when you are away, you do not have to come back. Just continue with your work, and remember me at Mass." Here again I witnessed the same unclinging love that I spoke about above.

Let me return to life in Zambia during those years that I was teaching in Kitwe. The economic situation in Zambia was very difficult during those years 1974 to 1977. The main reasons for this difficulty were the problems in our neighboring countries. Our biggest problem was caused by the closure of the border to the south. Rhodesia, under the rule of Ian Smith, had unilaterally declared itself independent of Britain. Since this was considered an illegal action by the international community, no one recognized this so-called new independent country.

Kenneth Kaunda, the first president of Zambia, closed the borders between Zambia and Rhodesia. This meant that Zambia lost her principal means of exporting her goods and receiving her imports since the rail link going south to the ports of South Africa was now closed. Zambia is a landlocked country and depends on peace in its neighboring countries for its exports and imports.

It was equally difficult to export through Mozambique because it was in the midst of a civil war. The same was true on the west with the country of Angola. So Zambia could not move its goods east, south or west. The only way that Zambia could receive its imports was by road through Dar Es Salaam. This was very inefficient since it required a large amount of fuel and the trucks could not carry as much as the train. In emergencies we had to rely on airfreight which was also very expensive. As a result of all this, there were many shortages in the shops and life could be very difficult. I can remember having to travel great distances to find some of the essentials of daily life.

Another problem faced by Zambia in those days were the occasional raids of the Rhodesian Air Force on the military bases of one of the freedom movements that was housed in Zambia. This was the Zimbabwe African

People's Union headed by Joshua Nkomo. It was humiliating and sad for Zambia as it was totally incapable of stopping these raids. It is said that the Rhodesian Air Force would communicate with the airport at Lusaka as it was entering Zambian air space to notify them that all planes should be kept on the ground. And when they were leaving, they would radio that their work was finished and the airport was free to be open. When these raids would occur, all white people were considered suspect, as they might be informants for the Smith regime. Then it was better to keep out of town and maintain a low profile. I never felt endangered as I knew the affection of the Zambian people and I was sure that I would never be suspected of such treachery.

The economic hardships were eased by the completion of the Zambia Tanzania Railway. This was a project undertaken by the Chinese government and they completed it in record time. The railway ran from Kpiri Mposhi, about midway between Lusaka and Kitwe, and the Tanzanian port of Dar Es Salaam. This railway was completed around 1975. Any objective person would have to admit that the Chinese did a great deal to assist Zambia in a moment of need.

The Chinese workers also had a reputation of being highly disciplined. They did not mingle much with the Zambian people and they were kept under close guard by their own government which probably feared defections. Their passports were taken from them when they arrived in Zambia and were only given back when they were leaving. The railway now made it possible for Zambia to export her copper and import her various needs. The railway was a great blessing for the country, and, as a result, Zambia has always felt a special bond with China.

Among the many happy memories of those years in Kitwe was the experience of my Jesuit community, especially in my last year there in 1976/77. Although I continued to live at the college so that I could be more available to the students, I did join the newly formed Jesuit community on the weekends. In my last year at the college, the community consisted of Fr. Peter Hannan, an Irish Jesuit, who was lecturing at the Kitwe Teacher Training College, Fr. Jim McGloin, an American Jesuit, who was teaching science at Kitwe Boys' School, a government secondary school, and myself. This was one of the happiest communities in which I have ever lived. We were only three. But we seemed to relate to one another very easily despite the fact that we were three totally different personalities. I never experienced any tension in this community and I genuinely looked forward each weekend to being there. We not only relaxed together, shared experiences of the week, occasionally went to a movie, but also prayed together. We even had the occasional day of recollection together. One of the hardest things about leaving Kitwe was leaving this community. As I look back after many years of various communities in which I have lived, I still recall this particular experience with special joy.

There is one special experience I had in this community which I will always treasure. It was the monthly meetings of the Kitwe Clergy Fellowship. This was usually held at the residence of the pastor of the Anglican Church. It was an attempt to build goodwill between the ministers of different churches. I always had an interest in ecumenism, and this was a concrete way of expressing that interest. The sad thing for me was the fact that Jim and I, both teachers, were the only Catholic priests present. No parish priest was ever present, and I thought this was a sad reflection of how little ecumenism meant to most Catholic priests.

Now I must take up the rather sad story of the end of my contract at the Copperbelt Teacher Training College. As I've mentioned earlier, I had caused a certain amount of unrest in the college because of the sad incidents surrounding the 10th anniversary Independence Day celebrations. Although that problem was resolved, it seemed in the mind of some that my presence was not helpful to the college. In my second year there I received a letter from the Ministry of Education reprimanding me for behavior that was not constructive. The letter informed me that I would be put on probation for six months and that if my attitude did not change, further action would follow. I approached the principal about this letter since I presumed that the information concerning myself was sent to the Ministry by him. He said I understood what the matter was all about and would say nothing further. I wrote a letter to the Ministry of Education in reply, asking for clarification as it was difficult to know what I was to do to successfully prove myself a useful member of the faculty.

There was no reply to my letter. So I simply continued doing exactly what I had been doing for the last year and a half. I was getting along very well with the students, the results of examinations were encouraging, and even my work as the chaplain was growing. I personally experienced no further tension in my relations with students. So I suspect that the problem was my relationship with the administration. In any case I just continued as I was since I'd no idea in what way I was supposed to change. The six months past, and nothing further happened. However, that letter of reprimand was in my confidential file and would remain there.

About five months before the end of my contract, the principal asked me whether I intended to renew my contract. I consulted my superiors in New York and they agreed to allow me to renew the contract for the sake of the continuity of my work. The principal seemed pleased with this decision of my superiors, and encouraged me to apply for renewing the contract. And so I made frequent trips from Kitwe to Lusaka to the Ministry of Education headquarters. It took several trips before I received a final answer from them. When the answer finally came, it was in the negative.

Along with the letter denying my renewal was a report on my performance for the past three years. It seemed to be very positive. I was given full marks for competence in teaching, for my professional qualifications, and only a slightly less grade for my general contribution to the college. I said to the person who gave me this, that if I was as good as his report said, then why was I not given a renewal of contract. He claimed it was because they wanted to Zambianise the position. I would've been happy if this were true, but in fact they hired an Asian to replace me. I believe the real reason was that the principal did not really want me there, despite his protestations that he wanted me to remain on the staff. This was a painful thing for me, for I felt a sense of rejection.I knew the students appreciated my lectures very much and also the many other things I did for them as a staff member and as a chaplain. In fact, when some of them realized that I would not be coming back to the college they were very sad and expressed this to me many times. I have kept in touch with some of the students for many years right up to the present.

At the college I was not sure of where I would be going the following year. My superiors had suggested that I return to West Africa. Since I was still barred from entering Nigeria, I was told to look for a place in Ghana. There was already one Jesuit in Ghana who had been there for about a year lecturing at the University of Ghana in Accra. I started writing to him immediately, and he began making inquiries as to where I might be able to find a position. All during the three months leave in the United States, I awaited some positive reply from him. Sadly he was not able to make any arrangement in time for me to go immediately there after my leave. I asked my superiors if I could return to Zambia since I really had no desire to remain in the United States. My provincial agreed, and I booked my ticket to Lusaka. I was warmly welcomed by the Jesuits there and one of my first thoughts was to see the provincial. He suggested that I spend a year at Canisius high school, a Jesuit secondary school in the southern part of Zambia. I was happy enough with this assignment.

It was 10 years since I last taught in a secondary school and that was my first assignment in Lagos teaching at a Catholic girls secondary school. Now here I was in a secondary school run by the Jesuits in a different country and in a rural area. I visited the school before since I stayed there with my parents when they were visiting me two years previously. It is about 8 miles off the main road that connected Lusaka to Livingstone. It was only a rough dirt road that led into the school.

At that time the school was largely a boarding school with about 700 boys boarding there. It was considered one of the elite government schools in the country and most of the students were very bright. Several of Kenneth Kaunda's own sons had gone to school there, as had many of the leading politicians of the time.

I was assigned to teach English to the first-year students, and religion to the second-year students. This assignment was a temporary one since we were in the final months of the academic year. It was the end of September and the academic year would end the beginning of December. I had never taught English or religion before, and so it was a challenge to me, but my consolation was in getting to know the students in my class. At the beginning of the new academic year in January, I was asked to teach mathematics to the fourth and fifth year students, equivalent in the American system of grades 11 and 12. Since the students were very bright this was to be a real challenge for me, but a challenge I looked forward to. However since I taught mathematics at a much higher level at the teacher training college it would not be difficult as far as the content went. The challenge probably would be in the methodology and holding the attention of less mature students. When I actually went into the classroom I found that this was no problem at all as the students were very eager to learn. I also found an empty room near the chapel and cleaned it up in order to make it into an office. In this way I could go over to the office every night and be available to the students while they were doing their studies in the classrooms.

A very great consolation for me during this year was the presence of Father Joe Hayes. He had just been assigned to the school, having just completed his tertianship. He was an Irish Jesuit who is now a member of the Zambia/Malawi province. He was named to be the chaplain of the school and also taught religion. We worked together very well in trying to deepen the faith life of the Catholic students. Joe is very open to new ideas and I was very anxious to be a bit creative in our approach to the liturgy. We even redesigned the sanctuary of the chapel in order to bring the liturgy closer to the students. That year the students would be in school for holy week. This gave us a wonderful opportunity to make the beautiful ceremonies of holy week relevant and unforgettable to the students. I think we succeeded quite well, and even the headmaster commented on this.

Another great consolation was the presence on the staff of John Sensele, one of my old students from the teacher training college who was then on the staff of the secondary school. He was a teacher of science, and I was happy to have him as a companion on the teaching staff. Since we had known each other quite well at the college, I visited his house quite often and we regularly went for walks on a Sunday afternoon which drew us even closer together. It was during the year that he introduced me to Christine, a young teacher in the neighboring primary school. He told me it was his intention to marry Christine. At first I had my doubts since they were of very different tribes, he being a Bemba, she, a Lozi.

I also wondered whether the relationship grew because they were both outside of their tribal areas and were probably feeling lonely. We had some frank talks about this and at times there were misunderstandings. I think I came to realize that the relation was a sincere one, and my mind was at ease. Since Christine was a Catholic, and John had not been baptized nor brought up in any specific church that I was aware of, he asked me if I would instruct him in the Catholic faith. Being convinced that this desire was sincere, I began his instructions and found him a very quick learner. He also asked me if I would be the priest who celebrated the nuptial Mass.

And so it was that at the end of July 1978 I baptized John in the community Chapel of the Jesuit residence. Present on the occasion were a number the Jesuits in the community as well as his fiancée. On the 16th of August of that same year, I presided at the wedding of John and Christine in the parish church of the Chikuni mission. It was a very happy occasion and I was very delighted to share in two important events in this young Zambian's life who had now become a friend.

A few weeks later John and I set out on a tour of the country since this would be my last chance to see something of Zambia. We took a train to Lusaka where we borrowed a vehicle from the Jesuit province.

We then set out, moving East about 450 miles to the city of Chipata, the capital of the Eastern province. We stayed overnight there in a Catholic school, and then moved on to the city of Lundazi where one of my former students was now a teacher, and then we moved on to the city of Chama where another former student was teaching. He was gracious enough to accommodate us in his home. Then we had to make a difficult decision as the road to the north was just a bush path. The only alternative was to return almost all the way to Lusaka and then head north from there.

That was not a very attractive proposition. After inquiring among the local people whether they thought we could make it with the old vehicle I was driving, we took our courage in our hands and set out. The road was just a dirt track through the forest that separated Zambia from Malawi. It could be quite rough at times as there were large elephant footprints in the ground that were similar to potholes. Fortunately this was the dry season of the year and we didn't have to worry about rain. However we did have to worry about sandy patches in which we could easily have gotten stuck. There was obviously no traffic on the road, and if there were I don't know how we would pass them or allow them to pass us.

We hardly ever passed any human habitation, and it could have been a bit frightening. If we had a difficulty on the road, I wondered how anyone would have found us. We put our trust in the Lord, and most consolingly we had companionship to help us forget the difficulties we might have encountered. I have often used this experience to teach others of the value of friendship. True friendship helps one to get beyond all difficulties. After several hours of driving on this difficult road, not even sure if we were going along the right way as we did pass several forks in the path, we finally reached a checkpoint with a bamboo rod across the road. It was set up to help control the tsetse fly infestation. I greeted the officer who sprayed under the car, and then asked him if he could find some water for me to drink.

He sent a young girl into the village who brought me a glass of water. After hours of a long and tiring journey I eagerly drank the water. My friend John also shared some of the water. We then continued on our journey and arrived in the town of Isoka. Not far from Isoka was the town of Chinsali, where another former student was teaching. From Chinsali we moved on to Kasama, where Sr. Illumina was now teaching. She was the sister who had been on staff with me at the teacher training college during all the unfortunate incidents of the 10th Independence Day celebration. It was good to see her again and to discover that she had settled in well as a teacher in a government secondary school along with several other Dominican sisters. We stayed that night at the Cathedral residence and spent the next day in the city of Kasama. The following day we started our journey back to Lusaka.

On the way back we began to develop car problems. The engine was overheating. At one point we pulled the car over to the side of the road, and I opened the bonnet (hood) of the car. I took out a handkerchief and tried to slowly open the cap of the radiator. It was a very foolish thing to do, as the cap flew out of my hand and I was covered in hot steam. I screamed in pain and John came running to help me. I was really in agony as I had been wearing only a T-shirt over my upper body. I tore off the T-shirt and tried to cool down until the pain subsided a bit. I was in no condition to drive. Fortunately down at the high school I had been teaching John how to drive though he had not yet passed his driving test. However he took over the wheel and we drove safely on to Serenje where we found a hospital. They gave me some pain killers and covered the extensive burns with some salve.

After a night's rest I was able to resume the driving on the next morning. We made it back to Lusaka where I was given further treatment and we were able to make our way back to Chikuni. It was good to be back.

Despite the pain of the last two days, I was very happy to have made the trip in the company of a good friend which gave me the opportunity of seeing a lot more of Zambia than I'd seen before. About two weeks after we returned I began to feel very sick. The color of my urine was turning to deep brown. I finally felt so sick that I went to the hospital in Monze. Sister Dr. Lucy O'Brien, a Missionary Sister of the Holy Rosary, a wonderful religious as well as a competent doctor, examined me and did some blood tests and immediately sent me to bed. She told me I was suffering from hepatitis and that I would not be able to leave the hospital for several weeks. In those days the only remedy for hepatitis was complete bed rest and careful control of the diet. I sent word back to Canisius and the superior came to see me the next day. I also communicated with Ghana to tell them that I would not be able to come by the end of September as I had originally planned.

And so I had to spend a month in bed during which I was able to do great deal of reading. I had to get used to a very boring diet as I was not allowed to have anything fried or cooked with oil. I could not eat groundnuts, eggs, beef, nor could I drink anything alcoholic. I would have to maintain this kind of a diet for several more months and would have to avoid alcohol for at least a year. At the end of the month of bed rest I was allowed to get up and take gentle walks around the grounds, and live a fairly normal life. I was not allowed to teach and was told to get plenty of sleep. By early December I was becoming very restless.

Fortunately my blood levels were back to normal, and so I could be considered cured of the hepatitis. Sr. O'Brien wanted me to return to the United States for further recuperation, but at this point I was anxious to move on to Ghana. And so I made arrangements for a flight to London and then on to Accra, Ghana.

Chapter Nine

A NEW BEGINNING FOR ME AND FOR GHANA

It was not easy leaving Zambia, as I really found a home there and had made many dear friends. I owed the people of Zambia, and especially the Jesuits of Zambia, a great debt of gratitude. They took me in when I thought I had no future in Africa after my expulsion from Nigeria.

As time would tell, this would not be the last time that Zambia would take me in when I thought my life in Africa was over. I had four very happy years there, and it would not be easy trying to make a new home in an entirely new country.

I already suffered the great pains of separation from Nigeria, and now I was going through the same emotional drama again. I hoped they would all end with Ghana. Ghana would be my third country in which I would have to find a home, build new relationships, and discover another family. And so on the sixth of December, I made my tearful farewell and flew off to London on my way to Ghana. The reason for stopping in London was to order a car since I was told by my fellow Jesuit in Ghana that it would be difficult to get one in Ghana, and a vehicle would be essential for my work.

I landed in Accra on an early December morning in 1978 just before Christmas. Pat Ryan, a fellow Jesuit of the New York province, was at the airport to give me a very warm welcome. At that time, he was a lecturer at the University of Ghana in Legon, a suburb of Accra not far from the airport. I stayed with him for a day or so, and he was able to fill me in on what I might expect in my new life in this country. He then drove me the 80 miles west to the city of Cape Coast. Cape Coast is a very old town and is home to some of the leading academic institutions of the country. It had the oldest secondary schools in Ghana. Wesley Girls, a Methodist secondary school for girls, was about 140 years old. Mfantsipim was a Methodist secondary school for boys, and it was over a hundred years old. Next in age was Adisadel secondary school for boys founded by the Anglican Church. The youngest of the elite secondary schools in Cape Coast was St. Augustine's College, a secondary school for boys founded by the Catholic Church about 48 years before I got there. This would be my home for the next four years. The chaplain was a Ghanaian diocesan priest by the name of Gabriel Mensah. On the staff of the school there were several Brothers of the Holy Cross who were also from America.

By the time I arrived in late December, the students had all gone home for the Christmas holidays. I was introduced to the headmaster and his deputy as well as to the brothers of the Holy Cross and the chaplain. The headmaster gave me a very warm welcome, by giving me a bear hug and telling me how glad he was to see me. I knew immediately that the Ghanaians were outgoing, affectionate, and welcoming people. I was shown the staff house that I would be living in, which was the house adjoining that of the chaplain. However, Pat Ryan was not happy with the condition of the house. I could understand this, as the mosquito netting on the windows was all torn, and the lock on the door was not working correctly, but I felt embarrassed to hear him reprimanding the headmaster for wanting to put me in a house that was not properly prepared. I said I would stay with the Holy Cross brothers while the repairs were being made. With that, I was given a room at the brothers and Pat took his leave. My new life in Ghana had begun.

The headmaster informed me the next day that I would be taking the fourth form and upper six classes in chemistry. There were two sections in the fourth form science classes and there was only one upper six science class. In the British system, the fourth form is the equivalent of grade 11 in the United States. The upper sixth form has its name from the fact that there were two years to the sixth form in the British educational system. It is called the advanced level, and is the equivalent of a bit more than the first-year university in the United States. I faced two immediate problems when the students returned. First of all, the sixth form students at St. Augustine's were extremely intelligent as it was a highly selective school. When they returned in January they would be preparing for their final exams in June. They would expect me to review the entire sixth form chemistry syllabus. The second problem was the fact that I had not been teaching chemistry for at least five years: the year of exile in London plus the four years in Zambia where I taught mathematics. I borrowed a chemistry book from the head of the science department and immediately went to work refreshing my mind on this subject. This would occupy my entire holiday.

When the students returned in early January I was both anxious and nervous about my first encounter with them. I was in a new country and I had not met any of the students before. My very first class was a chemistry class with a form four science group. They had heard that there was a new chemistry teacher and they were very anxious to meet me as they had not had any consistent chemistry teaching. They had the reputation of being a very intelligent class and very eager to learn.

When I reached the door of the classroom, I discovered that the room had not been swept. Without walking in the classroom, I announced that it is not my custom to teach in the midst of filth. I informed them that I would be in the staff room and that when the room was clean they could come and get me. I then walked off. This undoubtedly left them very puzzled and wondering what kind of the teacher they were getting. However they did immediately start cleaning the room and within 10 minutes came to the staff room to tell me that they were ready to begin.

I was in the custom of beginning all classes with a prayer since this was a Catholic school. However I would not begin the prayer until there was complete order in the classroom. I waited until there was complete silence, till all the students were standing straight, and showed they were ready to begin to pray. We finally said the prayer and the class began.

From that point on the classes went very well, and I soon had the reputation of being a very strict disciplinarian. I think this brought respect as well as improved the atmosphere of learning in the classroom. By the time I met the second section of the form four science group I had far less difficulty in finding the atmosphere that I desired in the classroom.

These two form four classes were composed of quite intelligent young men, and we got along famously together. I thoroughly enjoyed their company and their response to my teaching, and the results were obvious at the end of the school year. When I met the upper sixth form, I was challenged by a very gifted class. The sixth form science class at St. Augustine's had a reputation of being one of the best in the country. I knew I would have to be at my best to satisfy all their needs.

They asked very challenging questions and would not be put off by any kind of bluffing in the answers. I soon found that honesty was the best policy, and when I didn't know the answer to a question I would admit as much, and tell them I would bring them the correct answer the next day. In fact, we got along quite well and some of the students in the class are my friends even to this day. Their results at the end of the year in the A-Level examinations were quite impressive.

I was also allowed to take the sixth form students in classes known as General Paper. The syllabus for this paper was of a very general knowledge, including current events, logic, and religion. I thoroughly enjoyed this class as it gave me a chance to discuss very current issues with a very intelligent group of students. It didn't take me long to feel quite at home at St. Augustine's, and to find that I had fallen into a work that was thoroughly satisfying. It was an altogether different atmosphere from that in the college in Zambia, and I quickly felt very comfortable here. Living on the campus as I did, and the school being a boarding school with about a thousand boarders, I had frequent visitors from the student body to my house, and friendship grew quickly.

When I arrived in Cape Coast I was determined to live off my salary and not to expect anything from the province office in New York. I knew this would be difficult since I was only being paid a local salary and not the salary of an expatriate teacher. I also wanted to be able to save from my salary enough money to pay for my home leave in two years time. Because of this, I could not afford to hire anyone to work for me. This meant I would have to do my own shopping in the marketplace, prepare my own food, wash my own clothes, and clean my house. What made this a bit difficult was the fact that I did not have a car, since the one I had ordered in London had not yet arrived. And so every Saturday morning, after I moved out from the Brothers residence to my own staff house, I would walk to the marketplace about a 45 minute jaunt. Then I would buy the cheapest food available, which was usually vegetables, beans, and garri. Garri was the basic foodstuff of the poor, consisting of milled dried cassava which was lightly roasted. It was prepared by simply adding hot water and mixing it thoroughly with a wooden spoon to make a kind of cornmeal. This was usually eaten with some soup, prepared by boiling together all the vegetables and beans I had bought in the market together with some palm oil. I would make a big pot of this mixture every Saturday, and it would last me for the week.

My growing sense of contentment was strengthened on Saturday mornings when some of the young lads would come to my house to help me with the housework and laundry. I was very grateful for this and I considered it a sign of growing friendship. As they worked with me we were able to chat together and share more of our life experiences. In this way I came to know them on a more personal level, and they, in turn, were getting to know me. After my first year, some of the students who had left the school on completing their studies would occasionally come by my house when they happen to be in the neighborhood of Cape Coast. If they were staying overnight and had no other accommodation I would offer them a bed in my house. The fact that they were comfortable staying there, even sharing the same room, was proof that I had become a member of their family.

Those years at St. Augustine's were some of the happiest in my life, even though I probably have never lived a poorer or simpler lifestyle. The only other Jesuit in the country was Fr. Pat Ryan, who, as I said, was lecturing at the University of Legon in Accra. I would travel the 80 miles or so to Accra once a month on Saturday so that we could have lunch together and share our experiences. Pat would travel to Cape Coast two weeks later on Saturday so that we would be able to share time together at my house. Since I knew that he would not be able to eat the rather primitive diet that I lived on, I would save my money and take him out to a restaurant where we did have a decent meal. We changed this pattern after a few months so that we would not have to drive quite so far. We agreed to meet every other Saturday in the town of Winneba, which was about halfway between Accra and Cape Coast. This gave us more time together since we had less distance to travel back to our respective homes.

As assistant chaplain at St. Augustine's, with the permission of Fr. Mensah the chaplain, I started organizing a daily evening Mass. Father Mensah would celebrate a morning Mass each day before breakfast and I would celebrate a Mass each evening immediately after supper. I was given the use of an empty classroom as a small chapel and each evening the liturgy would attract 15 or 20 young men. It was a relaxed atmosphere, yet very reverent, and it seemed to make a deep impression on the students. Some of those regular attendees at Mass became very good friends. It also gave me an opportunity to share something of my faith with the young students.

In addition to my teaching at St. Augustine's, I was also asked if I would help out at St. Theresa's minor seminary in Amisano. They needed someone to help with the teaching of physics and chemistry, and I somehow managed to squeeze these periods into my busy week.

One of the greatest blessings that came from my time at the seminary was my first encounter with James Addo Nkum. At that time he would have been in form three, and he expressed an interest in the Society of Jesus. As a Jesuit, I was delighted to hear of this interest and encouraged him to be meeting me once a month so that we could discern together whether this was indeed God's will for him. From that first meeting in 1978 until the present (2008) we have remained friends, and I will say more about this later. It was from Addo-Nkum that I learned a lot about friendship.

On Monday morning the 4th of June 1979, while we were having a staff meeting, Jerry John Rawlings overthrew the military government of General Akuffo and installed himself as the head of government. He was only a Flight Lieutenant in the Ghana Air Force, and he had attempted to overthrow the government the previous May. That first attempt failed and he was put on trial for treason. He was imprisoned but somehow from the prison he managed to organize the second attempt. He was freed from the prison by some of the junior officers who took over the radio station and the seat of government. It was my first experience of living through a military coup, and, I must admit, that I was hardly aware that anything had happened. Cape Coast is about 80 miles from Accra and so our only knowledge of the coup was from the announcement on the radio. There was a certain amount of shooting involved and I cannot recall how many were killed in the attempt. Within a day Rawlings had full control of the country. His aim, he claimed, was only to clean up the corruption in the Army before the scheduled elections for return to civilian rule in September. He said he had no intention of putting off those elections but intended to use the four months or so at hand to purify the Armed Forces of all corrupt elements. One of his first orders of business was the execution of all previous military heads of state.

I remember that I visited the minor seminary at Amisano on the morning of the executions. I still recall at how shocked I was by the young seminarians rejoicing in the death of their previous military rulers. What shocked me then, and what has struck me so much in subsequent years, was how lightly we take the teachings of Jesus in the Gospels. All his teaching about loving your enemies certainly did not seem to have any practical application in this situation. Perhaps this was the beginning of my reflections on how we as priests, and I in particular, have failed to communicate to those to whom we preach the deeper meaning of the teachings of Jesus and how these teachings should affect our everyday lives. This reflection will come up on many occasions in future pages of this writing.

Jerry Rawlings' coup seemed to have little effect on the day-to-day life at St. Augustine's College. Classes continued as usual and all the extracurricular

activities functioned normally. I got the impression that coups occur only in
the capital cities of countries, and only in a few selective places of the capital
city. Unless there is a curfew imposed in the first days after the coup, you
would hardly know anything had happened. At least this was true of this first
Rawlings coup. His second coup would leave much deeper impressions.

Jerry Rawlings kept to his promise of returning the country to civilian
rule. After he had executed the previous heads of state and demoted many
of the senior officers, or even threw them out of the Army, he allowed
the organization of the elections to go ahead. They had actually been
in preparation for almost a year, and so there were clearly identified
candidates for president as well as organized political parties. He allowed
the campaigning to go on under his military rule until in the third week
of September elections took place. Hilla Limann won the election, and
Rawlings turned over authority to him. And so Ghana had its first civilian
president in a long time, and the Army had been purged of some of its
worst elements. There was hope for stability for the country.

One of the big events of 1980 occurred in March of that year when St.
Augustine's celebrated its golden jubilee of the school. It was founded and
opened its first class in 1930, and was the oldest Catholic boys secondary
school in the country. It wasn't a good time for celebrating since the country
was going through a difficult economic period. There were many shortages
in the country, including such common items as candles. This turned out
to be tragically significant.

One of the big items in any celebration in Ghana was what was called
"a picnic". A picnic, in this context, was a march to the town, usually
accompanied by a band. The school wanted a picnic to start at about 3
p.m., but many of the old boys, as the alumni were called, who wanted to
come to begin the celebration would have had to travel after work from
Accra. So it was agreed that the picnic would begin around 5:30 in the
evening. Since the march would probably take several hours, it would be
dark before they returned to the school.

As they began their march into the town a car passed them in the
opposite direction. The boys waved frantically at the car to indicate that it
should slow down since the road was narrow and the parade was quite long.
As the car passed along the way some of the boys slapped on the bonnet or
hood of the car to make clear to the driver that they wanted him to slow
down. Nothing happened. The car moved on, and the parade continued.
On the way back, only about a kilometer from the school, it was now dark.
A car was coming against them with its headlights on.

Some of the boys moved out into the road waving frantically for the car to slow down, since the car was moving at a good speed. However, instead of slowing down the driver speeded up. Boys quickly moved back into line, but the car swerved into the line of boys killing one instantly. Two of the boys were seriously injured. Since the hospital was nearby they were taken there. Some of the boys had noted the license plate of the car, and when the report was made to the police they gave this information to them. The driver was soon found. He was returning from a funeral where he undoubtedly had a good bit of alcohol to drink. The two seriously injured boys were in a coma. They were eventually transferred to Accra to the military hospital where they could be given better treatment. A few days later one of them died.

Since this picnic was the opening of the golden jubilee celebration, it was difficult to go on with any enthusiasm. But since the preparations had been made over a long period, and since many of the old boys had come for the celebration, we decided to carry on with the program but in a more subdued way. There was obviously a great deal of anger among the students since they had lost two of their friends.

The funeral was held shortly after the celebrations. The headmaster approached me and asked me if I would speak to the boys before the actual funeral. He felt that they were so angry that they may do something foolish at the funeral. I had to address the entire student body and it wasn't easy. I knew they respected me very much and would listen to what I had to say. I simply appealed to the fact that this was a Catholic school and everything we did should be marked by the spirit of Jesus. They observed silence as I tried to get them to understand that we did not know the condition or the motives of the driver of that car. We must give him the benefit of the doubt, perhaps he was frightened by this darkened crowd of boys singing and chanting. Perhaps he felt threatened. We would let the law take its course, and would behave in a manner befitting the students of the oldest Catholic boys school in the country. The funeral went off very well, and everyone remarked at the good behavior of the boys. In fact, the driver went to trial and was found guilty of manslaughter and served a prison sentence. Justice was done without any need for demonstrations or violence on the part of the students.

I traveled to Accra and went to the hospital to visit the student who was still in a coma. He had been in a coma now for about five days. And when I went to the intensive care unit to see him, I was amazed to find that he was able to hear, to understand, and to give a sign that he did understand.

I rushed back to Cape Coast and brought the good news to the assembled students who were gathered for an outdoor Mass at the closing of the week long jubilee celebration. The student eventually recovered, returned to the school and graduated in due course. I was impressed by the openness of the students to the appeal for reason and for Christian behavior.

After the excitement of the Jubilee celebration, life went on as usual. We were back to a civilian government. I continued to enjoy my teaching and my relationship with the students. Thanks to the very generous gift from one of my benefactors and good friends, I was able to stock all the science labs with sufficient equipment to allow us to run a very competent science department. As head of the department, I was expected to look after all the three sciences of physics, biology and chemistry.

One interesting experience that I had as head of the department was assigning classes to a new Peace Corps volunteer who had just come to us. He held a bachelor's degree in physics from an American University, and felt quite sure of himself. When I suggested that he takes on the physics classes of forms three and four, he seemed somewhat offended, as this seemed to be beneath him. He asked if he could not teach the sixth form, the equivalent of first-year college in the United States. I advised him that since he was not familiar with the British system of education that he begin with a lower grade until he becomes familiar with the syllabus and the quality of the students at our school. I told him that the sixth form students were a very select group and were academically very gifted.

A few months later, our senior physics teacher, an experienced Ghanaian, suddenly left us to go to Nigeria, which looked to him like greener pastures. I went back to my Peace Corps friend and told him that an opening had suddenly been created for a teacher in the sixth form. I asked him to take about two periods a week, though he would have preferred more. I asked him to cover the section of the syllabus on mechanics. Again, I warned him that the students were very bright.

On his first day in class, he tried to establish good relations with the students by introducing himself. After the introduction, a student raised his hand. When the teacher acknowledged him, the student said: "Since I have been in the school we have had five physics teachers. Only one knew what he was talking about. I hope you know what you're talking about." This certainly put the new teacher on the defensive. But I had warned him that he was dealing with very sophisticated young men.

A few days later a delegation of students came to me and said that they wanted me to change their teacher. They complained that he did not know what he was talking about. I tried to calm them down and told them to give him a chance. After all he had only taught them about three classes. I asked for some evidence that he didn't know what he was talking about. They took out their notebooks and showed me the notes they had copied from what he put on the chalkboard. I must admit, I was surprised to see that he failed to distinguish between force and energy, a very basic concept in physics. I told the students I would speak to him, and urged them to be more patient.

That evening I called the Peace Corps worker into my room, and gently explained to him what the students had told me. I reminded him of our earlier conversation, and why I was not anxious to put him into the sixth form from the beginning. I said I needed him to continue but encouraged him to be more careful in his preparation. I almost felt sorry for him when night after night I would find the lights in his house burning into the late hours. He did improve, and was no longer complacent in his degree from America.

What I learned from this incident is how often a stranger in a new culture underestimates the ability of the people in that culture. This is especially true, I'm afraid, when the culture is African. At this point, I had been in Africa for more than 10 years, and I had come to respect the great talent that was often hidden in the external poverty of some of the students. I can honestly say that they were as bright as anyone I had met during my limited teaching in the United States.

One of my responsibilities as head of the science department was to train the laboratory assistants. The assistant in the chemistry lab, where I normally worked, was in fact a very experienced assistant. He had been trained as a laboratory technician. Still, I had not completely shrugged off my own biases, and so, when I was preparing solutions for the experiments I did most of this myself. I knew how serious the practical exams were, and I didn't want the students to pick up any sloppy habits in the laboratory because of improperly prepared reagents. However, I would always have Henry, the lab assistant, be with me when I was preparing the solutions. I would carefully explain to him each step that I was doing. After a while, I would ask him to prepare a specific solution and I would be watching him. When I felt confident that he knew what he was doing, I left him on his own, and I was never disappointed. He was a very responsible and hard-working young man. He just confirmed what I've just written: the young African is as capable as anyone.

Chapter Ten

CHALLENGES AND ANOTHER COUP

At the beginning of 1981, I was asked by the headmaster if I would be willing to do the selection for the sixth form. He had asked that of me because there were many complaints by members of staff of corruption in the selection process. Our sixth form classes were overcrowded, and some of the students were not as qualified as they should have been. So I agreed to do the selection. Since St Augustine's had a very good reputation for its sixth form results, I knew there would be no great difficulty in choosing a very good class.

On the day for the selection, I traveled from Cape Coast to Accra where teachers from all over the country would gather to make their selection. It was all done in the school hall of Achimota high school, one of the oldest and most prestigious government secondary schools in the country. In the hall there were desks labeled for every sixth form school in the country. On each desk were the result forms of the students who had chosen that school as their first choice. When I got to the desk labeled St. Augustine's, I found a huge pile of such results, all arranged in order of merit. All I had to do was take the top cards, and I found a very qualified sixth form entry class for the new academic year.

When I reported all this at St. Augustine's during our next staff meeting, and had mimeographed copies of the selection I had made to give to the staff, I was first congratulated by the headmaster, who was seconded by one or more of the staff. However, there was a big "but".

"Headmaster, sir, Fr. Ugo has done an excellent job, but I notice that there are not enough students in the new entry class that are coming from our own school. This will make it difficult to choose prefects for the school because students coming from outside our school are not that familiar with our traditions."

I replied: "You asked me to make the selection, and I did so as honestly as I could. Perhaps if we had done a better job on our form five results there would've been more of our own students in the selection.

You are free to reject my selection, and make another."

"No, we would not think of doing such a thing, undoing the great work you have done. But perhaps you could add a few more names from our own form five graduates."

"If you ask me to do that, I will do it, provided we are agreed that we may expand our intake by a small amount for we do not want to overcrowd our classes. I will also insist that those we add to the list must have the same qualifications as the others and are only added because we have agreed to expand our numbers somewhat." At this point, one of the staff members raised her hand.

"I am told that Fr. Ugo is looking after a young man who wishes to be a Jesuit priest. He has not done his fifth form in our school, but in the minor seminary. Although we agreed that the names added to the list should be students who had completed their fifth form in our school, we could perhaps make an exception for this young man and accept him into our sixth form."

I shot back immediately: "There are no exceptions. He will not come to the school. I will find another school where he will be accepted."

I realized that if I had agreed to this proposal the staff would have been able to say that I am no better than the rest. I would've seemed to be as open to special favors for those close to me as they would have if they were doing the selection. I could not in conscience do this, and I felt I had an obligation to set an example for the future. The young man in question was James Kofi Addo-Nkum, whom I first met three years before when I was teaching in the minor seminary.

The incident at the staff meeting was not the end of this affair. I still had a lot to learn about the pressures on the one doing the selection. I would like to share just two further incidents. The first one occurred when a man drove up to the school one day and stopped in front of the chemistry lab, where I was working. I was called out, welcomed him, and he introduced himself. He asked me if I thought that his son would be able to find a place at St. Augustine's for the sixth form.

I politely informed him that I could not say so because the selection had not yet been made. Furthermore, I did not know his sons form five results. He then pulled out a slip of paper with his son's results. After glancing at them, I told him I did not think his son had much chance. The boy's results were average, but our school demanded much better than average. Furthermore he had not completed his form five in our school and so was not known to anyone.

He then changed the topic completely. He said: "I hear that you need tires for your car." I responded, "I do indeed need tires, but I do not need them badly enough to accept your son into the sixth form."

He protested that this was not his intention, and then asked if I thought his son should repeat form five to improve his results. I said I could not make a judgment on that since I did not know his son, but I was willing to interview the boy to try to discover whether his poor performance was lack of ability or simply the fact that he was in a poor school. A few days later he came to the school with his son and asked if I would interview him. I did so and told him I thought the boy had talent and that he probably could improve his results by repeating form five with the help of private coaching. He then presented me with two tires. I smiled and said that I thought I made it clear that I would not accept the tires in exchange for a place for his son. I offered to buy the tires from him and asked him how much he wanted. He insisted that he just wanted to help me as a missionary priest, and expected nothing in return. Fortunately, there were witnesses to this conversation. I did indeed need tires since my vehicle was on blocks and had been for some weeks.

Needless to say, I did not accept his son and jokingly said to my lab assistant that the man would probably be coming back to collect his two tires. It turned out not to be a joke, and about two weeks later the man came asking for his tires. Since the tires were already on the car, I offered to pay for them. I gave him a part of the money and told him to return at the end of the month to collect the rest. In between these two points, Jerry Rawlings was back in power and threatening many of the wealthy with inquiries into how they obtained their wealth. He came back before the end of the month and simply asked for whatever I could afford to give him since he was leaving the country.

The second incident also began before the final selection was made. A young student came to my house with a letter from Bishop Sarpong, the Bishop of Kumasi. The letter said that he was writing this while a woman was sitting in his office. The bearer of the letter was the woman's son, and the Bishop asked if there was anything I could do to get him a place in the sixth form at St. Augustine's. I asked the young lad for his results, and when he told me what they were, I gently tried to inform him that he probably would not be accepted in the school. I encouraged him to try other schools and that I was sure that with his results he would eventually find a place.

After the selection was made, and this young man was not on the list, I found myself one morning confronted by a gentleman who was the boy's father. He asked me if I had not received a letter from Bishop Sarpong. I said that I had. He asked me why I was not obedient to a Bishop since I was a priest. I told him I had done exactly what the Bishop asked me to do. He then asked for the letter, but I told him the letter was addressed to me and therefore I would not give it to him.

He shouted and threatened me. I politely requested that he speak in a more civil tone of voice and that if he insisted on shouting I would walk away. He continued to shout as I walked away: "you have not heard the end of this." In fact, it was the end. Nothing further came of his threats.

I learned a lot from this whole incident. I was much more understanding of those who give in to these pressures. I was a foreigner, unmarried, and fairly independent. But I wonder what I would've done if I had been a Ghanaian, married with a family, and finding financial difficulty in responding to all my responsibilities. It is not easy in a poor country to be completely honest. I am not justifying corruption or dishonesty, but I am saying that I can understand them. I experienced a lot of pressure during this whole selection process, and I told the headmaster I would not be willing to do it again.

On the 27th of December 1981, I traveled from Cape Coast to Takoradi, a city about 60 miles west of Cape Coast. I was invited to give a three-day retreat to a group of sisters. My friend James Addo-Nkum accompanied me on this trip. On the morning of the 31st of December, the retreat ended and I was preparing to make my way back to Cape Coast with James when the sisters told me that they had just heard on the radio that there had been a military coup. It seems that Jerry John Rawlings had come back into power and deposed the civilian government that had been elected just two years and three months before. His opening statements on the radio were very clear. The civilian government had disappointed the people of Ghana and it was necessary to take over and restore honesty and integrity to the country. He went further to say that he would never allow the Ghanaian people to sell their birthright through the ballot box again.

As we started our drive from Takoradi to Cape Coast I was a bit nervous, not knowing what to expect on the road since the military takeover. The amazing thing is that we met nothing along the road, and if we had not heard the news on the radio we would never have suspected that anything had changed. This was another lesson I learned about coups. They usually take place in the capital, and only in selected parts of the capital. It seems that as long as anyone controlled the state House and the radio station, the country is in the hands of those who hold them.

This second Rawlings coup would bring about radical changes in Ghana. It became known as the People's Revolution, and seemed to be strongly influenced by a Ghanaian academic who was a radical Marxist. Rawlings made it very clear that authority was to be invested in the ordinary people and not just in the rich and the powerful.

It soon became obvious that there were two kinds of people: the ordinary relatively uneducated people and the educated and financially successful people. The last were a kind of "non-people". Signs began to appear in the marketplaces and public squares which simply read "people power" or "power to the people". The effects of this kind of propaganda was soon felt in all social areas. For example, junior soldiers would be able to depose a senior officer if he was not to their liking; workers could sack a manager if they were unhappy with him; even pupils could dismiss a headmaster. In fact there was one tragic case in the early days of the revolution when an academic was actually killed by being badly beaten up by students who claimed he was unfair.

The new government labeled itself: "the Provisional National Defense Committee" or PNDC for short. It extended its influence through small groups of local people known as Peoples' Defense Committees. We found the same sort of structures that you would have found in a radical communist country. People's Tribunals were set up as a parallel judicial system to the courts of the former regime. It became difficult to know where authority in the local community resided. Even the police were uncertain of their role since these new committees seemed to be monitoring conformity to the revolutionary ideals. These committees would be allowed to go through the marketplace determining what was a fair price. If any marketeer tried to sell above that price they could be severely beaten in public. Since most of the marketeers were women, this resulted in public caning that was totally out of keeping with traditional African culture.

I recall one day when I went to buy a small traditional broom. As I came out of the market a member of one of these committees stopped me and asked me what I paid for it. I told him, and he immediately said it was too much. Even though I protested that I thought it was a fair price, he insisted on going back to the woman who sold it to me and giving her a severe warning. Fortunately, I did not have to see her caned in public.

The market women revolted against this attempt to control the prices of the objects they sold. They removed all their wares from the marketplace and for a time, it was difficult even to find a vegetable to cook. Rawlings was forced to back down and assured them of the security that they needed to sell their wares. However before they came to this resolution, Rawlings had bulldozed down one of the main marketplaces in Accra to express his annoyance with the power of the market women.

Bank accounts which were over the equivalent of about $1000 were to be frozen, and their owners would be asked to give an explanation as to how they got the money. The fact of the matter is that there was a flourishing black market in currency. Whereas the official exchange rate might be three cedis to the US dollar, on the black market you might get as many as a hundred. So those who had access to foreign exchange could become fabulously wealthy. I remember a Peace Corps volunteer who was able to fly around the world for the equivalent of about $200 by simply exchanging it on the black market and buying his ticket at a local travel agent using local currency. Even the church was affected by this decree, and it made life very difficult, for many of the church's accounts were built up from donations overseas that might have been exchanged at black market rates. If someone was dragged before one of these peoples tribunal's, they would not be allowed any lawyer, nor was there any appeal against any verdict given. They could confiscate all your goods, sentence you to prison, or even sentence you to death for economic sabotage. For many people, this was a very frightening time, especially for the educated middle classes. Many people simply fled the country.

Rawlings himself was very popular with the ordinary people, for he was one of them. He never promoted himself and kept the rank of Flight Lieutenant which he held in the Air Force before the coup. He was often found walking in the marketplaces, sitting down with the fishermen as they washed their nets, and never drove around in a big limousine. However, it was clear that there was a growing anarchy in the country with no clear lines of authority. And since these Peoples' Defense Committees were armed, it introduced an element of violence into the society.

There was one particularly tragic experience of the Rawlings Revolution. Some months after the revolution it was reported that a coup was attempted against Rawlings. The government then declared a curfew from sunset to sunrise. This all happened rather quickly and the word did not get out to all the people since it was only broadcast on the radio. The Archbishop of Cape Coast, John Kwadwo Amissah, had been out in one of the smaller churches in the rural area. He had not heard the news about the curfew. From his visitation to the parish he went to visit a convent of the Sisters of the Infant Jesus. They had put on a display of the works of some of the young sisters in formation.

As he arrived a bit late, the sister in charge suggested he stay there overnight since there was a curfew and he would not be able to get back to his house before dark. The Archbishop, known to be a rather stubborn man, refused their invitation and headed for his house. His car was stopped on the road by one of these young members of the People's Defense Committees.

The young man was armed with a rifle and demanded that the Archbishop turn over the keys to the car. The Archbishop refused and said he would take the young man where ever he wanted him to go. They ended up at the local police station where the young man told police that the Archbishop was under arrest for breaking curfew. The police were embarrassed and confused, but dared not go against these committees.

The Archbishop stayed overnight at the police station and then was brought back to his house and put under house arrest. The only person allowed to see him was his secretary. Some days after he was put under house arrest he received word that his mother was very sick and was probably dying. He asked permission to go to his mother so that he could anoint her, give her the last sacraments, and comfort her on her deathbed. Permission was refused, and within a day his mother died. The committee was very embarrassed by all this and immediately lifted the house arrest order. The Archbishop conducted the funeral for his mother in the presence of very many people and with most of the bishops of Ghana concelebrating with him. It was a sad moment in the life of the Archbishop and it took him a long time to get over the bitterness of not being allowed to see his mother before she died.

It did not take the PNDC too long to realize that some changes had to be made. One of the first things they did was to take the guns away from the People's Defense Committees, dissolve these committees, and form what they called the Committees for the Defense of the Revolution.

There were also clear guidelines as to just what these revolutionary councils were allowed to do. Things were beginning to get into some kind of order. Many of the more radical policies of the PNDC had to be modified.

During the early days of the Revolution, it was not only the marketplaces that were empty but also the shops. I could go into one of the supermarkets in town, and find just about nothing. Even fuel for the vehicles was very hard to get and some spent half their day searching for fuel, only to find that when you go to the pump you were allowed about 5 litres, probably the amount you used in moving from one station to another. I found it simpler and less strenuous to just forget about the vehicle and began walking. Longer journeys would just have to be put off.

To add to all this, Ghana suffered one of its worst droughts in a very long time. The rainy season from October 1981 to May 1982 passed with practically no rain. Almost all the crops failed, and we were totally dependent on donated rice from the European Community and the United States. Since there was very little wheat, bread became extremely scarce. A piece of bread was considered a luxury. People tried to make bread out of rice flour, but it was not very effective.

I must admit it was a very difficult time. When I returned from leave in September 1982, I still remember clearly the sharp contrast between the meal I had at the airport in London while waiting for my flight and the breakfast that I would prepare for myself the morning I arrived.

I had had a simple meal with the Nigerian friend of mine who met me at Heathrow Airport. Simple as it was, it was a nutritious and tasty meal. Some eight or nine hours later I landed in Accra and was met by a good friend of mine, Stephen Aikens, and we drove back together to Cape Coast. When we arrived we had a very simple breakfast. Stephen had found a small piece of bread, but there was no spread for it. So we had some ripe bananas which we used in place of margarine. For a beverage we had black instant coffee with no sugar. However, knowing the situation I would find I had brought back a few jars of saccharine tablets. That was our breakfast, and we had little choice since there was nothing else to eat. It's hard to believe that eight hours on a plane could take you from a land of plenty to a country which was on the point of starvation. I often wonder how many people living in America or Europe have any idea of what people are suffering only half a day's journey by plane away from where they are sitting.

The drought was so severe that many people died of malnutrition.

I remember a woman coming to the door of my house looking for a cup of rice. Strapped to her back was a young child and she was concerned about this child more than about herself. Since at the seminary I did not have a kitchen but took my meals in the common dining room for the staff, all I could do was send her to the kitchen and see if they could afford to give her anything. It was painful to watch people going around begging for food. It could shake one's faith in a loving God.

I remember once celebrating Mass with a group of students at a women's teacher training college run by a group of nuns. During the drought, we prayed each day for rain. On this particular day, I felt particularly emotional, and when I prayed for rain I interrupted my prayer, slammed the altar with my fist and said something like the following:

> "You are not listening. Each day we pray to you for rain and you mock us. When we wake up each morning we see nothing but bright blue skies and a hot shining sun. People are dying. We need rain. Are you listening?"

This prayer came out so spontaneously that I think I shocked even myself. When I calmed down I simply continued the prayer by adding in a calm voice: "Lord, hear our prayer."

Food and water are serious problems in the Third World because of the dependence of these countries on the climate. There are only two seasons in the year. In West Africa, the rainy season begins around May and extends until November. From November to the following April, there would be no rain. So, if you don't get rain during those six months from May to November, you have no hope of finding it after that until the following May. This is not only a problem for farming, but also a problem for drinking water, and electricity supplies. Most of the electricity in Ghana, as well as in Zambia, came from a hydroelectric dam. If there is insufficient rain the levels of the water in the dam fall to a point when they can no longer turn the turbines. As the water levels approached this point, there would be electricity rationing.

The problem with drinking water is similar. One year in Cape Coast, after I had moved to the seminary, we suddenly found our taps dry. When the rector went to the water company to inquire what was wrong and to ask when we might have water back, he was told quite simply that the reservoir was empty and there would be no water flowing in our pipes until the rains came. Many schools were forced to close, but we managed to keep the seminary open because the diocese had a water tanker which could travel each day about 40 miles down the road to pump water from a stream. This had to be done at least twice a day until the seminary closed at the end of the academic year. Again, these are problems the people in the first world can hardly understand. What always amazed me during these times of crisis was the deep faith of the people, their ability to smile in the face of suffering, and their willingness to help one another. It is the quality of the African people that never ceases to amaze me and for which I am grateful. I have learned how to be patient because of them. Now I can laugh when people in America complain when the electricity goes off for an hour perhaps once in five years. They have no idea of what it is to live with such limitations as we experience on a regular basis in Africa.

Chapter Eleven

AN ARCHBISHOP
AND A HERMIT

I would now like to share something of my relationship with the Archbishop of Cape Coast, Archbishop John Kwadwo Amissah.

When I first arrived in Cape Coast and moved into my staff house at St. Augustine's College, I was living practically next door to the Archbishop. The house I lived in was a double house, each with one bedroom. One end of this double house was occupied by Fr. Gabriel Mensah, who was a teacher in the school and also chaplain. In addition, he was the Vicar General of the Archdiocese. Next to Fr. Gabriel Mensah's house was a line of trees with a small path going through the line which led to the Archbishop's house. The distance between his house and our house was perhaps 100 meters.

When I was first introduced to the Archbishop by my fellow Jesuit from Accra, he received me very warmly and seemed genuinely happy to have me on the staff of the college. He would even occasionally come over from his house to visit me at mine, and we would sit on my veranda and chat. Within a short time I was asked to be a consultor to the Archbishop. I was one of the four consultors. I was also elected to be on the Presbyteral Council. This was a group of about a dozen priests who were called together twice a year to discuss in the presence of the Archbishop matters affecting the archdiocese. I felt very honored and privileged to be in these two positions as consultor and as a member of the Council.

There were several experiences that confirmed the character of the Archbishop as a very caring person and as a true father to his priests and his people. I think it was in 1982 that I was stricken with typhoid.

I didn't know what I was suffering from at the time, but I did know I was feeling very sick. I sent word over to Father Mike Blume, who was the vice rector of the seminary at the time. He was a good friend of mine and he immediately came over to see what the problem was. I explained to him how sick I was feeling, and he offered to drive me over to the Catholic hospital run by German Dominican nuns some distance from Accra. I was in no condition to argue with him, and I readily went with him. It was about a 2 hour drive to the hospital, and I was received very well by the sisters there. I was given a private room and one of the sister-doctors came to examine me and quickly saw that my problem was typhoid. She told me I was to stay in the hospital and would be there for at least a week to 10 days.

I thanked Mike very much and he drove back to Cape Coast. The very next day, the Archbishop was in my room. He had heard of my illness and immediately came to see how I was doing. I think this was very typical of his deep personal concern for his priests

When I recovered and was ready to be discharged, I sent a message to St. Augustine's College where I was teaching and living that they should send one of their drivers with my car to come and collect me. I did not want to inform the Archbishop of my discharge because I felt he would inconvenience some priest to come over to collect me. However, it was foolish of me to think I could keep it from him. The next day Father Gabriel Mensah arrived. Of course, he had been sent by the Archbishop to bring me back from the hospital. All my efforts to save him this trouble failed because of the overriding personal concern of the Archbishop.

Another typical example of the Archbishop's generosity was experienced when my provincial from New York came to visit me in Cape Coast. He was Father Vincent Cooke. One morning we were sitting on the veranda of my house in Cape Coast when the Archbishop walked over to greet me. I had already introduced the provincial to him as soon as he arrived in Cape Coast. He asked me if my visitor had seen the Elmina Castle. This castle is at least 500 years old and was used during the slave trade. It is one of the most significant monuments in Ghana. I told him that we had not yet gone there but had hoped to go there. He then insisted on taking us there himself, and, on arrival, organized a personal tour of the castle.

The Archbishop was not only a thoughtful person but also a thinking person. He was very gifted in intelligence and was trained in canon law. He had completed his doctorate in this subject, and had once taught in the seminary before he was named Archbishop. He was one of the first African bishops on the West Coast, being appointed the Bishop in 1957, the year of Ghana's independence. He claimed that he was the church's gift to Africa for independence. One of the limitations of the Archbishop was his quick temper and lack of patience. He did not entertain fools gladly.

Another limitation of the Archbishop was this tendency toward authoritarianism. It was clear that he was the chief Shepherd of the flock and had the ultimate say on any matter. This could extend to even the most trivial things. For example, he would insist on going over with the superior of the diocesan sisters, The Handmaids of the Infant Jesus, all the details of their habit and even the quality of the cloth that would go into making a habit. I observed the same tendency at every meeting of the Presbyteral Council. The members of the council were more or less asked to agree with decisions that he had already taken. There was never very much open discussion. No one could question his goodwill or his energy in doing the work of the Archbishop.

There are two activities in which I was involved during my years in Ghana that made a great difference in my self-understanding as well as in my opportunities to learn from my African friends. The first of these was the Young Christian Student Movement, or YCS as it is more commonly known. I mentioned how in my first days in Africa I was introduced to the national coordinator of the YCS in Nigeria, and how I worked with him on a small project. That was the beginning of a long commitment to the YCS in Nigeria, Zambia, and Ghana. The YCS was founded by a Belgian priest around 1930. It originally began as the Young Christian Workers as a means of counteracting the communist cells that were beginning to proliferate among the unionized workers in Europe. It then became applied to young Christian students who were also in danger of drifting from the faith.

Its structure is simple, dividing students up in a school into small groups of 10 or 12 who reflect on their daily experience and apply the light of the Gospel to that experience. One could have several of these small groups in one school, and they would be coordinated by a central committee, consisting of a president, vice president, secretary and treasurer. Each small group would have its own coordinator and secretary. The methodology of the group was a very powerful one that was summed up in three words: see, judge, act. Each meeting began with a prayer and then an application of this methodology. The students were asked to share the important events that they had observed and lived through since the last meeting. Then they would take one of those issues that seemed most prominent and urgent. They would judge that issue in the light of the Gospel by reflecting on the life and teaching of Jesus as it might apply to that particular issue. In the light of this reflection they would draw up a program of action which they would accomplish before the next meeting. At the subsequent meeting, the action program of the previous meeting would be discussed to see if it had been effective. If it had not been, they would reflect again and act again.

This methodology could be very effective and could accomplish a great deal. Let me give you one example from my experience with the YCS in Ghana. After the second Rawlings coup, the new military government put out some propaganda about how the majority of university students saw scientific socialism as the way forward for the country.

The YCS at the University of Science and Technology in Kumasi used this propaganda as the experience on which they wanted to reflect in the light of the Gospels. They saw it as a pernicious attempt to introduce a materialistic and atheistic way of life on the Ghanaian people. They decided to go around the dormitories and ask each student whether they knew what scientific socialism was. If the student said they knew what it was, they would then ask them if they thought this was the way forward to develop the country.

They found out that the vast majority of students did not even understand what scientific socialism was all about. And of the minority who did understand only a small fraction agreed that this was the way to develop the country. With their results in hand, all verified with signatures, they challenged the student leaders who first made the statement about the support for scientific socialism. They called for an open debate on the subject, and the YCS representatives won hands down. I was very impressed both by the leadership of the YCS, their courage in undertaking this challenge, and their intelligence in working out a methodology. It showed what the YCS at its best could do.

I was chaplain for the YCS at the diocesan level for almost my entire time in Ghana. I thoroughly enjoyed working with the young men and women in the secondary schools, colleges, and universities where the YCS existed. In the course of my many years association with the YCS, I think I met some of the finest young men and women who would turn out to be leaders wherever they happen to be. The methodology of see, judge, and act became a way of seeing the world and also a means of reflecting on that world throughout their lives. Of course, it was not always effective and sometimes the YCS sections in the schools could be disappointing. But no matter how disappointing individual sections or particular meetings were, there was absolutely no doubt about the quality of the men and women attracted to the movement and the effect that it had in developing the characters of these men and women. I could give many examples of how this worked out in specific cases.

When I was involved with the YCS in Zambia from 1974 to 1978 I witnessed the same kind of leadership quality in the members at the Copperbelt Secondary Teachers College. Each year in Zambia on the 12th of March the government commemorated a national holiday called "National Youth Day". On the week before that day the youth were to offer themselves in some kind of service to the community. I recall how the YCS members at the college would go off into the nearby shanty compound and assist the poor people there in various works from cleaning their homes to digging latrines.

Every year there would be a national YCS convention. At these gatherings, YCS representatives from the entire country would come together to discuss important issues and to come to know one another.

Every four years, there would be a national YCS Congress in which as many as 200 or more YCS members would gather together both to pray and to work with their hands. It was often intended to give the students, most of whom came from well to do families, to experience the life of the poor. They would go off into the villages and join the people as they went to the fields to work on their farms. In the evenings they would reflect on their experience and bring it to prayer. I was impressed both by the generosity of these young Africans as well as their ability to reflect deeply on the significance of their experiences.

There is another story that I would like to tell about some YCS students. One day two young men from St. Augustine's College, who were members of the YCS, went to the local hospital in Cape Coast just to visit the sick. When they arrived, one of the nurses informed them that an infant baby had been left there at the door of the hospital, abandoned by its mother. The students felt a great compassion for the child and wondered what they could do to help care for it. The nurses, whose salaries were very small, said that they needed some financial help just to get the milk the baby needed.

The boys immediately took out of their pockets whatever money they had, and handed it over to the nurse. They came and asked me what more they could do. I suggested that they take a collection from among their fellow students and bring the proceeds to the nurses. They did exactly this and I was so impressed by the maturity and generosity of these young men. I believed that it was their formation as Young Christian Students that inspired their action. They had been, almost spontaneously, following the methodology of see, judge, and act. They saw the abandoned infant; they judged that Jesus would have wanted them to show compassion; and they took the action that was appropriate. Since I had never encountered the YCS in the United States or in Europe, my very positive impression of this group was formed from the character of the people that I found involved in the movement in Africa. I was beginning to understand both the power of the movement and the wonderful character of the African people. I would find the same character many times, even outside the YCS.

Before I leave my reflections on my life at St. Augustine's, I would like to single out a few people whom I came to know quite well and whom I respected very much. One of these was Stephen Aikins. When I first came to know him, he was in form five, a year ahead of my opening class at St. Augustine's. Unlike the vast majority of students in the school, Stephen was a day scholar. He came from a very poor family in Cape Coast that was unable to pay the fees for his boarding. He could always be found at the evening Mass. He would often come up to my house to discuss personal problems as well is to get advice on his spiritual growth. I was amazed at his maturity. When he completed form five, he was offered a scholarship for the sixth form.

This enabled him to move into the boarding house, and because of his mature character, he was made a house prefect. One time, during the school year, the students went on a class boycott. I cannot remember the details of their complaint. What I do remember is that Stephen disagreed with them and refused to take part in their protests. This did not make him very popular with the majority of students. But Stephen was never very much influenced by what other people thought. He would reflect on his own position, and after much thought and prayer, would stick to that no matter what. He was a man of great integrity. For many years he considered the possibility of a vocation to the religious life, even before he was formally a Catholic. However, I believe that his responsibilities toward his extended family who were mostly poor influenced his decision to further his education so that he could find a position that would enable him to financially help his family. He is presently a lecturer in agricultural science at the University of Science and Technology in Kumasi, and is married with a family.

Another gift that I had received from God that began to be uncovered and developed during this time in Ghana was my ability to give retreats and become a spiritual guide to various people. I had given retreats in Nigeria, and even during my first four years in Zambia, but this work began to expand and develop during my years in Ghana. I found myself moving over the entire country during my holiday periods to give retreats. My retreatants ranged from bishops and priests to sisters, adult laymen and women, and on many occasions, young people. I had to develop many different approaches to these various groups, and I was reasonably successful in this work with the result that I was constantly invited to give retreats.

On two different occasions I was asked to direct the 30 day retreat. The first time was to two novices of the Society of the Divine Word. I was asked to spend the full month with them at one of the secondary schools run by the same society. There the three of us moved into a staff house, where we would be cut off from the world for a whole month. Each day I would meet individually with each novice and guide him through the Spiritual Exercises of St. Ignatius. It was a wonderful experience, and it gave me the confidence to attempt the same exercise again about a year later.

The second time I was asked to direct five young women who were preparing to take their final vows as religious sisters in a local diocesan congregation that had been founded by the local bishop. Since it was a new congregation, they were first formed by an expatriate sister from an older international congregation. She had been with this group for a number of years and felt it was now time for them to pronounce their final vows and take over the running of the congregation. Before they did so, she wanted to give them a deeper spiritual formation through the full Spiritual Exercises. I spent one month with them at a retreat house north of Accra. I had to see each of the five individually each day for up to 45 minutes. It was a very demanding exercise both for them and for me. But it went very well, and the sisters seemed very well prepared to take over the positions of responsibility in their new congregation.

Many years later I was teaching a group of young sisters from all over Africa at a formation centre in Lusaka, Zambia. One of the students was from Ghana and was a member of this congregation. It turned out that the general of the congregation was one of those young sisters whom I had directed in that 30 day retreat many years before. It was a very satisfying realization that I had at least some small part in the shaping of the spirit of that new congregation.

One of the great gifts of my life as a spiritual guide in Africa was my contact with Sr. Winifred Wilson, a member of the Society of the Holy Child Jesus, an American who had come to Africa long before independence for most countries. When I met her in1981 she would have been about

73 years old. She was living and working in Ghana at that time. Before that she had been for many years in Nigeria and was forced to leave that country after the Biafran war because she had been there during the war. Most foreign missionaries who were in Biafra during the war were forced to leave when the war ended. She came to me one day while I was still teaching at St. Augustine's College, Cape Coast. She introduced herself, and asked me if I would be her spiritual director. I readily agreed.

She revealed to me that she felt called to live out her final days as a hermit. Her superiors were not very enthusiastic about this since it was not part of the charism of their society for members to live a contemplative life alone. However, they gave her permission to discern this matter with the help of a spiritual guide for one year. As we met and talked each month I became more and more convinced that God was indeed calling her to the contemplative life. Her superiors eventually allowed her to pursue this vocation but she would have to find the means to finance the construction of a small hermitage. She managed to do this and by 1984 she had managed to construct a small, but very solid, building with one large room with two smaller rooms at one end. One of these was a toilet and shower, and the other a small kitchen. In the remaining space on that wall she had an alcove which was a small Chapel in which she kept the Blessed Sacrament reserved.

At the beginning of Lent in 1984, the Bishop came to consecrate the house and celebrate Mass there. She then moved in and began her eremitical life. She asked if I would continue being her spiritual director which involved visiting her each week to share her experience of prayer, hear her confession, and celebrate Mass with her. During the rest of the week she would attend Mass at a nearby convent. My weekly visits to her were some of the highlights of my time in the seminary. Once again, Africa had afforded me an opportunity I would not have easily found in the United States. Winifred was a very saintly person, and every visit was an inspiration. Her faith challenged me a great deal.

She was intensely happy in this life. She once even asked me if it were possible to be too happy. When a priest once asked if she became lonely in the hermitage, she just smiled and said she was never alone. Her sense of God's presence in her life and the power of her many prayers for others brought hope to many.

One time she shared with me that one of her disappointment in life was that she had not really experienced the cross of the Lord. It was hard for me to understand this, since she had lived a difficult life in Africa for 40 years, had set up rural industries and clinics, had remained in Biafra during the war, and was even imprisoned briefly after the war and, like myself, was a prohibited immigrant in Nigeria.

I didn't really understand what she meant until she was found with a fatal disease just three years after her entry into the hermitage. She was found to have contracted agranulocytosis which destroyed her white blood cells such that she had little immunity to any disease. In her final days, she had a bad sore throat and was in a lot of pain. She would not allow the doctors to give her too strong a pain killer. She was moved from the hermitage to the convent in Cape Coast. On the day she died, I had gone to celebrate Mass with her in her bedroom where she was surrounded by her sisters. At the end of Mass I bent over to her in her bed and said a few encouraging words. Then she said: "Now I am suffering, and I am so happy." That was the share in the cross. Her love for Christ was such that she wished to share all his experiences. I was very humbled by her love and commitment to the Lord. I had the honour of preaching at her wake-keeping and again at her funeral. She was buried near the hermitage in Africa which she loved so well.

I learned many things from this work of spiritual direction and giving retreats. I gained in self-confidence over the years. At times it frightened me to hear some of the very positive comments from those who have made my retreats. I felt unworthy of their comments, and often thought that I was a bit of a Pharisee, letting them think me a spiritual man, when, in fact, I did not feel I had a very deep spiritual life myself.

Chapter Twelve

A CALL TO THE SEMINARY

The retreat work was becoming an important part of my work in Ghana. There was hardly a school break when I was not asked to give some kind of retreat. In addition to that I found more and more people coming to seek spiritual direction. Apparently, the word was getting around that I had some skill in this work. At the same time, in the major seminary of St. Peter's in Pedu, a suburb of Cape Coast, they were experiencing some difficulties. I had hardly ever visited this seminary during my years of teaching at St. Augustine's and I knew little about it.

I had not had much interaction with any of the seminarians, and the only diocesan priests that I knew were those I met at St. Theresa's minor seminary. At St. Peter's major seminary, a regional seminary for the southern half of Ghana, the seminarians had protested against the small amount of money given to them for their holiday. The protest went so far as to physically damage the electrical system in the staff house at the seminary. There was a clear indication that something was going wrong in the formation of these men. After all, they were not high school students, but were the equivalent of university students. Their behavior was unbecoming for men of their age, and especially in their calling as future priests. Apparently, there had been no full-time spiritual director in the seminary for some time.

These are the circumstances that one day led the Archbishop to come to visit my house at St. Augustine's College. He had a proposal to make. He asked if I would consider being a full-time spiritual director of St. Peter's seminary. My first response was to tell him I had no experience or training in this field. His reply was that he had heard from many sources that I would be a good person for this work. I explained to him that I was not a free agent and that only my superiors could change my assignment. I was willing to propose this change to them since I understood how important this work was for the future development of the church.

I wrote my provincial in New York, and explained the proposition of the Archbishop. I also indicated to him my own limitations in this work, but I was willing to try it if he thought that was the better mission.

His reply came very quickly indicating his will that I should move to the seminary. This would dramatically change the work I had been doing in Africa since my arrival in 1967.

It was in the spring of 1982 that all this happened, and I was due to go on home leave that summer. This would give me an opportunity to do some preparation for this new work. It was not going to be easy leaving St. Augustine's or my work as head of the science department and teacher of the A-level chemistry. I enjoyed this work and I had come to like the students very much. Although Pedu was only about 2 miles or so from the school, I knew it would not be easy to be coming back frequently. At the same time I was unwilling to completely give up my teaching of chemistry which I enjoyed so much. I asked the headmaster if I could return on a part-time basis to at least complete the course for the students in the upper six class. He more than readily agreed and I felt that I would have at least some contact with the work in which I had some skill and which I enjoyed so much.

The staff at the college had a farewell party for me, and presented me with an African shirt, and expressed their appreciation for all that I had accomplished in my four years as a science teacher. I think their expressions of appreciation were quite sincere, and I would certainly miss working with them. But it was time to move on, and the Lord had made His will known to me through the decision of my provincial. With a certain amount of anxiety, I moved out of my house on the campus of the college and shifted my belongings to a new house on the seminary grounds. I then prepared to go on leave in the United States.

Before I leave my memories of St. Augustine's college, I would like to say that not everything I experienced was pleasant. First of all, there were the physical difficulties of living in a staff house at the college. One of those difficulties was the fact that we rarely had running water in the houses. I would have to use my bathtub as a storage tank for water. Whenever water was running, I would fill the tub to the brim so that it could be used for my various needs around the house. I would have used it to do my cooking, wash my dishes, or flush my toilet. Of course, this meant that I could not take a bath. The only way in which I could bathe myself was to get up early in the morning, take a bucket of water from the bathtub, and stand outside my house in the early hours of the morning when it was still dark. Using a cup I would take a small amount of water and pour it over myself, then lather myself with soap, and use another cup or two to rinse myself. This could only be done in the dark hours of the morning since I had to stand naked in the open air in the corner by the back of the house. When Kofi Addo-Nkum came to live with me during the first year of the sixth form, he suggested we clean out a simple storeroom in the back of the house so that we could use it as a shower room. This we did. Now we could take a shower at any hour of the day I would simply bring a bucket of water and a cup into the empty storeroom and then sweep out the water at the end of the shower.

When there was no running water for more than a week the reserve in the bathtub would be gone. Then I had to go down to the lower campus where there was more water pressure and carry large containers of water up to the house in order to fill the bath-tub.

It certainly made my life complicated, but it was amazing how quickly I adjusted to this new situation. I realized I had come a long way from my life in the United States where these kinds of inconveniences are hardly known in the big cities. I had become so accustomed to my life in Africa that these difficulties never tempted me to return to the comforts of home.

It was not only the physical difficulties of life of the campus that challenged me. It was also the occasional misunderstanding with the students that would be very painful. As I have said above, I was a very strict disciplinarian in the classroom and some students resented this. I still recall how one evening, when the students were expected to be doing study, I heard a great deal of noise coming from one of the classrooms.

I went over to find out what was the cause of all the commotion. When I identified the student I gave him a strong verbal reprimand. Not long after that, I received an anonymous note printed in a crude childish scrawl, threatening me with violence if I were to go down into the classroom area at night alone. In the body of this letter many abusive terms were used for me. I had to learn to accept these signs of immaturity in the students without reacting. I never felt worried about the threats, and continued my normal routine. It is true, that on one night when attending a meeting, I found one tire of my car had been punctured by a nail driven into the side. I had the tire repaired and nothing was said and nothing more happened.

All through my years in Africa I learned that there would be inevitable misunderstandings, but what I admired about the Africans, and still admire about them, is that they do not hold grudges for long and one can quickly find oneself back on friendly terms. I think that they are much better at this than I myself am, though I have tried to learn from them.

When I went on leave that summer of 1982, I set up a number of programs for myself to assis me in the new work that I would undertake when I returned. I had arranged to attend an eight day retreat/workshop on prayer given by the famous Father Anthony De Mello. That retreat was an extraordinary experience for me. I learned a great deal about prayer, and perhaps, even more about myself. I still recall about three days into the retreat finding myself uncomfortable with DeMello's conferences. It was not because he was in any way boring. On the contrary he was one of the most exciting speakers I have ever heard.

When I examined myself to try to discover the source of my discomfort, I first realized that I wasn't very happy with the way he used the Scriptures. But then I realized that we were not attending a course on Scripture. Furthermore, when I was preaching or giving a retreat, I would use the Scriptures in much the same way, choosing texts to illustrate a point I was trying to make, without worrying whether it was an exact scientific interpretation of the text. No, there was something more that was disturbing me. After much reflection, I realized that in much of what he was saying he was challenging my very concept of God. This was rather frightening and very disturbing. However, once I realized the source of my dis-ease, I was able to listen to him in a more objective way realizing that the problem was not in what he was saying but in the challenge he presented for myself. By the end of the retreat, I found myself thinking more and more about God as De Mello did. I have never looked back, and I thank God that he gave me the grace to look honestly at myself and to change. This lesson would be very important in my work as a spiritual director, being sensitive to how my words might be affecting others. I had to be open to many different interpretations of God's work in a human being and come to respect them all.

During that home leave of 1982 I was quite anxious and did quite a bit of reading about spiritual direction. I had never had any formal training in this field and felt that this was a very serious responsibility, requiring a certain amount of preparation. In addition to the workshop with Anthony DeMello, I also attended a workshop on the Progoff method of journaling. I learned a great deal on how to keep a spiritual diary and how to look into one's own life and especially, one's relationship with God. I also learned a lot about guided meditation which would be very useful in my work as spiritual director. Finally, I attended a workshop on the theme of church and authority. This was quite a challenging workshop since it was not a traditional schedule of lecturers and group sharing. Rather it was an opportunity to learn what is really going on in any group meeting when all agendas are taken away. It was emotionally and psychologically difficult, but very fruitful. It was known as the Tavistock workshop, and in the years since it happened I've come to appreciate more and more the value of those five days.

By the end of my home leave, I felt somewhat prepared to take on my new mission in Ghana. Just as I was preparing to depart for Africa, my father suffered a serious stroke. I immediately cancelled my return flight until I could be sure of what would happen to my father. He was in a coma, and I would go to visit him in the hospital even though he showed no response to my presence or my conversation. He died a few days later, and his funeral was to take place the very day I had originally planned my flight back to Ghana. I could not be present to celebrate my mother's funeral, but this time I had the privilege of celebrating my father's funeral Mass. I would miss him very much since he was a very caring and generous person who would have done anything for me. After the burial I arranged a flight back to Africa.

When I arrived in Ghana, I took up residence at St. Peter's Major seminary in Pedu. I was given a small cottage on the campus to be my residence. It was brand-new and very comfortable. It consisted of a shower and toilet, a bedroom and an office. Attached to the residence was a garage, and the residence also had a very nice veranda. I immediately invested in a bike so that I could cycle between the seminary and St. Augustine's College, where I would continue on a part-time basis teaching the A-level chemistry course to the final year students. I was introduced to the seminarians at the opening Mass of the school year. The rector, Father Thomas Mensah, was very welcoming.

Since I was a house spiritual director, my first responsibility was to be sure that every seminarian had a spiritual director. They had the choice of any of the staff in the seminary, and could, with permission, choose a priest from outside the seminary. That first year I found myself with about 80 seminarians for spiritual direction. The student body at the time was about 185.

My first task was to listen to the seminarians and try to discern their expectations of a spiritual director. As I began to see the seminarians who came to me for spiritual direction, I would ask them what they expected of me. I was also interested in learning about the various spiritual exercises in the program, and what they were actually doing during their time of meditation. I began to realize that they had very little understanding of prayer or the spiritual life. At first I got permission from the rector to use the half-hour between evening prayer and dinner to meet with individual classes so that I could speak with them about the spiritual life. With six classes of students, two years of philosophy and four years of theology, I would only get to meet them about twice a month. This was clearly insufficient.

I then proposed at a staff meeting that we introduce a course in spirituality. This course would be offered to the students in the first and second years of philosophy. There would be two periods a week for each class. At first the staff resisted this as it would crowd the academic program. I had to wait for the first meeting with the bishops at their annual visitation of the seminary. The bishops came and gave me full support, and the course was introduced. I insisted that it not be an academic course in the sense that there would be no exam at the end, and no grade would be given for the course. I felt that the success or failure of the student would be reflected in the way they lived their lives. This again was a concept not easily understood by the academic staff, but I finally got my way.

Although I seemed to have won my first battle with the academic staff, I could not feel comfortable with this as it seemed to put me at odds with the faculty. I would have hoped that we were on this team together to form good priests. There was always the difficulty with the academic staff who stressed the formation of students qualified in theology. This is not quite the same thing as forming qualified priests. However, I must admit with the goodwill of the faculty we were soon working together.

For the vast majority of the students my presence on the campus seemed to be a blessing. It took them a month or two to get used to me, but once they did, they accepted me warmly and I rarely felt more affirmed in anything I have done. I also began to appreciate more and more the importance of my position in the seminary. What could be more important for the growth of the church than the formation of good priests? I began to feel more and more at home in the seminary and enjoyed having a house of my own where I could entertain the visits of seminarians with perfect privacy. This was important if I were to gain their confidence and assure them of full confidentiality.

There was on the staff of the seminary another Jesuit. He was a Belgian Jesuit by the name of Joe Van Torre. I had known him even while I was on the staff at St. Augustine's. He had joined the seminary because he had known a young Ghanaian priest when he was a seminarian in the United States. Joe Van Torre had had an interesting life. After completing his doctorate in theology at Louvain University as a Jesuit, he lectured there for about nine years. Then, he taught philosophy at the Jesuit formation house outside of Kinshasa in the Democratic Republic of the Congo. From there he went to teach at a seminary in the United States in Rochester, New York.

It was there that he met the young Ghanaian seminarian, Peter Turkson, who was sent by his diocese to study in the seminary in Rochester. After being ordained, he invited Van Torre to come to join the staff in Ghana when it was clear that the seminary in Rochester would soon be closing for lack of vocations. He was on the staff for about a year before I came to St. Augustine's. And so when I heard that there was another Jesuit at the seminary, I drove over and introduced myself to him. At that time, I had James Kofi Addo-Nkum living with me in the staff house at St. Augustine's. One night we invited him to dinner, and I collected him at the seminary while Kofi did the cooking. We had a wonderful evening and I knew that I could be a companion to Joe and he to me.

My presence on the staff at the seminary was quite different from that of Van Torre. First of all, he was a rather conservative Jesuit in his theology and his role in the seminary was that of a lecturer. However, he was the spiritual director for a number of the seminarians. I felt very confident with this because I knew his Jesuit spirituality and I felt sure that the seminarians would greatly profit from their sharings with him. Although he was a much older man than myself, the fact that we are both Jesuits formed a bond between us.

By the end of the first semester at the seminary, I began to become busier than I've ever imagined possible. I found myself being personal spiritual director for about 80 seminarians. In addition to this, I was also teaching a course in spirituality. I would also meet each of the years of the seminarians about once a week so that I could get to know those to whom I was not teaching spirituality. Since the spirituality course was only taught the first two years, the final four years were unknown to me. Some did choose me as their spiritual director and so I got to know a few of them. They also encountered me when I was the celebrant at Mass, and when I led them in a day of recollection. To see each of my personal spiritual directees at least once a month required a good number of hours each day. I quickly learned that what was important in these meetings was for me to simply listen and ask leading questions that would help them to share more of their experiences in prayer and their encounters with God outside of prayer.

By my second year in the seminary I was personal spiritual director for close to a hundred seminarians. This required many hours each day in order to see them at least once a month. I was very encouraged by the progress they were making in the self examination of their daily lives. They began to see the many ways in which God touched them in the ordinary things they experienced. These became integrated into their prayer life in a very meaningful way. I also stressed a great deal the importance of a personal relationship with Jesus Christ, and I taught them the Ignatian method of contemplating the mysteries of Christ in the Gospels. As they came to share with me each month I could detect in their sharing a greater understanding of what they were doing in striving to become priests. In the large majority of them I found a great deal of maturity. What was most encouraging was the fact that most of them did not change spiritual directors from year to year. As a consequence, I found myself spiritual director to some seminarians for 3, 4, or more years. I came to know some of them very well, and I am very proud of the fact that five of those who had come to me for spiritual direction are now bishops in Ghana.

Despite the many hours that were occupied in the individual direction of seminarians, I was also asked to take on lectures in various subjects. And so I found myself at various times in my seven years there lecturing in quite a number of subjects. I would rarely have more than one subject other than spirituality in any given year. At various times, I taught logic, philosophy of science, Christology and catechetics. I was learning a great deal as I taught since each course required quite a bit of preparation and a lot of reading. I can say I was fully challenged during those years in the seminary.

One of the great challenges during my time in the seminary was being asked by the bishops to design a program for a spiritual year that was to be added to the formation of the seminarians. I thought about this a great deal and prayed over it. I proposed to the bishops a program that would help the seminarians to be introduced to a spiritual life as well as to the tools for discernment of spirits that would enable them to recognize whether God was really calling them to this vocation. I included in the program the full spiritual exercises or 30 day retreat. To my disappointment, this element of my program was not accepted as they felt I was trying to turn them into religious. Even though not all of the elements in my program were accepted I felt honored to be asked to design the program even if it were modified in ways that were not always to my liking.

In my contacts with the seminarians in the classroom, I began to appreciate the intellectual capability of many of them. The entrance requirements into the seminary were very high, and the seminary itself was affiliated to the university. The majority of the students did get a bachelor degree in religious studies. In subsequent years quite a few of them would go on to do advanced studies in theology or philosophy. Having such challenging students in the lecture hall kept me on my toes and made my task both challenging and interesting.

During the seven years that I lived in the seminary, I was also involved in some activities outside the seminary and also in extracurricular activities within the seminary. Within the seminary, I was asked to be chaplain both to the Charismatics and the Legionaries of Mary. On a personal level, I would not have been very inclined toward either of these movements, but I attended all the meetings, listened to what was being said, opened myself to see the positive aspects in them, and finally, came to appreciate the seminarians who were in these movements. As I came to respect them, I began to understand the value of the movements themselves, even if I were not inclined to join them. I believe this is something valuable that I learned during those years in the seminary. In past years, I would have prejudged both the movements and their members, and I realize now that I would have been very wrong.

In addition to my involvement with the YCS, I also found myself increasingly involved with the students at the Cape Coast University. I began to celebrating regular Weekday Masses in one of the hostels. These were usually celebrated at around six o'clock in the morning and so they did not interfere with my teaching and spiritual direction at the seminary. It did give me an opportunity to come to know some of university students and to try, in my limited way, to bring them something of the good news. Besides, I enjoyed this very much, and I found that it helped me even in my work in the seminary. I felt that the seminary was far too circumscribed a world in which to live and work. I needed some work outside the seminary to keep me in touch with the reality of the real world away from a house of formation. This contact with the students also brought me invitations to give days of recollection at the university. Looking back over this period, I realized I may have been becoming tired of my work in the seminary and was deliberately looking for the distractions outside. It once again brings me face-to-face with my own motivation in much of what I have been during my active life as a priest.

My work of giving retreats continued with growing involvement during my years in the seminary. Since I had the title of the spiritual director, people looked to me as some kind of a guru with regard to the spiritual life. During almost every holiday of the year in the seminary I would be invited to preach a retreat. Most of these retreats were between five and eight days in length. They were given to diocesan priests, religious sisters, secondary school students, and groups of laypeople. They would involve my travelling to various parts of the country. This brought me into contact with the church in just about every province of Ghana. I loved this kind of work and I valued the contacts that I made through the work. And the more work I did, the more invitations I got to do even more.

One year, I had two retreats to give back to back. One was a three-day retreat to the priests of the Sunyani diocese. The Bishop of the diocese, James Owusu, was a good friend of mine, and there was a great deal of mutual respect. I'd preached his diocesan retreat on at least two occasions. On this particular occasion that I am writing about now, I became quite ill during the first day of the retreat, probably with malaria. When I got malaria, I would often experience severe diarrhea and so I would simply stop eating and drinking in order not to be disturbed by the problem until the end of the retreat. And so I actually stopped eating and drinking for about three days.

I managed to get through the retreat quite well, and by the end of that period I hardly felt hungry anymore. The morning the retreat ended it was my intention to move on clear across the country to direct another retreat in team with a sister. This second retreat was to begin in two days. One of the young priests on the diocesan retreat had reported to a sister doctor at the Sunyani Hospital that I had not been feeling well during the retreat. She insisted that I come for an examination.

She found I was completely dehydrated, so much so that if she pinched my skin it remained in the pinched position. It showed no flexibility. She told me I had to be immediately admitted to the hospital to be rehydrated since this condition was quite serious. The fact of the matter was that I had not passed urine in almost 48 hours.

When I was admitted to the hospital, she ordered 10 pints of infusion. She told the nurse that she was to put the infusion into my arm at the rate of about one pint an hour. It was entering the body so fast that it actually caused discomfort. As pint after pint went into my body, I wondered where it was going since I experienced no desire to pass urine and detected no swelling in my abdominal cavity. Sister explained to me that my body was like a dry sponge, and it was simply absorbing all the liquid it could get.

After about the eighth pint I finally passed urine. Sister seemed relieved that my kidneys were working normally.

After completing the 10 pints, she said I could continue the rehydration orally. The next day I was allowed to leave the hospital, and I took my first solid food in almost 4 days. When my condition stabilized by the end of that day I was allowed to leave to travel to the other retreat location. Fortunately, the sister I was giving the retreat with was an experienced driver, and she did most of the driving. One thing I learned from this experience was that I had to be more conscious of the effects of my work on my body.

The second retreat was an eight-day directed retreat and it went very well. I fully recovered from the malaria and the effects of the dehydration. I've often thought that the Lord has been very good to me in looking after me, even when I wasn't looking after myself. I experienced this more than once during my years in Africa.

Another example of this lack of awareness of my own health occurred in 1986. In June of that year, I traveled to Nkawkaw where I would be collected by one of the young priests working in a small village. While I was waiting to be collected at the Mission Hospital there, I asked one of the sisters why my ankles seemed to be so swollen. She explained to me that there were many possible reasons and that they would have to do some blood tests to try to find out. I agreed to have these done as soon as I returned from visiting my priest friend in his mission. I had a pleasant three days in the mission which was in a remote rural area. When my friend brought me back to the hospital I had blood samples taken. When the doctor examined the results of the tests he first told sister that there must have been some mistake and that the tests should be done again. They were repeated with the same results. My hemoglobin count was about 4.8, when normally it should have been over 14. The doctor wondered how I was even able to continue going about my duties since I must have been lacking a lot of energy. He wanted me to stay in the hospital for a few days for further examination, but I had another retreat beginning the next night and I was going to be collected by car by some of the sisters making the retreat. we travelled together to the northern part of Ghana. The doctor gave me some vitamin B tablets, some iron tablets and cautioned me to get plenty of rest and to eat as much meat and fish as possible.

We traveled to the retreat and everything went well. I tried to be faithful to the suggestions of the doctor, and on my return to Nkawkaw after the retreat, the blood tests were repeated. Despite all my efforts to rest, to take the vitamin B and iron tablets, and to eat more than I usually would of meat and fish, my hemoglobin count was little changed. The doctor tried a few more tests, but could not diagnose just what the problem was. He urged me to see other doctors when I returned to Cape Coast.

Upon my return to Cape Coast, I informed my superior, and we traveled together to another Mission Hospital about 100 km west of Cape Coast. There was a reverend sister there who is also a doctor, and she repeated some of the blood tests done earlier at Nkawkaw. She got the same results and after further examination said that if she were my superior she would put me on the next plane for New York. I then began to realize that my condition was more serious than I had imagined.

My superiors did exactly as the sister suggested and within a few days I was on my way to New York. I informed the seminary staff and students and they were very disturbed. They promised to pray for me, and I knew they would unfailingly do so.

When I arrived in New York I went immediately to my general care physician, Dr. Kevin Cahill, who had been my general physician for about 20 years. He examined me and found exactly the same symptoms as were found in Ghana. According to his own first diagnosis, he told me that my problem was a genetic one and a serious one. According to him, I might have to have regular blood transfusions, would probably not be able to go back to Africa, and might only find myself with five or six years to live. However, he would send me to a hematologist who would be able to make a more exact diagnosis of the problem. I must admit that this conversation with the doctor made me quite serious, and for the first time I faced the possibility of death.

I was sent to a very good hematologist in Manhattan who told me that he would first like to do a bone marrow test. Those who had undergone this test always described it as a very painful one and so I prepared myself for the worst. He extracted the bone marrow then and there during that first visit. He had me lie down on the examining table on my belly, and then applied local anesthetic to an area of the skin just above the hip bone, and proceeded to drill into the hip bone and remove some of the marrow. It was all over before I even knew what happened. And I remarked that it was a rather painless procedure when I had been expecting a very painful one.

The nurse who, was dressing my wound told me that not everyone takes it as easily as I did. The doctor ascribed this to the fact that I was so thin. I had to wait several days for the results of that test to come in. When I went back to visit him for the review, he told me that, though the bone marrow had some few peculiarities, it was producing red blood cells as normal, but that upon entry into the bloodstream they were being killed off by my immune system.

The hematologist put me on a regimen of drugs and had me return to see him about every three days. It took several visits before we discovered some drugs that would begin to increase my hemoglobin count. However, once dosage was reduced, the hemoglobin count would immediately fall. Since it was not possible to remain on the high dosage, another solution had to be found. For weeks the doctor experimented with different combinations of drugs. At one point he even suggested that I undergo surgery for the removal of the spleen, as he was fairly certain that doing this would put an end to the destruction of the hemoglobin in the blood.

I said I was unwilling to undergo this operation for the simple reason that the spleen is the filter for the malaria parasite. To remove it would make me more vulnerable to regular attacks of malaria. In fact, the removal of the spleen may have meant that I could not return to Africa. I told the doctor that I would rather have a short life in Africa than a long life in the United States. This reflected my honest feelings. I realized how much I loved Africa and its people and how difficult it would be for me to give them up. The doctor fully understood my feelings and said he would continue to try various combinations of drugs. He did finally find a combination of three drugs that seemed to stabilize my condition. After observing my condition for a few days more, he gave me permission to return to Africa.

I was greatly relieved with this news, and was delighted to be able to return to Ghana in time to deliver a very important paper at the national meeting of the Knights of Marshall, an organization similar to the Knights of Columbus in the United States. I had been asked to give two papers at their annual general meeting some six months in advance, and I didn't want to disappoint them. Furthermore, I had worked very hard on the papers and the topic was one that I felt was very important to their own spiritual lives, and one which I wanted very much to share with them. The topic was "Christian Formation and Development".

I arrived back in Ghana just a few days before the convention, and after settling into the seminary again, I traveled to Kumasi to the university for the convention. The seminarians welcomed me back with great warmth, and shared with me how much they had been praying for me. They also revealed to me that they had had an overnight vigil of prayer for my healing. To this day, I attribute much of my healing to their prayers. The Knights of Marshall in Kumasi were equally happy to see me. I had mailed a copy of my talks to them so that someone could read them on my behalf in case I could not be there. I was delighted to be there and read them myself. It was an impressive gathering of dedicated men and women, numbering about 500. I think it was the largest group I had ever addressed in my life.

I had to go to the doctors about every two weeks for a blood test to check on the hemoglobin count. If the count was going up or remaining stable, I could reduce certain drugs. On the contrary, if the count was going down I would have to increase the dosage. This was a rather worrying time, since the condition did not seem to stabilize easily. All I could do was pray and ask the prayers of the seminarians. It took several months before I could begin to reduce my dosage on a regular basis. After about one year, I was down to a fairly minimal dose of drugs.

When I went on leave a year later, the hematologist took me off two of the very strongest drugs, since their side effects could be dangerous. When I returned to Ghana after that leave, I was taking only one drug. And by the end of another year, I was able to go off that drug completely. For the past 20 years, I have not had to take any drugs at all for any reason at all. The autoimmune condition seems to be in a state of permanent remission, and I'm very grateful for all the years that I've been able to work in Africa. Knowing the faith of the African people and the almost miraculous cures that I have heard about from dear friends which were the fruit of prayer, I have no doubt that my present good state of health is, in no small way, the fruit of the prayers of those seminarians and their love for me. And so my work in Ghana continued with its usual vigor and my own continued satisfaction in all the work I was doing both in and out of the seminary. But a large cloud was looming that would soon obscure much of the satisfaction and joy that I had been experiencing for more than five years in the seminary.

Chapter Thirteen

ANOTHER STORM BREWING

Before I take up the difficult topic of the looming dark cloud on the horizon, I would like to share something of the wonderful experiences of visiting the families of the seminarians in their villages during the vacation time. During the long break between academic years, I would almost always try to make a trip to visit the families of one or more of the seminarians. Sometimes I traveled by car, and other times with public transport. One particular visit stands out in my mind very vividly.

I was invited to visit the family of two seminarians from the Sunyani diocese. It was arranged that I should meet them in the city of Sunyani, and they would lead me to the village where I would be staying for a couple of days. We traveled west of Sunyani to the town of Dormaa-Ahenkro, and then still further west to a village close to the border with Cote D'Ivoire. It was the smallest village I had ever visited during my time in Ghana. I believe there were only five houses, two on one side of the road and three on the other. I was given accommodation in the largest house, which was that of the chief. There was neither electricity nor running water.

There wasn't even a latrine inside the house. They showed me to my room, which was probably as comfortable a room as they could find. Then they took me outside and we walked 100 meters or so down the road and then turned off into the forest and another 50 meters or so. This, they told me, was my toilet. They assured me no one would disturb me here or embarrass me. If I needed to have a bowel movement, I would carry a small hoe with me, dig a small hole, relieve myself, and then cover the hole. For washing up, they left a bucket of clean water outside my door. Believe it or not, I was not at all disturbed by the simple conditions. In fact, I was very happy to be there since these two seminarians were very close friends of mine.

One of the first things a visitor must do when arriving in the village is to greet all the people in the village. As we moved from house to house, we were very warmly greeted, and the people expressed surprise that a "professor" from the seminary would come to visit them in their village. I was very humbled by this as I did not consider myself as doing anything very extraordinary. We also made a visit to a neighboring village which was the home of the family of another seminarian who was not with us at the time. When we came to the house of his mother, she danced for joy at our visit and presented me with a gift: three small guinea fowl eggs. These were probably her most precious possession and would have been used to prepare a meal for special guest. I will never forget that gift. In monetary terms it was worth very little, it was the widow's mite. The joy of the woman in receiving me into her house, and the joy it gave her to present me with a gift meant more to me than any amount of money. We said Mass in that village in a small mud block church.

The next day, the two seminarians asked me if I would cross over into Cote D'Ivoire to celebrate Mass for part of the extended family. Going from Ghana to Côte d'Ivoire was a simple process of riding a bicycle about 2 or 3 km on a path through the forest. There were no immigration or customs controls. You hardly realized that you had crossed from one country into another. The standard of living in Côte d'Ivoire was obviously higher than that in Ghana. We visited the house of the chief to present ourselves to him upon entering his village. I still treasure a photograph of myself with the chief and his entourage.

After visiting the extended family of the seminarian, I celebrated Mass in a small chapel. We had a wonderful day there, and the people were reluctant to let us go back to Ghana.

When it came time to leave to return to Cape coast, I was invited to a farewell meal at the family of one of the seminarians. After the meal, I was presented with several gifts which all had symbolic meanings. I was presented with a torch (a flashlight) to symbolize the desire of the people that I should always have a light to guide me in my path. I was then presented with a pair of shorts (underpants) because that is the garment that is closest to your body, and symbolize the desire of the people to be always near to me in my heart. I was then presented with a pair of sandals, to symbolize their desire to give me the means to one day return to them. Of course, I also departed with a car trunk full of foodstuffs.

There were several other visits to villages similar to this one, and they made up one of the greatest treasures in my memory of my years in Africa. The warmth of the people and their extraordinary spirit of welcome are qualities that I will always treasure and hope to imitate.

What always touched me so much was the fact that I could not even speak their language. It made me very sad that I could do no more than utter a few greetings. It never seemed to bother them too much that I had to always work through an interpreter. My presence in their midst meant a great deal to them. One of my seminarians tried to encourage me by assuring me that some missionaries could speak the language fluently, but could not relate to the people in a loving way, as I apparently had done. Although this eased my mind a bit, to the end of my days I will always regret not having learned the language of the people.

There were many things I learned from these visits. One of them was a deep admiration for the faith of the people. I never ceased to be amazed at how much the church meant to them. Their love for the Scriptures and their zeal in spreading the good news to others were beyond anything I had ever experienced before. One man in the village I went to visit was responsible for bringing the faith and establishing the church in five other villages. I once visited a village deep in the forest area where the parish was celebrating the 75th anniversary of its founding. This was at a time when the church in Ghana was only a little over a hundred years old. I wondered how the faith could have gone from the coastal region where the missionaries first landed into this remote interior region in just 25 years.

The answer is simply the faith of the people. Some representatives of the village had gone to the coast to trade for salt, found the faith of the missionaries, were converted, and brought their new faith back to the people. Too many people think that the work of propagation of the faith was largely the work of the missionaries. I do not want to underestimate the extraordinary sacrifice and suffering of the early missionaries, but they could not have been as successful as they were without the zeal of the lay men and lay women who first came to the faith.

Now I must come to one of the most painful of my experiences during my life in Africa. I had already suffered two very serious setbacks in my work in Africa. The first I have already spoken of when I wrote of my deportation from Nigeria. That was an extremely painful experience because it separated me from the people I'd come to know and love. At that time, I wasn't even sure I would go back to Africa.

I thank God that he opened a door for me to go to Zambia. Then came the experience of not getting a renewal of the contract at the teacher training college in Zambia. This again was due to a misunderstanding between me and the principal of the college which resulted in my being put on probation; thus assuring that the Ministry of Education would not renew my contract. And so, after a transitional year teaching in a Jesuit school in Zambia, I moved on to Ghana. But what I was about to experience in Ghana, was far more painful than either of my other disappointments.

I will have to begin with the background to the events that were about to unfold. In 1985, the New York province made a very significant decision to establish a community in Ghana. Up to that time, we had just been two or three Jesuits working more or less independently in different apostolates. With the kindness of the Archbishop, two neighbouring houses were made available for us as a temporary residence until a permanent residence could be built.

The temporary residence belonged to the Archbishop and was situated on property adjoining St. Augustine's College. The Belgian Jesuit, Father Joe Van Torre, had even asked if he could become a member of this community. His heart was in Africa and he wished to remain there. Unfortunately, he was suffering from a brain tumor, and when he went on leave during the summer of 1985, the doctors told him that the situation was quite serious. However, he insisted on returning to Ghana and to the seminary. He arrived back on the campus in time for the new academic year in September 1985.

One day, in early February of 1986, I was summoned by the Rector to go quickly to Father Van Torre's room since he seemed to be suffering from a seizure. When I arrived there it took three of us to hold him down while we arranged to get him into my car and take him to the hospital. There he was sedated and put to bed. He was not fully conscious nor did he ever regain full consciousness. The rector assigned seminarians to be with him round-the-clock. They would go on several hours shifts throughout the day. In this way, he was never without a companion. The doctors did what they could to make him comfortable.

But there was little they could do about the cause of the problem, which was the tumor in the brain. On one of these shifts during the night when I had joined the seminarians, I was praying by his side and holding his hand when he quietly slipped out of this life. I immediately informed the Rector and the Archbishop. We transferred his body to the mortuary and arranged for his funeral. He was waked at the Cathedral and a large crowd of people stayed with his body throughout the night, singing and praying.

The Archbishop presided at the funeral Mass the next morning, and I was invited to preach the homily. Since Fr. Pat Ryan had returned to New York to take up a position at Fordham University, I was the only Jesuit in Ghana at the time from the New York province. When the news circulated that a Jesuit in Ghana had died, the superior of the mission, Father Eamon Taylor, presumed that I had died. When he came to Ghana and I met him at the airport, he was happily surprised to learn that I was still alive.

Father Taylor's visit to Ghana at that time was to confirm the arrangements for the setting up of the new apostolic community. He met with the Archbishop and confirmed the Archbishop's desire to have the Jesuits working in his archdiocese. He seemed quite content with me and my work both when I was at the secondary school of St. Augustine's and since my move as spiritual director to the major seminary. I was also a member of the Presbyteral Council of the archdiocese, and was also one of the consultors of the Archbishop. We also visited the two houses near the Archbishop's house that would be the temporary residence of our first Jesuit community. The new members of that community were due to arrive in a few months time.

That summer I had been asked to give a series of retreats to the various communities of the SVDs (Society of the Divine Word). This would occupy me for the better part of two months of July and August. When I arrived back in Cape Coast I found that my new community had arrived. It consisted of two priests, Father Ray Adams and Father Bob Dullahan, and two scholastics. Fr. Adams would take a position as a lecturer at the University of Cape Coast, while one of the scholastics would teach in the seminary and the other at St. Augustine's College. Father Dullahan would join me as a spiritual director at the seminary. He would live in the new community, while I would continue living in the seminary but having a room in the new community where I could stay on weekends.

Before the new Jesuits arrived, most of the priests and religious in the area presumed that I would be the superior since I had been living in Ghana at that point for about eight years; Father Adams had never lived or worked in Africa. But the New York provincial appointed Father Adams as the new superior in Ghana, working under the regional superior, Father Eamon Taylor, whose office was in Lagos, Nigeria.

I would be less than honest if I did not admit that I was a bit disappointed, being overlooked after almost 20 years in Nigeria, Zambia and Ghana. In subsequent years, I came to appreciate more and more the wisdom of this decision. Experience has taught me that I am not a very effective superior, nor would I have had the skills to deal with the building of a new house on the property acquired with the help of the Archbishop. It would take me a bit of time to adjust to the reality of a superior with little experience in Africa. However, Father Adams proved to be an able administrator and wasted no time in initiating the building of the new house. The difference in our experience of Africa and his position of authority in a new community created a bit of tension between us. Although this was never expressed outwardly, there can be little doubt that it existed and at times, made our relationship in the community a bit uneasy. This undoubtedly had an effect on the events that would follow.

Each weekend on Sunday morning I would cycle from the seminary to the Jesuit residence to share dinner and a bit of socializing with my brothers. I did this every Sunday, as I thought it was important to maintain a regular relationship with a Jesuit community. I had lived alone for the past six years, and I had to get used to being with a community. I decided to maintain my regular residence at the seminary in order to be more effective in my work as a spiritual director, since every evening after supper I would be having meetings with my spiritual directees. Father Dullahan, on the other hand, lived at the Jesuit residence and commuted each day to the seminary.

Sometime toward the end of 1988 I was summoned to the Archbishop's office. He told me that he was not entirely happy with my work in the seminary. This came as quite a shock to me since, as I wrote previously, I was a member of his Presbyteral Council as well as one of his consultors. In my many interactions with him he had never mentioned anything like this before. He said there were three things that were brought to his attention which disturbed him a bit. The first was that I did not always concelebrate Mass with the staff each morning in the seminary chapel. I admitted that this was true but that I was saying Mass each week on several days at the University campus for the students. I also honestly admitted that there were times when I just wanted to be alone and so celebrated Mass privately.

The second item that disturbed him was similar in nature in that I did not always take my meals with the staff community in their dining room. This was also true, but there was at least one other priest who never took lunch or breakfast in the dining room and, as far as I know, this did not seem to present any problem. In the evenings, at times when I went to the dining room at the appropriate time I found that I was the only one there and was eating alone. However, I did not try to justify my actions and I accepted his criticism.

The third point he had to make was that the seminarians were afraid of me and therefore could not be completely open with me especially on matters of celibacy. This was the most incomprehensible of the three items because I always had the largest number of seminarians for spiritual direction, and my experience with them was that they were always very open with me. So I could not understand where this last point was coming from.

I found it hard to believe that the seminarians themselves who were coming to me complained to the Archbishop since most of them found him rather unapproachable. I apologized for the failings in my life at the seminary and said I would sincerely try to correct my behavior in accordance with the items he had brought to my attention.

I did try to change. I was more frequently a concelebrant at the seminary Mass and more regularly at the evening meal in the dining room. As of the third point I was a bit puzzled since I had never shown any harshness in my dealing with the seminarians during our private chats and spiritual direction. Life went on for another few months and sometime early in 1989 I was again summoned to the Archbishop's office. This time I was accompanied by the superior Father Adams. The Archbishop repeated his three complaints in the presence of my superior and said that he wanted me removed from the seminary staff. This was a complete shock to me and I found it emotionally very difficult. There were only a few months left before the end of the academic year. I kept the news to myself for a long time, reflecting on just how to break this news to the seminary students. I presumed that the rector had already been informed by the Archbishop so that he could make arrangements for someone to replace me. As we approached the end of the academic year, I asked to see all the seminarians in their dining room because I had a short statement to make during the meal.

I carefully prepared my statement so that it would not reflect negatively on the Archbishop or the seminary. I explained to the seminarians that I always taught them that an important part of the life of a priest was to form communities with his fellow priests. I explained to them that I had not always lived up to what I had taught them, and this inconsistency made my work at the seminary less effective. Aware of this inconsistency, the Archbishop had rightly asked me to terminate my work in the seminary.

I expressed appreciation for the friendship and trust the seminarians had shown me, and also expressed my appreciation for the cooperation of the staff and the trust the Archbishop had shown me up to this point. By the end of my statement I was in tears and so were the seminarians. They could hardly believe what they were hearing, and I tried to help them to accept this and to see the reasons behind the Archbishop's decision.

That June of 1989 was the 25th anniversary of my ordination. The rector of the seminary, Father Thomas Mensah, wanted to have a farewell celebration for me and also an opportunity to celebrate my silver jubilee as a priest. I must admit I didn't feel like celebrating anything. I told the rector that it seemed inappropriate to celebrate my life in the seminary when I was being asked to leave precisely because my behavior had been inappropriate to my work in the seminary. However the rector said that it would be very much out of keeping with the African culture for me to leave without some kind of expression of appreciation. I accepted his decision and I did celebrate a Mass with the seminarians in which the rector thanked me publicly for all my contributions to the seminary in the past seven years. He also presented me with a beautiful stool and a kente stole, the latter of which I have treasured even to this day.

In the early part of that year, aware of the Archbishop's dissatisfaction, I had, with the permission of superiors, begun to prepare for an alternative apostolate. I had been in touch with the Bishop of Sunyani, James Owusu. He had always been very friendly with me and showed great affection for me. He had wanted me to move up to his diocese to direct a new pastoral center and retreat house that he was building. I had already discussed this with Father Eamon Taylor, and he told me to continue exploring the possibility. When it was clear that the Archbishop no longer wanted me in the seminary, I wrote to Bishop Owusu to fill him in on this development.

He wrote back to me and said he would explore precisely the reasons behind the Archbishop's decision to remove me from the seminary. It was a policy in the Episcopal conference that if one Bishop rejected a priest no other Bishop would take him up. He inquired among those who were at the last meeting of the bishops. He himself was not at that meeting but had sent a representative, his vicar general. He was told that my name had not even come up at the meeting, and nothing was said about my being dismissed from the seminary. He concluded that this was a personal matter between me and the Archbishop and therefore, he could invite me to come to his diocese.

In the meantime Father Eamon Taylor was also exploring the possibility of my coming back to Nigeria. He discovered that after 16 years my name was no longer on the list of prohibited immigrants. He suggested that I make a trip to Lagos from Accra and see if I could be admitted. If they rejected me it was only a 45 minute flight back to Accra. I travelled with Father Adams when he was going to Nigeria for a consultors meeting. I was very anxious as I approached the immigration desk at the new Murtala Mohammed Airport in Lagos. As the man typed my name into the computer I said a silent prayer. The next thing I knew he was stamping my passport and welcomed me to Nigeria. Father Taylor met us at the airport and drove us to 4 L. Agosto Close. It was a strange experience returning to the very house where I first lived in Africa some 22 years before. Many things had changed in the 16 years since I had left Lagos. The city had expanded greatly, and the new ring roads around the city were a vast improvement over the congested streets of the past. There was also a new bridge connecting Lagos Island to the mainland. I slept soundly that night and woke in the morning to celebrate Mass with the others.

I had only one full day in Lagos, and while Father Taylor, Father Adams and the others were having their consultors meeting, I was given a driver and was able to move around to visit old friends. When I went down to St. Gregory's College, I was surprised when a mature man called out to me. It turned out he was at one time a student there and remembered me after all these years. He gave me a big bear hug, and I suddenly felt very welcome. He was now a teacher and invited me to come to his house to meet his family.

The day passed very quickly and the next day, in the morning, I was flying back to Accra, happy in the fact that I could return to Nigeria and work there if it proved to be impossible to continue working in Ghana. I was now somewhat confident that I would be able to remain on the Nigeria—Ghana Mission. When I arrived back in Accra I was busy giving a day of recollection to the community of the Society of the Divine Word. I returned to Cape Coast quite content.

When I returned to Cape Coast I found that my personal situation had only grown worse. It was becoming increasingly clear that the Archbishop did not want me in his diocese or even in the country. This was revealed when he refused to give me the necessary letters for the immigration authorities in order to renew my work permit and my right to remain in the country. When Father Adams brought me this news, he also added his own comment. He said it was his desire that I leave Ghana and forget about any work in Sunyani. This was a devastating blow to me. I had come to love Ghana and its people very much. The thought of abandoning any hope of working further in the country was very painful and put me in a deep state of depression.

The last two or three months of my stay in Ghana were very busy ones. I tried to occupy myself as much as possible in order not to have to face the reality that I would be leaving the country and not returning. I had been asked to give several retreats and I traveled around the country going from one retreat to another. But the day came when I had to leave. It was late August 1989. It was a very sad day. Once again I was being banned from the country that I had come to love and found myself facing an uncertain future. There was a slight possibility that I could return to Nigeria. But Father Eamon Taylor was going out of office as the superior of the mission and would soon be replaced. The new superior did not know me very well and I had no idea what his plans for me might be.

Chapter Fourteen

ONE DAY ENDS AND ANOTHER DAWNS

I traveled to New York and began my leave by getting a complete physical checkup and visiting friends and family. For the first time since I left Nigeria I had no idea when I would be returning to Africa nor what I would be doing. I took up some temporary work at what was then the Jesuit Seminary and Mission Bureau. On November the 12th 1989 we received word of a great tragedy in Cape Coast that would darken my whole future. Father Ray Adams had been brutally murdered in his own bed in the early hours of the morning by an unknown assailant. His dead body was discovered by members of the community when he failed to show up for Mass. Immediately a suspicion fell upon a young student from Togo who had come to Ghana as a political refugee about a year before. His name was Jacques Attaklah.

Jacques first appeared on my doorstep a year before when I was living at the seminary. He came to me with a letter of introduction from the Catholic Secretariat in Accra. He had gone to them to seek assistance since he had escaped from prison in Togo and could not return to that country. Since he had come to know the Jesuits in Cotonou, Benin, he was sent on to me who was at that time the only Jesuit in Ghana.

I welcomed him and listened to his sad story, and was impressed by his sincerity and the difficulty of this present situation. I arranged for him to stay at a hostel in Accra while attending classes in the English language while we considered his future. Actually, his English was quite good, as he was a university major in modern languages. I would finance his housing and studies. When the Jesuit community was established in town, I introduced

Jacques to the community. During school breaks from his course in English in Accra, he would come and stay with the community. Thus, he became known to Father Adams and the other members of the community.

As time went on Jacques expressed more clearly just what he hoped to do with his life. He wondered if I could find financial help for him to pursue his studies at the University of Ghana while waiting for political stability in his own country. It was at about this time that we had a very important visitor from Rome. He was Father Galli, an Italian Jesuit who had worked for years in Africa and was the general's assistant for the continent. He had words of encouragement both for me and for Jacques. For me, it was the invitation to become the spiritual director of the diocesan seminary in Malawi. The episcopal conference of Malawi had asked the Jesuits to take over the administration of their major seminary in Zomba. The provincial of Zambia had already identified someone to be the Rector and another person to be the dean. They wanted at least one other member of staff as a lecturer and another as a spiritual director.

Father Galli claimed that he had heard good things about my work at the seminary in Cape Coast and wondered if I would be willing to carry on the same work in Malawi. This meant that I would have a job to do even if I left the seminary in Ghana. The good news for Jacques was the offer of financial aid from the Society of Jesus to assist in furthering his education until someday he could return safely to his own country. Like myself, Jacques now had something to look forward to.

I started receiving communications from the provincial of Zambia about the possibility of my coming to Malawi to work in the seminary. I could not give him a definite answer since it all depended on my superior in Nigeria who had expressed an interest in my returning to Nigeria for an assignment there. Since the superior of Nigeria was ending his term of office he was busy about many things. I never could get a specific assignment from him, and the months dragged on without any clear idea of what I might do if I should leave Ghana. It was very clear at this point that I would not be able to return to Ghana. At the same time, the opportunity to work in Malawi was slipping away as the superior there had to make a decision to confirm the staff appointments at the seminary.

And so I return to the tragedy of 12th November and its implications for me. On that day, death not only struck Fr. Ray Adams in Cape Coast but also my brother-in-law in Brooklyn; both were in their 50's, and both deaths were completely unexpected. Fr. Adams was brutally murdered in his bed; my brother-in-law died within minutes of a massive heart attack. Arrangements were made for the body of Fr. Adams to be returned to the United States, and I attended the funeral Mass at Fordham which was attended by the Archbishop of Cape Coast. I also had celebrated the funeral Mass for my brother-in-law. It was a difficult time for me: personal tragedy and an uncertain future affected me deeply.

Since it was not clear when I would return to Africa, I began working at Mount Manresa retreat house in Staten Island. I helped with the high school retreats during the week, and occasionally assisted by celebrating Mass in one of the nearby parishes on weekends. I was in a very supportive community and this helped me at this difficult time in my life. On the ninth of December the new regional superior of Nigeria/ Ghana phoned in the morning to say that he would like to come by in the evening to see me. I looked forward to meeting him in the hope that he might be able to give me some idea of my future in Africa. It was a very difficult meeting, and at the end of it I felt completely crushed.

He made it very clear to me that there was no future for me in Africa. He implied that I had been a negative influence and that it would not be in the interests of the mission for me to return. I tried to clarify the reasons for this rather harsh judgment, but I never received an answer that satisfied me. It may have been because I was too disturbed to hear clearly what was being said. I wrote a letter trying to give a more positive judgment to the work I had done in my 22 years in Africa. I quoted from the letters of bishops and priests who seem to find something good in what I was doing.

I admitted that the opinions expressed in some of these letters were probably a bit exaggerated, but I also felt that the negative judgment on my life and work in Africa was also a bit exaggerated, I suggested that the truth lay somewhere in between. I went to see the retired superior, Father Eamon Taylor, and asked if he could help me to understand why I was not being allowed to return to the mission. He said he could not help me since he was not aware of what the present superior had in mind. A few days later I received a reply from the new regional superior confirming his original decision and that there would be no further appeal. I must admit that I was in such a state of depression that I had even considered leaving the Society in which I lived for the last 39 years.

I spoke to one of the priests in the community at Mount Manresa who would talk sense into me and dissuaded me from making any foolish move.

Shortly after the devastating news from the regional superior, when I was at my lowest point in spirit, I had an experience that will remain with me for the rest of my life. It was a cold wintry morning and I was on my way to celebrate Mass with the Baptistine sisters at their school near Mt. Manresa. There was snow on the ground, and as I trudged my way to their school feeling very sorry for myself, I suddenly felt a lightness of spirit that I cannot explain. I felt that God had somehow touched me and assured me that I would be happy whether in Africa or in the United States. I found myself stopping in mid-course and almost saying aloud to myself: "It doesn't really matter whether I go back to Africa or not. I can be happy here." That was a kind of turning point which bought me a great deal of peace. However, my trials were far from over.

I went to see the provincial about my future. He not only confirmed what the regional superior had said but even showed me a letter written by another Jesuit in Africa who more or less repeated the same judgment that I should not return to Africa. More seriously, the provincial suggested that I was not well and that I should undergo psychiatric therapy. He suggested that I go to Boston to consult a Jesuit psychiatrist who is also a friend of mine.

The Jesuit psychiatrist in Boston, who was a longtime friend, could not personally undertake such therapy but said he would recommend a good psychiatrist in either Boston or New York, depending on where I would have preferred to live. I suggested I would like to remain in New York so that I could be near my family, especially my sister who had just lost her husband. And so he suggested Dr. John Donadeo who had his office on the upper West side of Manhattan. I would move from Mount Manresa in Staten Island to St. Ignatius residence on the Upper East Side and continue doing some part-time work at the Jesuit Mission Office.

And so I began my therapy. At my first meeting with the psychiatrist he suggested I come twice a week. After my first two meetings he suggested once a week would be sufficient. After five meetings, he told me he was not quite sure why I was coming since he could not detect any serious problem in me. We talked at length about my experience in Africa and the depression I felt at suddenly being told that I would not return there. The doctor felt that what I was experiencing was perfectly natural and did not require psychotherapy.

I asked to see him one more time so that we could explore other possible flaws in my character. We did meet again and I tried to dredge up as many possible flaws as I could conceive. He rejected almost all of these. I then suggested that I allow my provincial to speak with him and that I absolved him of all confidentiality so that he could tell the provincial exactly what he had learned from his meetings with me. I thanked him very much for the help he had given me.

I then phoned the provincial, told him what I had learned from the psychiatrist and asked him to phone the psychiatrist. That was the end of my psychotherapy, although the provincial had told me when he first suggested this that it might continue for at least a year. Of course I had to explain to my sister why I was not returning to Africa. She was very encouraging to me and affirmed me by telling me there was nothing wrong with me, but that, like her, I was going through the pain of loss. She had just lost her husband with whom she had lived for 34 years, and I was losing a relationship to Africa and its people which I had nourished for 22 years. And so, with the help of family and Jesuit friends, I knew that I would be able to continue the life I have always lived as a Jesuit for so many years.

In the spring of 1990, my sister and I jointly shared a common loss with the death of my younger brother Joseph on Good Friday, 13th April. He was only 53, and had had a rather troubled life and neither of us seemed able to help him, though we tried many times. We had a consoling funeral as I was accompanied by over a dozen fellow Jesuits at the requiem Mass. He was laid to rest in the same plot with my parents.

To compensate for this sorrow, it was about that same time that I received a letter from the provincial of Zambia, Father Jim McGloin, inviting me to return to Zambia to work in Kitwe as chaplain to the university, the Copperbelt Secondary Teachers' College, and a private secondary school run by the mines. I was delighted to receive this invitation, for it meant I could return to the continent which had meant so much to me for so many years. After all, it was the Africans who constantly affirmed me and gave me a sense of self-worth that I had not known in most of my life. When I spoke over this proposal with the provincial, at first he was not very enthusiastic about it, but then agreed that I could go.

It was when I was beginning my preparations for my journey back to Africa, that I began to understand what had colored the thinking about me on the part of my own province. I had booked a ticket to Lusaka via Ghana. I was once again summoned to the provincial's office, and told that I was very insensitive to want to go through Ghana.

I explained that some 70 seminarians who had been my spiritual directees for five years had been ordained and I wished to see them to congratulate them. After all I had lived in Ghana for 11 years, and I would've thought it natural that I would want to return there for a visit.

I presumed that my superiors in New York, referring to my insensitivity, were concerned about my going to Cape Coast where I was not in favor with the Archbishop. I told my superiors that I would not go to Cape Coast but that I would remain in Accra, staying with diocesan priests friends of mine. I was told that the insensitivity referred to the recent death of Father Adams and the feelings of the Jesuits in Ghana. Did my superiors really think that I was in any way associated with Fr. Adam's death?

I began to realize that because of my relationship with Jacques Attaklah I was somehow considered partially responsible for the death of Father Adams. Subsequently, there were other indications that this was indeed the thinking behind the decision that I should not return to Nigeria or Ghana. Jacques Attaklah was never found again and thus never tried for the crime, although there was circumstantial evidence that he had done it. I have personally never heard from him again, and I pray for him, for, if he did this, he had to be a very disturbed young man.

Looking back over this year, I have to admit it was very difficult. I had lost all self-confidence and even a sense of self-worth. I suffered a good deal of depression during that year, but was encouraged by friends both inside and outside the Society of Jesus. I had to rely more on faith than reason, and I even found that difficult. But I have learned on more than one occasion that when things seem darkest, it is just before the dawn of something much brighter than what had gone before. I experienced that when I was deported from Nigeria, and experienced it again when I could not get a renewal of contract at the teacher training college in Zambia, and had to move on to Ghana. Why should I not expect the same thing again? Is this not the meaning of my faith in the death and resurrection of the Lord? We do not always find the new life on this earth; but I have been blessed with finding a new life on this earth after a kind of death on this earth. I have much to be grateful for, and I have never really doubted the love of God.

So at the beginning of October 1990, I began my journey back to Africa. I had a wonderful week in Ghana seeing young priests whom I'd known so well, and who were so happy to see me. Once again, I felt as if I were somebody who could win the respect of others, and felt reassured about the future that lay ahead of me.

At my arrival at the Lusaka Airport, I was given a warm welcome by the provincial of Zambia. When I left there 12 years before I thought I would never see it again. It was a wonderful surprise to find myself back in Zambia. After a few days in Lusaka, I made my way by road to Kitwe and took up residence in the new Jesuit community which didn't exist when I left there in 1978. I was again given a warm welcome in my new community, most of whom I had not known before. During my early years in Zambia I was cut off from most of the Jesuits in the province because I lived almost alone in the Copperbelt.

The superior of the community, Father Colm O'Riordan, offered to show me around the university, which again had not existed when I was there first, and also Mpelembe Secondary School, which was run by the copper mining company. The Copperbelt Secondary Teachers' College was already known to me since I had lectured there and lived there for three years from 1974 to 1977. He also took me around to the various religious living in the area, and brought me to be introduced to the Bishop of Ndola, who was made Bishop when I was first in Zambia. I had known him well at that time, and he had wanted me to remain in the diocese when I was asked to return to West Africa.

Within a few days I began to get down to work. I celebrated my first weekday Mass at the University and met some of the student leaders in the Catholic community. I also set up my office hours on the campus so that I could begin to see the students individually. The first Sunday I was there I also celebrated Mass at the training college and was introduced to the Catholic student body there. The previous day I celebrated Mass at Mpelembe Secondary School I saw that I would have plenty to do at the three institutions. For the first few weeks I did not celebrate Mass with the university student body because that Mass was also a parish Mass. The Bishop had asked the Jesuits to establish a parish in the Riverside area of Kitwe. The church was just about finished, but until it was formally consecrated Mass continued to be celebrated in the sports hall of the university. University students generally attended this Mass.

On the eighth of December 1990 the new church was dedicated and the parish Mass would no longer be held on the University campus. I consulted the student body to see if they would prefer to continue attending Mass with the parishioners, or would prefer to have their own Mass in the sports hall. They overwhelmingly voted to have their own Mass, and so now we would begin to form the Catholic community on the university campus. This meant that I would celebrate Mass every Saturday afternoon at Mpelembe Secondary School, and then on Sunday morning I would celebrate first at the university and then at COSETCO. I also had a weekday Mass every Wednesday evening at the University, and every Thursday afternoon at COSETCO. I also organized and structured classes at all three institutions for those wishing to prepare for the sacraments of baptism and confirmation. I began to feel very much at home in this new work, and also found it very satisfying.

In addition to this work, I had always desired to be somehow directly involved with the poorer people in the neighborhood. Father Colm O'Riordan had taken me on a tour of a shanty compound very close to our residence and directly behind the university campus. I met with a missionary, Sister Celine, who was doing social work among the poor. I asked her what I might be able to do to assist the poor, considering that I did not know the vernacular language. She suggested I work with the grade 7 pupils to assist them to get into secondary school. In the Zambian educational system grade 7 was the final grade of primary school and there was a screening exam to determine who goes to secondary school.

Children from the shanty compounds rarely do well in this exam and so their education stops at grade 7, hindering any opportunity to raise themselves out of the poverty of the compound. Sister said that she would make an announcement in the church to find out what pupils would like some extra coaching on a Saturday morning. There were four young people who began coming to classes. Every Saturday morning, I walked down to the shanty compound and sat with them going over old exams. I enjoyed this work very much as it put me in touch with the reality of the poor people of Zambia who make up the majority of the population. Presently, advancement to grades 8 and 9 is still determined by a grade exam. There is another screening exam for advancement to grade 10.

Before I begin describing my pastoral work with all these various institutions, I want to mention an event that deeply influenced my life and, I think, made me a much better person. It was a Saturday afternoon, the 26th of November 1990. I had spent most of the day at a private Catholic school attending a regional meeting of the Young Christian Students. When I returned home that night before supper, Father O'Riordan informed me that there had been a serious accident involving some of the university students. He told me he had already been to the hospital to see them and I could go there the next morning. One student, a woman by the name of Euridyce Bubala, was killed in the accident, another student, Leonard Chisala, had a fractured neck and was paralyzed. Other students had broken limbs or serious abrasions.

On Sunday morning, even before I celebrated my first Mass, I went to the hospital to see how the students were doing. All I had time to do was to introduce myself, to say a few comforting words, and to depart with the promise of returning later in the day. I did come back in the afternoon when I had finished my Masses. Now I had more time to talk with each of the students individually. The one whose injuries touched me most was obviously Leonard Chisala. He was paralyzed from the neck down and had neither movement nor feeling below the neck. He was on a special bed called a Streicher bed, which allowed them to apply traction to his neck and spinal column.

Within one week, all the students were discharged from the hospital except for Leonard. Many of them had limbs in casts, but were otherwise okay. I felt I could not stop visiting the hospital to see Leonard just because he was the last of the victims to be in the hospital. He remained in the hospital for 9 1/2 months, and I began visiting him every day, and sometimes twice a day. It was a very lonely life for him in the hospital. During the first two weeks, many students from the university came to visit him; but they seemed to get bored with the whole idea as his stay in the hospital became prolonged.

A member of his family was almost always with him, but he didn't seem to have that much to share with them. There was another reason why I continued to visit him so often; and that was because he was a member of the Seventh-day Adventist church which prohibits any activity on the Sabbath. The accident happened on the Sabbath as he and the other students were on their way to a volleyball game against a team in Ndola. Leonard was the captain of the volleyball team, and I was afraid that he might judge that he was being punished for going to play a game on the Sabbath. I wanted to communicate to him that he is a very good person and that God is not one who punishes.

As the weeks and months passed, Leonard became much more open with me, and I came to know him and his family better and better. As he slowly recovered some movement of his limbs, I was always able to assist him when he wanted to move, take a bath, or just sit up in a wheelchair and go out for some fresh air. The nurses accepted my service of him and never attempted to stop me from doing any of these things because I was not professionally trained. I can't imagine being allowed to do that in an American hospital. Once again I am grateful to the spirit of Africa that allowed me to do these things and so draw ever closer to Leonard. I became a father, an older brother, and a close friend. I don't know if I ever felt closer to anyone than I did to him at that time.

I also had to learn to put up with his varying moods which could go from hopeful to almost despair. There were times when he would not wish to speak to me or to anyone else. These were difficult moments but they never broke the bond of friendship between us, because I could understand what he must have been going through. Here was a young man in his 20s, who was a first-class athlete and would probably never walk again. I once shared with him, at a particularly low point in his recovery, how I too had suffered a great loss that would change my life forever.

That loss was the decision of superiors that I would never return to Ghana or Nigeria again. That meant that there were many friends whom I would never see again. It also meant giving up a country and culture I had truly come to love. But, I went on, that perhaps it was necessary that this decision be taken by superiors. For without that decision, I would never have come to Zambia. And if I had not come to Zambia, I would never have met him nor he me. This seemingly chance encounter opened up for me a whole new understanding of myself and my life.

I truly believe that my life was greatly enriched by my friendship with Leonard, a friendship which was the fruit of an experience which initially brought great pain. I wanted to assure Leonard that his future was no less bright. That from this great tragedy something good would come. I believe he reached such an understanding when one day he told me that he felt this accident was a great blessing. I am not sure what he had in mind when he said this, but most assuredly his life at the university would have been very different had he not suffered.

On two occasions, I went with Leonard to Harare in Zimbabwe to consult a highly respected urology specialist surgeon. He was a Ghanaian, who had worked in Zimbabwe for many years and was considered one of the best in his field in southern Africa. It had become clear that Leonard would probably have to live with a permanent catheter unless a surgeon could make it otherwise. After two visits, it was clear that any constructive surgery would have been risky and its outcome uncertain. I left the final decision to Leonard. He chose to live with his present condition.

I admired his courage and acceptance of the present. One of the things I've always admired about this man is his ability to smile in the face of difficulty, and to find hope in all circumstances. After a while, it was Leonard who was encouraging me and not the other way around. I suppose it would take many pages to write about the ways I have grown through my relationship with Leonard. However, I would like to limit this selection to one more beautiful event in his life.

Sometime in 1996 he informed me that he was going to be married. We talked at great length about this. His future wife, Gwendolyn, was fully aware of what was involved in marrying a man who was handicapped. She was not a young girl, but a woman of his own age, a college graduate with a degree in accounting, and employed by Standard Chartered Bank. As a mature woman with a career of her own, she accepted to marry Leonard, and I was very happy about it. I admired the love that she showed in making this decision, and I also knew that the man she was marrying, though physically handicapped, was a man of many talents and a wonderful person.

A few months before the marriage, Leonard invited me to a traditional ceremony that is common among the Bemba people before marriage. The ceremony is known as "Amatebeto". It is a gathering of all the male friends of the bridegroom. I felt honored to be among them as a guest of honor. During the ceremony the family of the future wife prepares various dishes that are common in her tradition. The future husband is to try all these different dishes so that his wife-to-be will know the food that pleases him most. Another part of the ceremony involves the women of the wife's family giving him instructions and counsel about married life. In the third part of the ceremony, the future wife must wash his feet as a sign of a desire to both love and serve her future husband. Of course, all the guests also get to taste the various wonderful dishes that have been prepared. This brief description is in no way an adequate one for the richness and joy of the occasion.

On the 22nd of December 1996, Leonard and Gwen were married at the Civic Center in the city of Mufulira. It was a simple ceremony, but a very happy one, attended by friends and family of Leonard and Gwen. After the ceremony and the picture taking, we proceeded to the reception which was held in the hall of a nearby school. The hall had been beautifully decorated for the occasion. I went there as a guest of honor, and was asked to say a few words after the meal. To be asked to be the guest of honor at the wedding of a friend is indeed a very great honor. I knew from my participation in the Amatebeto ceremony and from my position as guest of honor at the wedding that I was indeed a very close friend of Leonard. It is not as if I needed this, but it was satisfying when it came.

In my short speech I recalled my long friendship with Leonard and my deep admiration for him and for his wife. I reminded the guests of the

scene of just a few moments before, as Leonard and Gwen processed out
of the council chamber. Leonard had walked into the chamber using two
crutches. As he processed out of the chamber he gave one of the crutches
to a friend to carry while he had put his arm around the arm of his wife.
As they proceeded down the aisle, Leonard lifted the one crutch into the
air and continued walking. To me it was a beautiful symbol and a sign that
with Gwen he would be able to walk, and no longer be totally dependent
on crutches. Over the ensuing years I have remained very close to Leonard,
and I am still learning from him.

Chapter Fifteen

A CHAPLAINS WORK

To return to my work as chaplain in the University, one of the most satisfying aspects of this work was the existence of the small Christian communities. This is a structure within the Catholic church in Zambia and East Africa generally which provides for every large parish or Christian grouping to be divided into small communities. These communities meet on a very regular basis usually every Sunday or every other Sunday at the home of one of the parishioners. There might be 20 or 30 members of this community who will gather together to share the readings of the day's Mass and reflect on them together in the light of the priest's homily during the morning Mass. They also share the needs of the members of their community: who is sick, who has suffered a bereavement, who is in financial difficulty, where is there a marriage problem, et cetera. And as they gather in this way every Sunday they grow in their knowledge and love of one another forming a true small Christian community.

By 1990, this concept had been in existence for almost 25 years. It was mandated by all the bishops of Zambia for all the parishes in the country. Even in the university, the students had formed themselves into small Christian communities. These were normally based in the various student hostels among the students living there. During my time as chaplain at the Copperbelt University there were about 10 of these communities. Each community had between 12 and 14 members. This meant that we had about 140 very active Catholic students in the university.

Of course, there were many more Catholic students than this, but many of them were no longer active in the church or rarely did anything more than attend Sunday Mass. As chaplain, I would visit each of these communities about three times a year, that is, once a term. I was always impressed by the seriousness and sincerity of the students in these groups. Out of these close social encounters came deep friendships that would last for years after the graduation.

Another activity of our catholic community as a whole was the organization of a day of prayer during each of the three terms. These were usually conducted off the campus to give the students an opportunity to be free of the atmosphere of study and have a chance for some serious prayer and reflection. Sometimes these days were directed by the students themselves, other times by myself as chaplain, and at still other times by an invited priest or sister. There were rarely more than 20 or 25 students who came to these but they formed the heart of the leadership in our Catholic community.

To assist in the formation of good Christian leadership, I managed to raise sufficient money to be deposited into a fixed deposit account in the bank such that the interest on this account would be enough to finance a weekend leadership training course at a residential retreat center. I was always impressed by the 10 students who attended these courses and showed themselves very mature and reflective persons. I not only did this for the students at the Copperbelt University, but also for the students at the Copperbelt Secondary Teachers College (COSETCO).

Another important aspect of my work as chaplain was my availability to meet individually with the students for more personal discussion. For this, the university provided me with an office which I could use. I came to know a fair number of students in a much deeper and more personal way through these meetings. In addition to these meetings were my encounters with the students in their small Christian communities. In this office I built up a small library of books that could be borrowed by the students to deepen their understanding and knowledge of the faith and of themselves. It was also my ambition to build up a library of videocassettes of thoughtful movies and documentaries that could become the basis of serious discussions. Unfortunately, the pressure of studies prevented this latter dream from being realized.

Finally, I would like to comment on the liturgies that were at the heart of our Catholic life at the campus. In addition to the Sunday liturgy, which was always very well attended, we had a weekday liturgy on Wednesday evenings, which was almost as well attended as the Sunday one. I still look back upon those liturgies with great joy. The enthusiasm in the singing and the participation in the liturgy generally was most encouraging to me. It was obvious that the students enjoyed being there. They came not because there was an obligation to attend Mass, but because they simply enjoyed the experience. And their joy in the experience was an incredible encouragement to me and was a true spiritual experience each time I celebrated this Mass.

On the feasts such as Easter or Pentecost, I would try to bring together the various student communities for which I was responsible. I would organize the transportation of the COSETCO Catholic students and the Mpelembe Catholic students to come to the University or to the Jesuit house to celebrate Mass together. These were always happy occasions and forged bonds between the students of the three institutions. From these interactions, students sometimes found their future spouses. I have presided over several of these weddings. The combination of the small Christian communities and a great sense of family that the students found in the Catholic community at large was a powerful force in forging friendships and bonds that would last a lifetime. Even now, years after graduation from these institutions, I still find that many of the friendships that began at that time have persevered over the ages.

The enthusiasm of the students in all these institutions for their faith, and a willingness to make sacrifices to express that faith, constantly inspired me as a priest to be the best that I could for them. I don't recall ever going to Mass without having carefully prepared my homily. I could usually depend on the students to make some comment about my preaching. I always appreciated their openness in expressing their likes or dislikes about what I was preaching. In a very profound way they were shaping and forming me as a priest as much as I was influencing their formation as growing adults.

Some of the most memorable liturgies that I celebrated with the students occurred during Holy Week when the students happened to be on campus. The liturgies of Holy Thursday, Good Friday, and Holy Saturday are particularly moving. I recall one particular Good Friday. In the morning we had an outdoor Stations of the Cross right on the campus. We simply marked off 14 stopping points as we moved around one of the back roads of the campus. These stations were prepared by the students themselves. That afternoon we had the traditional liturgy for Good Friday which was adapted to some of the cultural practices of the various tribal groupings in Zambia on the occasion of the funeral of a chief. I was often moved to tears by the emotional power of the celebrations. That same evening we gathered outside the chapel around the large fire. We simply shared our experiences and memories of Jesus, as the Zambian people would do at the wake of anyone who died. It was quite spontaneous and sincere, and made our commemoration of the death of Jesus something that links them to the death of any person close to them.

For the Easter vigil, we would begin again outside the chapel around the large bonfire. You could almost feel the anticipation among the students who came to the celebration. The blessing of the fire, the lighting of the Paschal candle, and the entire liturgy was filled with extraordinary joy and enthusiasm. The vernacular Easter hymns are particularly touching and carry the sense of joy. At the end of the liturgy, the students walked back to their dormitories carrying their lighted candles and continuing to sing some of the Easter hymns in the vernacular. It was a deeply moving site to see the line of candles moving from the chapel into the various dormitories. It was a vivid symbol of the students carrying their faith and their hope to their fellow students.

I mentioned earlier that one of my first experiences upon my return to Kitwe in 1990 was my visit to the shanty compound under the guidance of Father Colm O'Riordan. I also wrote about my own personal involvement in coaching the children in grades seven in the compound to prepare them for their exams that would qualify them for secondary school. Some months after I had begun this work, I realized that so much more could be done in that compound. It had always been one of my dreams even while working in Nigeria and Ghana to involve students in the works of social justice. Here was an opportunity which I had not found before to implement this dream.

At that time I was the chaplain for the Young Christian Student Movement, also known as the YCS. Since one of the goals of the YCS is action on behalf of those in need, I suggested to the university group that they take up the challenge of beginning literacy classes in the shanty compound. They agreed. Within a few weeks I had organized a program with the help of Sister Celine. She had made announcements in the churches that there would be classes teaching adults to read and write. It was an ecumenical endeavor reaching out to churches of various denominations. We had a preliminary meeting to decide how many adults wished to be literate in English and how many in the vernacular. There were about seven or eight University students who were willing to be involved in this work, and they were soon organizing their classes.

I would go down and watch them at their work, and I was very impressed both by their commitment and their ability as teachers. None of them had had any formal training, yet they quickly learned how to communicate the basic skills of reading and writing. To encourage the university students, I contacted the producer of a local television program called, "Focus on the Copperbelt". I had come to know her because of her involvement in the parish. She agreed to make a segment of a program on the work of the students in the compound, and she would do this free of charge. The program was aired on national television and created a very positive image of the university students, who are often pictured as selfish and troublesome.

Unfortunately, the YCS disappointed me and after a few months, seemed to lose interest in the project. Part of this was due to the fact that attendance at these classes began to dwindle because many of the adults were too busy tending to small garden plots or their farms to find time to attend class on a regular basis. As they were continuing with the literacy program, I continued with my work with the grade 7 pupils. With the failure of the literacy program, I decided to expand the work with school children. I formed a new group in our Catholic community and gave it the title, "Christian Action Group".

I invited any university students who wanted to live out their Christianity to join this new group which would have two outlets: working with school children in the shanty compound and visiting the sick poor in the hospital. A good number of students joined our group. Each Saturday morning I would drive a bus, which we had acquired for the chaplaincy, from the campus to the shanty compound and the students would break up the children into classes from grade 1 to grade 12. Of course this required preliminary advertisement through the various churches.

I then proposed that one of university students take responsibility for this project and discuss with his/her fellow students how they would divide up the work. I promised them the financial support they would need in order to purchase blackboards, chalk, notebooks, biros, and textbooks. The classrooms were simply benches scattered under the trees around the local Catholic Church. By the end of the first year, the students were so well organized that they would even appoint one of themselves as "headmaster"/"headmistress", who would then organize the assignment of classes.

At the end of each academic year the students would contribute from their own money in order to have an end of year party for the young pupils. I found that as the students became more and more involved with the poor pupils that they matured greatly. Some even took on the responsibility of sponsoring some of the poorer pupils to attend government primary or secondary schools. This project also turned out to be a kind of therapy for university students who were suffering personal disappointments. I would suggest that they join their fellow students on a given Saturday morning in the compound and see if they could not get somehow involved in teaching the poor. This invariably had a positive effect in their lives.

The other half of the mission of the Christian Action Group consisted of students who made visits to the Kitwe Central Hospital on Sunday afternoon to visit the wards of the poor during the visiting hours. If they found patients with no visitors they would spend some time talking with them. This often led to acts of charity when they found the patient in need of some food, a request to contact a relative, or even the finances to pay for their journey back home. Again, I was impressed by the compassion and love that university students showed towards these poor patients. Every Sunday afternoon 12 or more students would go down to the hospital and spend two hours there.

In 2000, I had been missioned to Lusaka. By this time the project had been in operation for almost 8 years. It continued even after I left as university chaplain, and continues to this day as I write this in 2008. I was always very proud of this accomplishment. The only regret I have is that I did not have regular meetings with the students involved in this project to help them to reflect on just what the project was saying to them. I think I could have deepened their understanding of themselves and their relationship with God and people through these kinds of reflection. I was certainly impressed by the generosity of these African students and their genuine compassion for the suffering poor.

Another memorable event in my work as chaplain and my desire to awaken the social consciousness of the university students was a trip we made to a refugee camp at Maheba, about 200 km west of Kitwe. The camp had been opened by the United Nations around 1970 to cater for the thousands of Angolans displaced by the civil war in their country.

Around 1990 the Jesuit Refugee Services, more commonly referred to as JRS, began a pastoral social program in the camp. The Jesuits who were assigned there were attached to the community in Kitwe. As superior of that community from 1993 to 1999 it was my responsibility to pay occasional visits to the camp to see the Jesuits there. I consulted the Jesuit who headed the team to see if it would be possible to bring some university students there for a visit. We planned to stay there for three days and three nights.

I believe it was eight students who volunteered to make this journey. They knew that their time there would not be easy, but would be undoubtedly fulfilling. We left early in the morning on a Friday and arrived at the camp somewhere after noon time. We were warmly welcomed and given something to eat. Then Father Salvatore, an Indian Jesuit who had worked for many years with refugees in Africa and elsewhere, gave us a tour of the essential parts of the camp. He told the students that they would spend much of Saturday morning working in a part of the camp where there were a lot of old people. They would help them by chopping firewood for them and doing any of the tasks that they needed to be done. The students spent four or five hours with these old people and accomplished a great deal of work for them. They were quite tired; and they were fed by the people themselves.

On that same afternoon I accompanied the students with Father Salvatore to a remote part of the camp where new refugees were just beginning to settle in. We walked among them. Almost all were living in very makeshift shelters constructed from branches and plastic sheeting. The conditions in which they were living and their personal appearance revealed the great suffering that they had gone through. It was becoming emotionally quite difficult for the university students to see so much suffering. Father Salvatore had the brilliant idea to organize a quick football match between university students and young people of that area. There was a bit of open space where they could play soccer, and they did so with great enthusiasm. At one point the ball was kicked in the air and got caught in a branch. This ended the game; but it broke the tension and sadness that the students were feeling. As it was getting late, we returned to the central part of the mission.

The next day, being Sunday, Father Salvatore had organized Mass for the community. There was a large crowd of several hundred refugees. The Mass was held out in the open under the trees in the forest. Our benches were simply long logs. The altar was a simple table.

The Mass was conducted in several languages as Father Salvatore was a gifted linguist. He used English, French, Swahili, Portuguese, and Luvale, a local language in that area. In this way he catered for the Angolans, Rwandans and Congolese, as well as for other refugees. The singing was wonderful and the enthusiasm of the people infectious.

After the Mass, the people, with the help of JRS, prepared a meal for everyone present. It was a very happy occasion. That night, university students met with the JRS workers and shared their experiences. Early Monday morning we returned to campus.

I suggested to the students that they write down their experiences in the form of a small booklet which we could distribute to their fellow students so that the experience could be shared with many. We had a meeting and organized the writing of this pamphlet. Each student wrote a short essay on one or other of the various activities in which we had engaged. I wrote a general introduction and a conclusion, we called the little book "Meeting Christ at Maheba".

This was not the end of the project as the university students who went to Maheba wanted to extend their involvement by asking permission to go to the various parishes to share that experience and beg for old clothes, foodstuffs, or anything else that might assist the refugees. I encouraged them in this project and gave them letters of introduction to the pastors of the various parishes around the university. The students were welcomed in these parishes and ended up collecting quite a large amount of material which was turned over to the JRS for distribution to the refugees.

The compassion shown by the university students in their work in the compound, their visiting of the hospital, and their visit to Maheba made a deep impression on me. It was just another example of the incredible ability of Africans to reach out to their fellow human beings who are in need. I saw this over and over again, not only in the university and teacher training college, but also in the parishes all over the country.

The problem of AIDS has deeply affected the countries of Southern Africa. I am personally acquainted with several Zambians who have lost more than one sibling or more than one parent to this dreaded disease. In practically every church of Zambia, Catholic and Protestant alike, there are Home-Based Care groups who go around their parishes visiting the sick and dying and catering for their many needs. They carry out this extraordinary work of mercy on a regular basis for years on end, receiving no financial recompense for their dedicated service. It deeply touches anyone who witnesses this. I have personally experienced that love and compassion many times in my 40 years in Africa. I will certainly mention a very significant one on a later page.

Of course, life on a university campus, especially in Africa, is not always easy. I recall a time when the university students were boycotting classes because their monthly allowances were not paid on time. I had heard rumors that they would be taking this action, and, at this time I was a part-time lecturer in mathematics at the University. I'd cautioned my students that if they boycotted class I would continue conducting lectures as normal for those who did not wish to observe the boycott. If no one showed up for the lecture, I would simply outline the material that I would have covered and put it on the board. If they were interested, they could go into the class, and copy the topics and study them on their own. I would not cover those topics again. Whenever they decided to resume class, I would presume that they already knew the material that I would have covered.

When they did go on to protest and boycott the classes, I went one morning to my classroom to find no one there. I did as I had cautioned them. I wrote down the topics I would have covered during that class, and I walked over to the bookstore to greet a friend, Christine, a woman who worked there. While there, a few students came to me and asked if there was going to be a class. I told them that indeed there was a class but no one had showed up. They asked if we could go back to the classroom so that I could resume the lecture. I went back with them and began lecturing for the four or five students who came with me. When word went around and reached those who had organized the boycott, they began moving toward the classroom beating drums, and chanting. The students in the classroom became a bit nervous. I told them to simply sit there, that they had nothing to worry about.

The demonstrators reached the classroom, barged in, and erased what I had on the board, and ordered the students out. All except one student moved out. One sat there to keep me company and give me courage. They tried to force him out but he refused. When they threatened physical violence, the leader of the group told them that there was to be no violence. I never forgot that student and the courage that he showed.

Earlier in this book, I wrote about a similar incident at COSETCO in 1974 when a small group of students showed great courage in going against the general trend of their fellow students. This is another characteristic of the African people that I have admired very much. It is hard for us as Americans and individualists to appreciate the pressure of the group on an African person. There is an African proverb among the Bantu people that says: "I am because we are". The individual finds his or her identity in the group. To go against this requires far more courage than it would for an American.

Lecturing in mathematics at CBU was never an easy task. The new course I was teaching was a first year degree course for those studying in the Department of Built Environment. It was considered an important auxiliary course for those studying construction, quantity surveying, and architecture. Because it did not seem to be directly connected with their area of specialization many of the students did not take it seriously. In all my years of teaching in this department I don't think I could count more than a handful of students who seemed to be genuinely interested in mathematics. Every year that I taught this course, I always found a certain number of failures. This meant preparing a supplementary exam and hoping that they would pass.

I prepared a problem set each weekend for them to work on, but I believe few did so. It took great patience to try to teach with enthusiasm to a class that had no great interest in the subject. However, being a lecturer in the university gave me a certain standing in the eyes of the students that I would not have had if I had only been chaplain. It also gave me exposure to students who were not Catholics and whom I might never have met otherwise.

I discovered another limitation in the teaching at the university when I was asked to teach a course in physics in the same department. I was only given two periods a week. I suggested to the head of Department that I make the course a practical one since its main purpose was to introduce to students the skills of taking measurements in their own specialized fields. I put together a series of experiments in heat, electricity, sound, light, and mechanics. When I went to see the laboratories where I would be teaching the course I was appalled by the lack of equipment. This made the teaching very difficult, and I only taught this course once.

Another serious limitation in whatever I was teaching was the library. In mathematics, most of the books were very old and very few copies were available. It was for this reason that we had no textbook and so I had to produce these problem sets every week to give the students something to work on. I was once asked if I wanted to become a full-time member of the staff, but I refused, partly because of the limitations of teaching there, and partly because it would interfere with the time I needed to be chaplain.

In addition to lecturing at the university, I was also lecturing at the teacher training college. Again, I was lecturing in mathematics. Although the students were not as academically qualified as the degree students in the University, I found them much easier to teach because they were training to be mathematics teachers, and therefore, had some serious interest in the subject. I must admit now that I do not quite understand how I managed to carry on lecturing in two institutions, being chaplain for four institutions, and still find time to be with my community.

Lecturing at COSETCO was, in many ways, easier than at the University. First of all, I had been on the pioneer staff of COSETCO from

1974 to 1977. So I was familiar with the physical structure and spirit of the institution. The university didn't even exist in 1977. In addition to this familiarity, I was lecturing at the advanced diploma level to a relatively small groups of students. These classes would have numbered no more than 30. The students were almost all teachers who were upgrading themselves to the advanced level above the first diploma they had received. Therefore, they were highly motivated people who were more mature. To my great surprise, on two occasions I found students in the class who had been in my class for the first diploma between 1974 and 1977. It was wonderful meeting them again and renewing friendship. The syllabus of mathematics at the advanced diploma level was about the same as that of the first year degree course at the University. I enjoy teaching this level of mathematics.

From 1997, I had asked the administration to allow me to teach the first diploma program since I had been teaching the advanced diploma program for the last six years and wanted a break. At this point in the history of the college the first diploma classes were huge. This was due to the financial needs of the college. The government would sponsor about 40 students, but to supplement the fees paid by the government the college opened enrollment to students who came as private individuals willing to pay the tuition fees and to find their own accommodation. Since there was a great desire for higher education beyond secondary school, people were willing to make the sacrifice to attend the college at their own expense. This resulted in classes of 75 or more students, trying to sit in a classroom that was built to accommodate less than 40.

Another way of supplementing income in the college was to run advanced diploma courses for teachers already in the field who could not afford to leave their work. During the three school breaks in the academic year, in April, August, and December, school teachers would come to the college for a period of three weeks and do this for three years. This gave them nine sessions of three weeks each, supplemented by assignments they would do between sessions. I did not want to be involved in this program because I felt I needed a vacation to relax between terms.

Many lecturers took part because it meant a substantial financial reward for the three weeks work. On two occasions the administration asked me to please help them since they could not find an adequate staff. I reluctantly agreed, but did find the experience rewarding. The students were often older teachers who had been teaching at the primary level for many years. At best, some of them taught at the junior high school level. Considering the background of these students, I felt the syllabus was totally unrealistic.

On one of the occasions when I was asked to teach in this program, I was told to cover topics in integral calculus. Shortly into my first lecture, some of these students who are 30 and 40 years old complained that this was too difficult for them to understand. I sympathized with them but assured them that they were quite capable of comprehending this matter. I tried to do my best to be as simple and as clear as possible. By the end of the three weeks they were amazed at what they were able to do. And this gave me a great sense of satisfaction. Over and over again in my experience in Africa I found people who had a rather low opinion of themselves, but were quite capable of accomplishing great things. In addition to my academic lectures in mathematics and science, as chaplain to these institutions, I also conducted classes for the Catholic students who wish to be prepared for the sacraments of baptism or confirmation.

Both at the University and the training college, as well as at Mpelembe secondary school, I ran these classes. Toward the end of each academic year, I would invite the Bishop of Ndola to come and celebrate the sacrament of confirmation at the university. He never refused this invitation, and it was always a source of great joy to have the Bishop among us for an evening. After the Mass, there would be a reception during which the students had an opportunity both to meet the Bishop and to raise questions for discussion. These were always very happy occasions. These instruction classes introduced me to another development in my life and a mission I never even dreamt of.

Chapter Sixteen

A FATHER AND HIS FAMILY

In 1998, I was able to give up my chaplaincy at Mpelembe secondary school because another Jesuit had joined our community and he would take on this responsibility, as well as assisting in the local Catholic radio station. Before he began his work at Mpelembe, he asked me about the confirmation and baptism classes. I described what I had been doing and what material I had covered. However, I had no notes or textbook. I knew in my mind exactly what I wanted to do, and I simply used the Bible to illustrate the various points I was making.

I told him that my basic plan was to give the students a simple picture that would help them to understand the nature of the Church and her sacraments. And this image was simply that of Jesus Christ himself. As I expounded on this, Joe Hayes, our new member of the community, who would be taking on the work of chaplaincy and assisting at the Catholic Diocesan radio station, said that he thought what I had proposed was rather unique. He asked me to think about preparing a series of radio programs on this material. At first I said that this would be too difficult for me as it would require a lot of time to write out the programs and then, with the help of the radio technician, record them for broadcasting.

As he persisted in this request, I finally agreed to try a few programs. I ended up making 13 half-hour programs, which were broadcast and heard all over the Copperbelt. The programs were so successful that they were broadcast again, and I was requested to make a sequel to that series. Now that I was accustomed to writing these programs, I agreed a bit more readily to do this. And so I prepared 13 more half-hour programs following up on the theme of the original 13. As I had introduced the people to encountering Christ in the sacraments of the Church, I went on to outline for them in the next 13 lessons how their lives should be affected by this encounter. It was a short course in Christian living. This second series was as popular as the first, and people started asking me for the transcripts of these talks.

Sometimes I wondered just what affect these talks were having on people. I came to realize just what they meant to at least some people when, one day the front doorbell rang at our Jesuit residence. I went down to answer the door and found standing there a middle-aged woman. I didn't know her and she obviously didn't know me. After greeting her I asked her if I could help her. She said she wanted to speak to Father Ugo. When I told her that I am he, she simply said, "I want to thank you". Curious as to what this might mean, I invited her in and we sat in the visitor's parlor while I listened to her story. She told me that her husband had died of AIDS some months before, and that she had recently lost her job. She wondered how she could take care of her family, and was at the point of despair. She had considered committing suicide. While these thoughts were going through her head, she heard her neighbor's radio which happened to be tuned into one of the programs that I had made. What she heard gave her a new understanding of the meaning of her life, and so she could put aside any thought of suicide and took up her responsibilities for her family, putting her trust in God. This gave her such consolation that she was anxious to know the source of this program. So she asked her neighbor what program she was listening to, and when she discovered that I was the speaker, she made up her mind to find me and say thank you.

I don't know how many people were touched by the programs I made. I know that it was listened to by tens if not hundreds of thousands of people. If these broadcasts touched no one else than this woman I would feel it was all worthwhile. This taught me in a very dramatic way that we can never judge the value of what we're doing by any mere simple external criterion. Sitting in a small room at the radio station with only a technician as company and speaking to a microphone may not seem very important, but I soon learned that it had consequences far beyond my imagining.

As people asked me more frequently for copies of the scripts, it became a financial burden to me. For the full text of the scripts even when printed in small font with narrow margins ran to over 45 pages. To photocopy these each time cost a lot of money. Fortunately, about this time, the Missionary Sisters of Our Lady of Africa, more commonly known as the White Sisters, were given some money for the publication of materials for the spiritual growth of young people. One of my friends among the sisters said that my programs seem to be suitable material. They were willing to fund the printing of these talks. And so I made contact with the Mission Press in Ndola, and began the work of putting together a book. This would be my first publication. We printed 2000 copies, and the book ran to about 180 pages. I decided to sell it at cost so that as many people as possible could read it. The cost per copy was the equivalent of two US dollars. It was published in the year 2000, my golden jubilee as a Jesuit, and my final year in Kitwe as chaplain to the university and teacher training college.

I don't know how many copies of the book have been sold to date. I suspect that most of the 2000 are gone. I used it for several years as a textbook in training senior sisters of many congregations from all over Africa in the course I taught at the Kalundu Formation Center in Lusaka between the years 2001 and 2007. The book was also used in the instruction classes for a number of years at the Copperbelt University and other institutions. I also gave copies each year to our Jesuit novices to help them in the preparation of their own catechism classes in the nearby parish. What made it attractive to many people was simply the fact that I referred to the Scriptures a great deal.

This was one of my motives behind my approach to this task. One of the frequent criticisms of Catholics in Africa is that their beliefs are not found in the Scriptures. It was my goal to try and show that almost everything that we believed and practiced was solidly based in the Scriptures. I suppose if I were to rewrite the book there would be several things that I would change and other things that I would add. But I thank God that I was able to bring this project to completion.

One of the unusual unexpected byproducts of this publication was my relationship with a prisoner on death row in Kabwe, Zambia. One day, I received a letter from one Peter Cassam Kunda. It was dated 22nd February 2002. The return address was: Maximum Prison, Kabwe. The letter opened with: "Dearest Fr. Ugo, Greetings and Prayers from Death Row! Surprised you'll be to receive a letter. The information age is upon us and this includes your precious book, 'Encounters With Christ'."

On the back cover of the book was my photo and short statement about me that included the fact that I was a chaplain at the Copperbelt University. He sent the letter through the university, and it reached me in Lusaka after I had moved to the seminary. He went on to tell me that he had been on death row for 22 years. He had been sentenced to death for aggravated robbery with a weapon, though no one was killed. In Zambia any robbery with a weapon—even a sharpened stick is enough—means an automatic death sentence. Peter was only approaching his 18th birthday at the time. So he was just 40 when he first wrote to me.

We continued correspondence for the next 5 years. A daughter was born to him just before he was sentenced. Her name was Noria, and she came to visit me shortly after my correspondence with her father began. I listened to her story, and eventually financed her training as a seamstress. As my friendship with her father grew through the correspondence, I sent a letter to the office of the president to ask for a re-evaluation of Peter's case. In prison, he had been a model prisoner. Although he hadn't even completed secondary school before he went to prison, he had educated himself in prison, and read just about everything in their small library. The quality of the English in his letters, as well as the thoughtfulness of the content, convinced me that he was a gifted person who might have gone on to the university, had circumstances been different. I mentioned all this in my letter to the president. Nothing came of the letter. I did write again with the same silence following.

I consulted one of the priests at the Catholic Secretariat, who was involved with social justice issues. He suggested I write to the Chief Justice of the Supreme Court. Since he is a very devout Catholic, I had the letter given to him by hand through one of the priests at the cathedral where he worshipped. He did give me a response, and told me he had copied the letter to the Attorney General. I then received a letter from the Attorney General, who was very encouraging. I even met the Chief Justice at the cathedral on the occasion of the funeral of one of the former Archbishops. This all resulted in an amnesty for Peter, and in November of 2007, two months after I left Zambia, he was discharged. He sent a photo of himself and his daughter taken on the day of his release. I was very happy with this outcome.

Because I find it difficult to say no to any request for my help, I found myself with another obligation to my work in Kitwe in addition to my being chaplain at the university, teacher training college, and Mpelembe Secondary School. This obligation came from my friendship with the Baptistine sisters in town where they ran a private primary and secondary school. They had asked if I could come once a week to celebrate Mass for the children. This quickly became twice a week because it was almost impossible to celebrate any meaningful liturgy that would appeal to both the primary and secondary school children at the same time. So once a week

I was to celebrate Mass for the primary school children, and on another day for the secondary school children.

Once again, this minimal contact with these young people seemed to forge bonds that lasted far beyond their years at school. I would occasionally encounter them in later years, and they would remember those Masses. I never cease to be amazed at how God works in us to touch people's lives. But I also believe that part of this effect is simply the openness and sincerity of the African people in any activity that has to do with God.

One day, while waiting in the university car park in Lusaka for someone, a young man approached me, greeted me, and said: "You probably do not remember me; but I was a student at Mpelembe secondary school when you use to come each week for Mass. The sermons you preached each week have changed my whole life, and I just wanted to let you know." It was encounters like these that made my whole life seem very worthwhile. It encouraged me to try even harder to bring the Lord's message wherever I was sent.

I thank God each day for the wonderful people of Africa who constantly affirmed me and encouraged me by their expressions of appreciation for whatever little I did for them. Perhaps it would have been the same anywhere in the world. I cannot say; all I know is that it was the people of Africa who did so much to help me to grow in my self-understanding and the appreciation of my vocation as a Jesuit priest.

Another example of an individual whose life I touched and who touched my life was Moddy Ngambi. I first met Moddy when I started going to the shanty compound to coach those five young people who were in grade 7. At that time, Moddy was in grade 11. I decided to take him on as an extra student to coach. I worked with him in almost all the subjects. Even in literature, I would buy the books needed for the course and I would read them to him. He was quite capable of reading them himself but I knew that the listening would make a deeper impression on him than reading. I also assisted him in maths and science, and purchased whatever history books he needed to do well. He was a very gentle and sincere young man.

When he completed grade 12 and sat the exams, he did not do well enough to advance for further education. He did pass everything, but not with sufficiently high grades to qualify him for teacher training or technical school. He asked me if I could teach him to drive so that he could at least get a license and find work to help support his poor family.

I would not normally agree to teach someone to drive since it is very time-consuming and requires a lot of patience. But I didn't want to see this young man with practically no prospects for his future. So I did teach him to drive. He turned out to be an excellent student, and a very responsible driver.

When it became time to take him for his driving test, I brought him to the road traffic office and we booked an exam. The day we showed up for the exam, we waited patiently for the testing officer. When he arrived he asked me to point out the vehicle that would be used for the test. I pointed to my double cabin pickup, which was fitted out with the required L. plates. The officer pointed out that the plates were made of cardboard covered in plastic. He said they were not proper L. plates.

I asked him what were proper L. plates. He gave me no answer except to repeat that mine were made of cardboard. I insisted that he show me where it was stated that the L. plates could not be made of cardboard. He obviously was beginning to become annoyed but, having no answer, he took Moddy out for the test. As I sat waiting for them to return, I knew Moddy had failed, not because he would not drive well, because the testing officer was very annoyed and would look for even the smallest mistake to fail him. This was exactly what happened, and Moddy was quite discouraged.

As we were driving back to the house, I noticed some kernels of maize on the passenger seat where I was going to sit. I asked Moddy how they came to be there. He then told me that the testing officer had asked him to stop on the road during the test so that he could buy a cob of roasted maize. I asked Moddy what else he did. He also asked Moddy to pick up someone outside the gate and give her a lift into town. Furthermore he asked Moddy to stop at some point in the market so that he could do some shopping. I knew that none of this was appropriate behavior for a testing officer during the testing of a candidate for a driving license. I sat down immediately and wrote a very strong letter to the Officer in Charge.

This was not the first time I had written a letter to someone either to complain or to commend. I have already spoken of my correspondence on behalf of Peter Cassam Kunda. In this case, my letter brought an immediate response from the chief testing officer, who invited me to come by and meet him. One day, I did just that. He was full of apologies for the behavior of one of his officers, and when I said I did not think my friend would want to come back there for another test, he assured me that if I brought him back he would be given a fair test.

At first, Moddy was hesitant to return to the same place for his retesting. I finally encouraged him and he reluctantly agreed. When we went for the second test, the same testing officer approached, Moddy was about to get up and walk off, saying he would not be tested by the same man. Fortunately, at that point the chief testing officer was returning from another test. He recognized me and came over and greeted me. He then asked me if Moddy was the one who had come for the test. When I said he was, he agreed to take him out himself. This time, as I sat waiting for them to return, I was pretty sure Moddy had passed, not because the officer would be too lenient on him, but simply because he was a good driver and would be given a fair test. And this is how it turned out.

My next task was to find work for Moddy. I knew the head of an NGO, and I had heard that she was looking for a driver. I asked her to consider Moddy, to interview him, and let him be tested. I didn't want him to think that he got the job because of my influence and not because of his own qualifications. This has been a policy of mine almost all my life. As I said earlier I would not use my influence to find a place at a school for someone who was a candidate for the Society of Jesus and a good friend. Moddy did get the job and the NGO was very happy with him because he was not only a responsible driver but an honest one; he would never use his position to make extra money taxiing people around. I often used Moddy as a driver whenever he was free and I had to travel to Lusaka. I always felt very safe with him.

From the time that Moddy acquired the job with the NGO as a driver, he began coming over to the Jesuit residence every Sunday morning after Mass. I would usually chat with him for a while, and then would bring him a video to watch while I went to my room and did some work. When the video ended I would rejoin him, prepare him some lunch, and then have him take me out for a drive while we continued our sharing. We would usually stop somewhere for a Coke, and then I would drive him to his house.

This went on for many months. I once asked him why he continued to come over to our house each Sunday. I thought to myself: what do we have in common? I am so much older than him, of a different race and culture, and of a far higher level of education. His answer to me that day was one that I will never forget. "During the week, when I am at work, I am simply a driver. People call after me, "driver go here" or "driver go there". I feel I am just nobody. I don't even have a name. But when I come here, I feel I am somebody."

I think that that is one of the greatest compliments I have ever received, and I have often told others that it is no small achievement if someone feels in your presence that they are somebody. I wish I could say that I always treated everyone in this way.

About two years after Moddy began his work, he started feeling quite sick. He went to many doctors, but they rarely were able to do much for him. When he had first started work, he got married and had a child. When his sickness began, the child also became sick, and by the age of two had died. I realized that Moddy was probably dying of AIDS. It was painful for me to watch him deteriorate like this. By this time I had been transferred to Lusaka, but I took every occasion to come to Kitwe to see how he was doing. In 2002, I went to Kenya to make a 30 day retreat. When I returned in the middle of June I met the news that Moddy had died. It would be impossible to describe how I felt on getting this news. I wished I could have been there at the end. He had been like a son to me, but not only as a son but also as a friend. I went to see his widow and tried to help her find some financial security. I realized that it was very likely that she was also HIV-positive and probably would not live long.

Another individual who touched my life was another AIDS orphan by the name of Simon Matende. His mother died when he was in grade 7. He lived in the shanty compound where I had been coaching the children. Simon was one of those I coached when he got into secondary school. When he reached grade 9, he took the screening exam that was common for all pupils in this grade. This exam determined whether they would move on to upper secondary school, that is grades 10, 11 and 12. Just before these rather important exams, his father became very ill, and I would visit him in hospital quite often. His father died just before the written exams.

I assisted in the funeral for the father. Simon was now a double orphan, and was the firstborn of the four children in his family. I knew I had another responsibility. Simon managed to pass the exams and was promoted to grade 10. At this point, I began working intensively with Simon, another classmate of his, Bruce, and a third, Charles, who was a younger brother to Moddy. I wanted them to do well in their grade 12 exams so that I could try to get them places in a teacher training college to ensure them a position in the civil service.

One of the challenges of these three young men was simply the fact of geography. The shanty compound in which they lived was about 5 miles from the secondary school where they were enrolled.

They would spend about an hour and 40 minutes walking to school every morning, and then a similar amount of time walking home each afternoon. When they left the house in the early morning they would have had no breakfast since their family could not afford three meals a day. At school, they were given nothing and so attended all their classes on an empty stomach with nothing more than a bit of water to drink. When they return home in the late afternoon they would have their one meal of the day. This was the pattern of their school life for the five years that they were in secondary school. As the final exams approached at the end of grade 12, I invited them to the Jesuit house early each morning to give them a proper breakfast, and then I would drive them to school. I wanted them to be rested and alert during their final exams.

Unfortunately, the exams Council in Zambia took several months to grade the final exams since they had to be done at a national level. These three young men completed their final exams in early December 1996. The results would not come out until March or April of 1997, and only then could they apply to the teacher training college for acceptance in January 1998. While they were waiting for the results to come out they managed to find work as untrained teachers in a community school in the shanty compound. This enabled them to earn a very small amount of money, but also gave them some experience for their future profession. When the results did come out, Bruce and Charles did well enough to qualify for entry into COSETCO to be trained as secondary school teachers. Unfortunately, Simon did not do well enough to be admitted to COSETCO, but I worked hard to try to get him admitted to Kitwe Teacher Training College, more commonly referred to as KT TC. They continued their teaching in the community school until the end of the year.

In January of 1998, Bruce and Charles began the studies at COSETCO, while Simon moved to KT TC. Of course, with the help of benefactors, I would have to pay all the expenses for these three young men throughout their training. For Bruce and Charles, they would have both academic work and teaching practice and would complete their training by December of 1999. Simon, at KT TC, would have only one year of academic work followed by a full year of in-service teaching. Bruce and Charles completed their program successfully and were assigned by the Ministry of Education to secondary schools. At the end of his first year of academic work, Simon failed two minor examinations.

According to the regulations at KT TC, failing any subject at the end of the academic year meant being excluded from the program. These were the conditions set down by the Danish aid agency that set up this program at the college. I went to the principal of the college and asked him what I could do since this young man is an orphan. He took pity on me and told

me that the only thing that could be done would be for me to enroll him
again in the course and pay the fees a second time. Once again I relied on
my generous benefactors in the United States to pay the fees so that he
could re-sit the course

Toward the end on the academic year, Simon told me that he was
informed by the principal that, in fact, he would only have to re-sit the
exams that he failed at the end of his first effort. I thought this was very
good news since he did rather well in all the other papers at the end of the
previous year, and they would simply accept the marks on those papers. He
completed all the papers, at least that is what he told me.

A few weeks later he came to celebrate the fact that he had finished
the course successfully and that he was being sent to a school in northern
Zambia. I was absolutely delighted to hear this and looked for some money
to help him travel and settle down at his new assignment, which would
begin his year of in-service teaching as a necessary requirement for the
certificate.

When, two weeks later, he was seen to be still in the shanty compound,
I asked to see him to discover what was going on. He gave me some story
about waiting for an allowance that would be given him through the college
for his travel. The next news I heard was that Simon was in the police cells.
It turned out that he had been caught in association with a young man who
was convicted of stealing. When I went to see him in the cells he looked
terrible. I managed to get him released from the cells since they had no
evidence against him. When he was released he had obviously been beaten
and was quite sick.

I brought him to a private doctor for a complete physical checkup and
finally got him back into shape. I told him to go to the principal to get a
letter explaining what had happened so that he could move into the school
to which he had been assigned, even though he would arrive late. It was
only at this point that Simon came to me in tears, explaining that in fact he
had never taken one of the exams because he had been drinking the night
before and was in no condition for such an exam.

I did not become angry but only sad. Generous friends overseas had
managed to pay for his schooling for so many years, only for him to waste
the opportunity. But I had to try to understand the background of this
young man, and I did not want to give him the impression that he was
being rejected by me for what he had done. We sat and talked for a while,
and then he asked if I could help him to obtain a driver's license. Once
again I had to call upon the generosity of others to put him through a

driving school. He never successfully obtained a driving license, although he told me that he did and was looking for a job.

I began to realize how difficult it is for a young person brought up in a shanty compound, whose parents had both died of AIDS, who was the oldest of the four children who are now orphans, to succeed in life. It would take an extraordinarily strong person to overcome all these obstacles. At this point I had been transferred to Lusaka to become the spiritual director at the major seminary. I tried to keep in touch with Simon but it was more difficult. On my rare trips to Kitwe I would always look him up. He had found work as a security guard, but the pay was very small and the work dangerous. After being beaten up badly by thieves breaking in to the home he was guarding, he quit that work and wanted to return to his village to do farming. I offered to finance this move.

The only times I would see Simon after that were on two occasions when he came to Lusaka, claiming he had some business to do there. It seemed an odd coincidence that these occasions always occurred around his birthday. I always remembered his birthday and would give him a gift of some money so that he could get something he needed. After the second time this happened, I became a bit suspicious that he had never returned to the village and would only come down to Lusaka on the occasion of his birthday to try to get some money.

On that last trip I told him I would only pay his return fare to the Copperbelt. He became quite annoyed and said that I did not trust him and that he would not return again. In fact, he never did, and I have always felt a bit guilty. I realize that he had much deeper problems than even I knew about. One time, after I had moved to Lusaka, I received a telephone call from England from a woman looking for Simon, claiming he was the father of her child. I worried a great deal about him and felt helpless to do anything more for him and I still wonder if I had failed in my love for him.

The story of Charles, the younger brother of Moddy, is also a tragic one. He was assigned to teach in a secondary school in Kitwe, and seemed to be doing well. After only one year of teaching, he became quite sick and died very suddenly. I could hardly believe the news when I heard it because I had not known him to be a sickly person, though he was never very strong. He seemed to be doing well as a teacher, and looked like he had a happy future. I never did find out the cause of his death, but sudden deaths are not unknown in Zambia, sometimes the result of cerebral malaria, meningitis, or stroke.

Of the three young men that I tried to help train as teachers, only the story of Bruce has a happy ending. Bruce completed his training in 1999 in December, and by March of 2000 was teaching in a secondary school in Kasempa where he has been teaching until now, 2008. At first he found it difficult teaching there because it was far from his family in Kitwe, who needed his help. He was also among a people whose language he did not know. Because of his young age he was not given much status, though he worked very hard and was one of the most dedicated teachers in the school. Now, more than eight years later, he seems very happy there. He is now respected by the administration of the school as well as by the pupils. He has been given a decent house and is able to look after a younger sister who he keeps with him and puts through school. I am very proud of the kind of person he is, being a man of great integrity and dedication.

When I look at the experience of these three people and my role in their lives, I thank God for the privilege of knowing them, trying to understand them, reaching out to empower them. Obviously, I wasn't always successful, and that is very humbling. It also is troubling, if I, in any way, were somehow responsible for the unhappy ending in the case of Simon. This experience of assisting young people, both men and women, was a very enriching one which I probably would not have had if I had not gone to Africa. It was there that I found so many people in need and who were so open and trusting. These people were teaching me how to be a true father. After all, I am given that title as a sign of respect by most people who know me as a priest, but in Africa, I had the opportunity to experience both the privilege and responsibility of being a father to many.

Chapter Seventeen

TWO VISITS AND A JUBILEE

It would take many pages to put down all my efforts to reach out to the poor and find ways to empower them. The tragedies of poverty are countless, and I could only touch a few lives. One of the saddest experiences of poverty, where I felt completely helpless, occurred while I was in Kitwe. One day, the doorbell rang at the Jesuit Residence, and two men were there. They were obviously poor. They introduced themselves and said they were from Chipata Compound, the shanty compound where I often visited and began my work of tutoring some pupils there.

They told me a woman was about to give birth, and they needed to get her to the hospital and the hand of the fetus had already come from the womb, but she couldn't deliver the child. I got my vehicle and rushed down with them to the compound. We took the woman to the Kitwe General Hospital.

When we got there, I went to the nearest entrance, and it was locked. When I pounded insistently, someone finally opened the door. Once I was sure she was to be taken care of, I returned home. The next day, I went down to find out how things turned out. The child was dead when she got to the hospital, and the woman died some hours later.

I asked: "But why didn't you take her there sooner, before the delivery began?" The simple and tragic answer was: "We didn't have the money to get a card at the hospital to see the doctor." The card would have cost them the equivalent of about two dollars. Two lives were lost because of the lack of two dollars. Is that all human lives are worth? What is wrong with a world where some people can spend at least that much on a cold drink, and others cannot find that small amount to save a life?

I think it was in 1997, while doing some shopping in town, that I met Dr. Chola Mutale. He was the doctor who had looked after my dear friend Leonard Chisala after the accident that left him crippled. He greeted me warmly and told me that there was another student from CBU who had been in a serious accident and needed my help. His name was Anthony Mwansa. Like Leonard, he was a very capable athlete, and had fractured his neck during a game of rugby. His injury was very similar to that of Leonard. I started going to visit him and found that he needed a lot of encouragement. Once again, he was a bright athletic young man who would probably spend the rest of his life in a wheelchair. Anthony came from a very gifted family. His father was a chartered accountant who had worked for the mines for many years, had taken voluntary retirement, and was now an accountant for a law firm in Kitwe. His mother was a lecturer in religious studies at a teacher training college in Mufulira where the family lived. He had four junior brothers all of whom were destined for the universities and professional careers.

Anthony is one of the most intelligent people that I had met in Zambia. He was knowledgeable about many things and very well read. Conversation with him was easy since he could discuss with me politics, science, and even the latest movies. His accident also occurred during his studies at the university and after recovering some movement returned to the university for his final years. He graduated with honors from the business school. It was difficult for him to find work since he could not move on his own outside of a wheelchair. Once again, I was faced with the difficulties of living in the Third World. Had he been in America he would have received all kinds of special help and probably would have found a good job. What always amazes me about the people of Africa, no matter what their difficulty, is their ability to find something positive in life. As I write this, Anthony is trying to organize some sort of service for counseling and encouraging young people like himself.

In 1998, my sister phoned me early in the year to tell me that she was thinking of making a trip to Africa. I was quite surprised to get this news but extremely happy to think of her coming to spend some time here. As the time approached for the visit, she told me that my niece, the daughter of my late brother, also wanted to come, as well as two of her grandsons, the sons of her daughter. They would only be with me for about 12 days, and I wanted to give them a wonderful experience of Africa.

And so on July 24th, I drove from Kitwe to Lusaka to welcome my sister, my niece, Gina, and Justin and Timothy. It was hard to believe they were here in Africa with me. We spent the day of their arrival in Lusaka to give them a chance to recover from the long journey. We did take a short trip to Kasisi, a 20 minute drive from where we were staying. I wanted them to see the orphanage and the agricultural training centre. They were very touched by the orphans, who were so anxious to be held and played with. The next day, Saturday, we drove to Chikuni, a small village in the bush, which is the origin of the Jesuit mission work in Zambia. I wrote of this when I told the story of the visit of my parents. We spent a night there as guests of the Jesuit community. The next morning, Sunday, was a very special celebration of thanksgiving for the harvest, and people came from all the nearby villages to attend a special outdoor Mass for the occasion. The students from the secondary school and teacher training college also attended. It gave my family an opportunity to share in a real African liturgy, full of life with singing, dancing and drumming.

Later that morning we continued our journey south to Livingstone and to Victoria Falls. When we arrived at the falls, my family were overwhelmed by their beauty and the natural surroundings. It was very impressive. It was a good season for viewing the falls since the flow of water was not so great as to make viewing difficult, but more than sufficient for the family to be awed by the spectacle. We stayed overnight as guests of the missionaries of the Divine Word.

The next morning, Monday, we drove over the border to the town of Victoria Falls in Zimbabwe. It was a highly developed tourist centre compared to Zambia, but lost some of the naturalness of the setting. Still we enjoyed seeing the falls from another viewpoint. After lunch we returned to Zambia and in the late afternoon took a dinner cruise on the Zambesi River. On the cruise we saw may hippos in the river as well as quite a few elephants on the shore, and even had the opportunity of seeing elephants swimming across from the shore to a large island in the middle of the river. While the sun set over the river, we were served a lovely meal.

The next morning we began the long drive back to Lusaka, and spent the night there, guests of the Christian Brothers. On Wednesday, we flew to Mfuwe, a town near a large game reserve. We put up at the Zambia Conservation Society camp. The accommodation was simple but comfortable. That same evening we went on an evening safari.

We saw a lot of animals: crocodiles and hippos in the river, and on the land, elephants, zebras, lions, mpala, hyenas, puku, and warthogs, as well as loads of chimpanzees and baboons. The next morning we were on a morning safari to see the animals as they went for water. In the afternoon, we took a walking safari. The next morning, Friday, we were back on the plane to Lusaka and drove up to Kitwe.

The week we spent in Kitwe was less touristy, but just as memorable. My students at the university and teacher training college put on wonderful Masses for my family. So they had to attend two Masses on Sunday morning, but it was well worth it. The singing and drumming, and the sincere warmth of the welcome was most moving.

The university students even presented each member of my family with a beautiful gift. During the week they met many of my friends and parishioners. Of course, I took them to Mufulira to meet my good friend, Leonard Chisala, and the other handicapped friend, Anthony Mwansa. They certainly learned what African hospitality is all about.

On the Sunday evening that they were in Kitwe, my grandnephew, Justin, fell out of a tree just outside the front door of the Jesuit House and managed to break his arm. Even this turned into a wonderful introduction to Kitwe Mine Hospitals. We went on Sunday evening, and a doctor and radiographer were called out from their homes, and an x-ray was immediately taken. The doctor saw that the radial bone was not only broken but displaced. It would require taking Justin to the operating theatre the next morning to set the bone. They gave him a temporary cast, and we brought him home.

The next morning, my sister and I went with him to the hospital where he was given a total anesthesia. The doctors and nurses were so friendly, that Justin felt very comfortable and seemed to have no anxiety. Twenty minutes later he was out, with a cast on his arm. We took him home once he was fully conscious and able to stand. The next day we were back for another x-ray and to see the consulting specialist.

The arm was declared to be set as well as could be. When he returned to New York, the specialist orthopedic doctor there looked at the x-rays and said he couldn't have done better. The most amazing thing was the cost. When we went to pay the bill, we had to pay the equivalent of $35, and this included everything, even the pain-killers he was given.

On Friday, 7th August, I drove them back to Lusaka to see them off on the evening flight to London. It was a memorable two weeks.

Sometime in the summer of the year 1999, I was invited to address the bishops' conference in Lusaka to report on my work as chaplain to the university and the training college. I received this invitation each year since I was financed by the bishops' conference. In 1991, my first full year as chaplain, I did accept the invitation and presented my report. In the subsequent years I merely mailed to the bishops my report in sufficient copies to provide each bishop an opportunity to read what I was doing. But, in 1999, I wanted to personally present my report since it would be the last year that I would be sponsored by the bishops' conference. The bishops had decided that in the future a chaplain working in institutions in a given diocese would be sponsored by the diocese. After my presentation, I was invited to share tea with the bishops.

One of the bishops, Noel O'Regan, who was the Bishop Director of seminaries, approached me and asked if I would be willing to move to St. Dominic's Seminary as the spiritual director. I said that in principle I was willing but that these decisions are not made by me but by my religious superior. We then approached Bishop Denis De Jong, the Bishop of Ndola, the diocese where I was presently working. He also agreed that the work in the seminary was more important than the work I was doing as chaplain in the university and teacher training college. I told them I had no objection to their approaching my provincial about this mission. About a week later, they did so.

I received a letter from my provincial in Lusaka outlining the proposal of the bishops. He asked me if I were willing to go to the major seminary as the spiritual director. I answered his letter, outlining the advantages of remaining in my present position and also the advantages of moving to the seminary. I left the final decision to him. I received a reply shortly after that saying that he would prefer that I move to the seminary at the beginning of the academic year 2000/2001.

Three very significant things happened in that summer of 2000 before I made my move to the seminary. The first of these was a visit of three American friends. On Saturday, the 20th of May, I was at the Lusaka Airport to welcome them to Zambia. It was their first trip to Africa and they were quite surprised as the weather was quite cool since we were approaching the winter of the southern hemisphere. We stopped briefly at the novitiate for a bit of breakfast, and then started off by car to Kitwe. I wanted them to experience Mass in the university before the students left at the end of the term on Friday.

Sunday morning they attended the university Mass and were quite impressed by the enthusiasm and the warmth of the welcome given them by the students. That evening, the students put on a bit of entertainment for my visitors. The entertainment included a short skit in which one of the students took on the role of myself. This was quite amusing and reflected the love of the students for me as well as for my visitors. I showed them around the Copperbelt before we flew off to the Mfuwe game park, the same place where I had taken my family. We all thoroughly enjoyed the view of the animals and of the birds, since my friends were all keen birdwatchers. After two days there we flew back to Kitwe so that I could celebrate.

This celebration was the second significant event that happened before I left for my home leave in my new assignment. The celebration was for my golden jubilee as a Jesuit. I had entered the Society of Jesus on the 30th of July 1950. So we anticipated my golden jubilee celebrating it on the night of the 27th of May. Joe Hayes, the superior of the community, had organized an evening outdoor Mass and a dinner for a large group of friends from the Copperbelt. It was a very happy occasion.

It is a tradition in the Jesuits that Father General writes to each golden jubilarian on this occasion. Sadly, I never received this letter on time. And it was only about a year later that I finally made inquiries as to what happened to the expected letter. It seems to have gotten lost in the mail somewhere but a copy of it was found in the provincial's files both in Lusaka and in New York. I wish I had had that letter on the occasion of the celebration since it expressed so beautifully much of what I felt about Africa. I will print a copy of that letter here.

Curia Generalizia della Compagnia di Gesù
Borgo S. Spirito, 4
C.P. 6139 / 00195 ROMA-PRATI (Italia)
Tel. 06/689.771—Fax 06/686.8214
30 July 2000
Rev. Ugo R. Nacciarone, S.J.
c/o New York Province Offices
39 East 83rd Street
New York, NY 10028-0810
U.S.A.

Dear Father Nacciarone, P.C.

It is a pleasure to greet you and to offer you my heartfelt congratulations as you celebrate fifty years as a Jesuit. I join you in thanking the Lord for the countless moments of grace that at first enabled you to respond to His call and then have

kept you faithful to your commitment for half a century in the Society of Jesus.

Most of your years of apostolic work in the Society have been spent on the African continent, in Nigeria, in Ghana and in Zambia where you are currently working. You are often quoted as saying that you have received much more from the people of Africa than you have ever given. While this might be true, your service to the African people in many different areas is remarkable: teacher training in Nigeria and Zambia, teacher of chemistry in a secondary school and later spiritual director of a major seminary in Ghana, university and college chaplaincy work (with many side apostolates) at present in Zambia. You have left a deep impression on many young teachers, priests, and professional people. Your care for young people and your enthusiasm in working with them, your willingness to share your faith in word and deed, has drawn many to enquire about priestly and religious vocations and some to enter the Society. These same qualities have also attracted many young Jesuits in formation to seek you out for retreats and counseling. You have been blessed by the people of Africa, but you have also been a great blessing for them.

And so at this time, I also join with your fellow Jesuits and friends in thanking the Lord for the blessings that have filled both your life and theirs and in wishing for you His special blessings in this time of jubilee. To mark this occasion I am happy to apply, from the treasury of the Society, fifty Masses for your intentions. I commend myself and the whole Society to your prayers.

Sincerely in Christ,
Peter-Hans Kolvenbach, S.J.

When I look back over that letter and recall my 50 years as a Jesuit I feel very grateful to God both for my initial vocation to the Society of Jesus as well as for my vocation and call to work in Africa for most of those 50 years. Certainly one of the greatest blessings of my life as a Jesuit has been the invitation of my superiors to work on the continent of Africa and so to meet an extraordinary people who have shaped so much of my life.

The day after the party I celebrated Mass at the main church in the center of Kitwe. I brought my friends to that Mass, and they would certainly have been impressed by the enormous crowd that packed the church so that there was standing room only. The enthusiastic singing during the Mass would have rocked the walls. The Mass was certainly unlike anything they would have experienced in the United States. It lasted for over an hour and a half but the time passed very quickly.

After Mass, we began our journey south toward Victoria Falls. We stopped overnight in Lusaka, and then moved on to Chikuni where we stayed another night. We finally arrived at Livingston, moved into our accommodation, and almost immediately took a trip to the Falls.

As it was for my family when they came two years earlier, so, too, for these friends from America: the sight of Victoria Falls was truly awesome. When they came at the end of May the Falls were in full flood. After three days in Livingston we made our way back to Lusaka and the next day I was at the airport to see them off after a memorable visit.

The third significant event before I went on leave was the surgery I underwent to repair an inguinal hernia. I decided to have this operation done before I went to the United States because I knew it would be much cheaper, as competently done, and with much less red tape and bureaucracy. I was admitted to a hospital in Mufulira, where I was given a private room. The surgeon was a very competent one and the operation successful. I stayed in the hospital for about three days and was then moved back to Kitwe.

Although I was somewhat incapacitated because of the operation, I had to begin the process of packing my things for my move to Lusaka. I had the help of several friends, and before the end of June I was ready to move. I carried all my belongings to Lusaka where they could be stored until I returned from leave. A few days later, I was on my way to the United States for my three month home leave before taking up my new assignment. Back in the United States I had two further celebrations for my Golden Jubilee. One was with my fellow Jesuits, classmates of the year 1950. We had a wonderful evening together, concelebrating Mass, enjoying a social hour of relaxed reminiscences, and then going out for a fine dinner in a nearby restaurant. It was a wonderful celebration of our being together. The other celebration was put on by my sister, and it was a catered affair for family and friends. It was another very happy occasion. One of the gifts my sister gave to me was a beautiful photograph album that recorded the various stages of my life from my entry into the novitiate until my most recent photos in Africa. I treasure this collection of memories very much.

Chapter Eighteen

BACK TO SEMINARY LIFE

Part of the time of my leave in the United States was spent preparing myself for my new position as spiritual director of the major seminary. I had been told that I would be teaching several courses and I used my time to do some reading in preparation for those courses. As usual, during my home leave I took advantage of the occasion not only to visit my family but to renew contact with old friends and to express appreciation to my many benefactors who have assisted me over the years to reach out to the poor in whatever countries I was in. The months passed very quickly and by early October I was back in Zambia, settling into my new home at St. Dominic's major seminary in the Woodlands area of Lusaka.

Although I had worked for seven years in a major seminary in Ghana, I felt a bit uneasy moving to this new seminary in Lusaka. One thing I learned over my years in Africa is that there is no such thing as African culture. Each country and each ethnic group within a country has its own traditions and culture. There was certainly a great difference between the peoples of West Africa in general and the peoples of southern Africa. So I approached my new position with a certain amount of anxiety. However, my long years in Africa also taught me of the warm welcoming nature of African people in general. I knew it would only be a matter of a relatively short time before I began to feel at home among them. After all I had lived and worked in three different countries and in various positions and never once felt unwelcome.

The academic year had actually begun toward the end of August. And so when I arrived at the end of the first week of October the academic year was well under way. I was a total unknown quantity to almost all the seminarians since I had little contact with any of them during my years in the Copperbelt. Before I begin speaking about my many experiences, I must take a little time out to talk about the differences in the structures of the major seminary in Zambia and that in Ghana.

The seminary in Zambia, like the seminary in Ghana was a regional seminary. In Ghana the seminary catered for all the dioceses in the southern part of the country. In Zambia the seminary catered for all the dioceses in the country. This meant that seminarians came from many different language groups and therefore the language used in the seminary was English. In contrast with this common nature of the seminaries there were quite large differences in the two seminaries, both regarding the academic program as well as in the social structures of the seminary itself.

Let me begin by looking at the academic programs in the two seminaries. In Ghana, there was a very heavy emphasis on the academic. As I shared in an earlier part of this writing I had to struggle as spiritual director to include into our program a course in spirituality as well as regular days of recollection. The seminary in Ghana was affiliated to the national university in Legon, Accra. Most of the students would complete a bachelor's degree in religious studies. There were very few courses of a pastoral nature in the curriculum. For example, there was no course in the practice of spiritual direction or in theological reflection. In Zambia by contrast both of these courses were offered and, although the seminary was affiliated to an ecclesiastical university in Rome, the academic program was not as rigorous or demanding. I felt that the course in Zambia was more clearly focused on the life of a diocesan priest. Of course, we wanted them to be academically qualified but most importantly, we wanted them to be good priests with a clear understanding of their identity as priests. Besides the different emphases in the academic program there was also a difference in the social structure of the seminary.

The structure in Zambia was very much influenced by the structure of the church in Zambia which was organized on the lines of small Christian communities. This concept of the small Christian community dominated the life of every parish and was also installed in every other institution. For example as chaplain in the University, as I have already mentioned, the students were broken up into small Christian communities. The same structure was found even in the seminary. The seminarians are broken up into small communities of about 14 seminarians each with a staff member as the facilitator of the community. When I arrived in the first week of October as I had already said, the academic year was underway and the small communities already in place. I attended my first small community meeting and was introduced to this community.

The members of the community were selected from the various year-groups in the seminary and also came from different dioceses. I felt very welcomed by them but it took me some time to understand what my role was in the community. We would meet just twice a month, and, in the beginning, I found these meetings quite boring because they tended to focus on rather trivial concerns of the day-to-day life in the seminary. As the year progressed I was able to move the students to a deeper understanding of the purpose of this community and we began to share at a more personal level. Before Christmas, we had a social evening when we took our meal together as a community and had a chance to relax together. I made a very real effort to get to know the names of each of the members of the community, and began to feel at home with them. By the end of the year, we had a farewell outing and went away from the seminary for the day and had a picnic as a community. It was a wonderful experience and I began to appreciate the value of this structure.

At the beginning of the new academic year, I discovered that all the small Christian communities had their compositions changed. It meant that I was now with a completely different group of seminarians. By this time I really did understand my role better as the house spiritual director, and I called in the secretary-general of the student body and told him that in future years I would like to see a change in the way the small Christian communities were organized. I suggested that we keep the same composition through-out the four years, replacing those who leave, but leaving all the others in place. It took a bit of convincing, since the seminarians do not like changes without understanding them. He did agree. By the following academic year, I found myself in the same small Christian community and began to feel immediately at home since I knew more than half of the members from the very first meeting. My community was called Blessed Anuarite small Christian community. It was named after an African saint from the Congo. Over the course of the next five years, I was always associated with this community, and I became very close to most of its members.

In addition to the meetings we had twice a month, we met twice a week for morning and evening prayers together as a community. On Tuesday mornings, we also celebrated Mass together as a community. During these Masses, one of the members of the community shared a reflection after the readings instead of the priest giving the homily. Those assigned to this particular work always took the assignment seriously, carefully preparing their reflection, and delivering it with great sincerity. I was impressed by how seriously the seminarians took the Scriptures, and always took the occasion to encourage them in their desire to share the word with others.

As our bimonthly meetings began to grow in openness as we got closer to one another, I introduced the concept of faith sharing. This gave any member of the community the opportunity to share some experience in their lives where they felt that the Lord was somehow speaking to them. I was always very touched by the personal nature of these sharings. Over the course of years I gained a great deal of insight into the character of most of the members of my community, and, I am sure, they also came to a deeper understanding of myself. Of course this kind of openness with one another leaves one vulnerable, but happy. In leaving the seminary, I felt my greatest loss was my membership in this small Christian community of Blessed Anuarite.

As a spiritual director of the seminary, I was responsible for organizing anything to do with the spiritual formation of the seminarians and with the general spiritual atmosphere of the house. One of the structures that was in place at the seminary was that of the monthly spiritual conference. When I first arrived at the seminary the dean of studies suggested that I take all the monthly conferences in order to give the seminarians an opportunity to get to know me. I was a bit nervous about this, and probably prepared better than I would have normally done for such an exercise.

The response was very positive and very encouraging. This enabled me to carry on with the monthly conference until the end of the academic year. However, I decided that I did not want this to be the pattern for the rest of my time. I planned that each year there would be a theme for the monthly conferences. Since one of the courses I was teaching the third-year theologians was: "Spirituality and States of Life", I set as a theme for my second year this very topic. I invited persons of various states of life to talk about their own relationship with God. I invited a diocesan priest, a religious sister, a professional unmarried lay man, two married couples, and finally, a young person who was very active in the youth groups of his parish. These talks far exceeded my expectations and the seminarians were very pleased. They took many occasions to thank me for inviting these people. This again encouraged me to continue with this idea for the rest of my time as spiritual director of the house.

The following year I chose as a theme: "Non-Christian Spiritualities". I invited in a Jain, a Muslim, a Hindu, a Buddhist, Sikh, and finally a professed atheist. I felt this opened the seminarians to a whole new way of understanding people and a greater tolerance for those who were different than themselves. There was a great deal of interest shown in the speakers, and I hoped that this would encourage seminarians to explore other religions more seriously.

The next year I chose as a theme: "Lay Movements in Parishes". I invited in representatives of the various movements in the parishes such as the St. Vincent DePaul Society, Catholic Women's League, Legion of Mary, and many others. My reasoning in choosing this theme was that the priests would one day be chaplain to these various movements and they should come to know them and the people who live and work in them.

I have not mentioned the fact that I did bring into the seminary various Protestant ministers, a Coptic priest, and an Anglican priest to share with us during our evening prayer at the time of the octave of prayer for Christian unity. In all of this, I felt it was part of my responsibility as the spiritual director to form the most open and broad minded priests possible for the future church in Zambia.

As a lecturer in the seminary, I was asked to teach various courses which helped me to come to a deeper understanding of myself, my faith, and my role as spiritual director. One of the courses I taught which was as instructive to me as it was to the seminarians, was Theological Reflection. Since I had never had such a course in my own training, I had to read widely to come to some understanding of what it was that I was to present to the seminarians. This course helps someone to reflect more deeply on their everyday experience, and to find in that experience a revelation from God. I had undoubtedly been doing this informally through much of my life, but now I began to see even deeper meanings in my everyday experiences from the reading of the newspapers, watching television, to casual conversations with friends.

In our Jesuit spirituality, we have an exercise known as the examination of conscience, which, in more recent times, has been better labeled examination of consciousness. It encompasses one aspect of theological reflection as it applies to my own relationship with God. But the course in theological reflection was also asking the seminarians to see in their experience revelations about the nature of the church, the understanding of God, and the meaning of their vocation.

One of the spinoffs of my teaching this course was the invitation on several occasions to assist in the formation of lay prayer guides by giving a workshop on religious experience. I began to recognize how just about any experience can be a religious experience when looked upon with the eyes of faith.

Another course that had influenced me a great deal was the course I taught on Inculturation. I drew upon the wide experience of the seminarians themselves to come to understand how God speaks to us in any culture. I came to appreciate more and more the beauty of African cultures which vary from tribe to tribe. It is one of my hopes that I may one day write up all that I have learned on this very significant topic to encourage the African people themselves come to a deeper appreciation of their own cultures.

One of the many reasons I feel so grateful for the opportunity of working in Africa, and in particular, for the privilege of working in the diocesan seminaries, was my frequent encounters with the bishops of the country. They came to the seminary from time to time since we were training their future priests. I came to know the bishops in a much more personal way than I would have otherwise. On one occasion, I asked for permission to address the Episcopal conference on the question of the spiritual formation of the seminarians. I was granted the permission, and I addressed all the bishops of Zambia on this important issue. Having come to know them through their visits to the seminary, I was not afraid to challenge them on certain issues. Subsequently, I was invited to preach the Episcopal conference retreat where I was able to share with the eight bishops of Zambia on a deeper level. I was most impressed by the seriousness with which they took the retreat; their silence was truly edifying, and the spirit of prayer was obvious. When I returned to the seminary after this retreat I assured the seminarians that, though they may have their criticisms and complaints about their bishops, they should know that their bishops were men of prayer, even if imperfect in many ways. One of the joys of Africa is a more informal way in which we encounter the bishops of the church. My impression is that here in the United States and in Europe the relationship is much more formal and the bishops are a bit more removed from their priests and their people.

At the end of my fourth year in the seminary the bishops had appointed an indigenous diocesan priest to be the house spiritual director. This was something I had asked for several times in the past, and I was delighted to welcome Father Jude to replace me. I moved into a small office and agreed to be his assistant for the next year or so in order to help him find his way in this position which he was occupying for the first time. At the same time that he was moving into the staff of the seminary, my own provincial had appointed me as the Rector of the Jesuit novitiate. Since I was to be the superior of this community, I could no longer reside full-time at the seminary. I kept my small office, but I commuted each day from the novitiate. I continued teaching as well as doing personal spiritual direction, and I was like any working father. I was available to my community each evening after five o'clock, and would be with them most of the weekends. During the working hours, I was at the seminary.

I felt very honored to be named as the Rector of the novitiate, which was a rather large community consisting of about 16 novices, 11 priests and a brother. It was always a joy to be in this community as the presence of the young novices from Zambia, Malawi and Zimbabwe gave me great hope for the future of the Jesuits in Africa. I learned a great deal from their idealism and generosity, and was sure that most of them would make fine Jesuits. One of the things that touched me so much in the life of the novices was their great concern for the elderly Jesuits in our community. The respect for the elders in African culture is deeply embedded in every African, and it's certainly meant a great deal to the elderly missionary Jesuits who were in their declining years.

One of the sidelines of my life in Lusaka was my involvement with the training of prayer guides. This was a program originally created by a Franciscan Sister from the United States. It began as a program that would last for 18 months, requiring the participants to be present Monday through Friday, from 8 in the morning until noon time. They were offered courses in spirituality, psychology, Bible, and dogmatic theology. The first group of students consisted of seven religious sisters, six lay people (four men and two women) and one diocesan priest.

I gave a one-week course on the practice of spiritual direction, and a two-week course on dogmatic theology. I was most impressed by this group of mature people so interested in trying to assist others in their relationship with God. Although the course was subsidized through generous gifts of the American church, the students themselves had to pay some tuition, and, for the lay people, it meant re-organizing their work day. The people who graduated from this course showed great skills in guiding others in retreats and spiritual direction.

After this first group graduated, it was difficult to continue offering the same program to others. Under the leadership of a young Zambian sister, the program was restructured and simplified so that it would involve the first three Saturdays of every month for 10 months.

Each Saturday would begin at about nine in the morning and end at about four in the afternoon. The syllabus of the program was also simplified.

I continued assisting in the program by taking two of the Saturdays: one on the topic of religious experience, and the other on the formation of conscience. By the time I left Zambia in 2007, the program had trained over 50 men and women who are doing wonderful work in their respective parishes. Except for the first group, when we had seven religious sisters, almost all the participants were lay men and lay women.

There were two other programs outside of my seminary work that I enjoyed very much and which also taught me very much. One of these was teaching at the Kalundu Formation Center. This was founded about 30 years ago to help form African sisters to become future superiors, novice mistresses, and formation personnel. The sisters came from all over Africa and represented many different religious congregations. Each year a class of about 30 of them would come for a one-year program.

Ever since my move to Lusaka, I was asked to teach them for about three weeks. I taught them courses in the practice of spiritual direction, Christology, and moral theology. These were very impressive women, and often challenged me with very perceptive questions. It was a real honor to meet them and to have the chance to share with them my own understandings of my Christian faith.

The other program that I enjoyed very much was teaching the various religious novices from the Lusaka area. The various novice mistresses and novice masters had organized a program of courses, each lasting about one week, open to all novices, both men and women.

There were many religious houses in the Lusaka area, and not all of them would have had the personnel to give instructions in so many different areas. So they called upon the personnel in the city to offer these mini-courses about twice a month.

I was asked to give three different courses: introduction to the New Testament, moral theology, and ecumenism. I would have between 70 and 80 young men and women religious. It was another great sign of hope for the church to see all these young people training to become priests, brothers, and sisters. The church in Africa is a very young church, filled with enthusiastic people whose faith would touch even the greatest of skeptics.

One of my regular routines during almost all my years in Africa was to go once a month to see my spiritual director. From the time I was appointed as a spiritual director in the seminary, I felt I could not in conscience encourage seminarians to have a regular spiritual director if I myself did not have one. If it was important enough for them, it was important enough for me. And in fact, I have always found this practice extremely helpful. One of the fruits of this regular sharing for me was a growing awareness in myself of the question of my future in Africa.

Chapter Nineteen

AN ACCIDENT AND A PAINFUL DECISION

In the year 2000, as I celebrated my Golden Jubilee as a Jesuit, as I have written of earlier, I began to question my continued stay in Africa. I cannot fully explain why this thought seemed to slowly infiltrate my mind. I wondered whether it were not time to return to the home province after so many years. I discussed these thoughts with my spiritual director at the time. I proposed that I make the full 30 day retreat, as a retreat of election, to ask the Lord's guidance in discerning my future. In the spring of 2002, I received permission from the provincial of Zambia to travel to Nairobi to make the 30 day retreat at our Jesuit retreat house in Mwangaza, a suburb of Nairobi in the Ngong hills. It is an incredibly beautiful place and was the setting for the movie "Out Of Africa".

Although I had made the full 30 day retreat as a novice in 1950 and again in my final year of formation in Austria in 1965, I really felt I had never made the spiritual exercises as they were originally intended. In both of these retreats I was part of a rather large group, and so the retreat was a preached retreat with only occasional opportunities to speak to the retreat master. I wanted to make a 30 day retreat as a fully directed retreat. I was given a fellow Jesuit at Mwangaza retreat house to be my retreat director. There was a certain amount of anxiety as I approached this long period of silence and prayer. But as I moved into the retreat I found a deeper and deeper peace. I don't know that I have ever found meditation and prayer easier than at this time. I went through all the exercises that Ignatius suggests to make a good election.

At the end of the retreat, I felt the Lord was leading me to return to my home province, although the feeling was not as strong or as clear as I might have wished. From that time on I began sharing these thoughts with my spiritual director as well as with my provincial in Zambia and the provincial in New York. They all respected my own mature judgment.

I realized that it would not be an easy decision. I knew how fruitful my work in Africa had been, and I had no idea of what I might do if I returned to New York. My discernment on this issue went on for several years because I knew how painful it would be to leave Africa which had become truly home for me and whose people had shown me so much love and affection. As these thoughts continued to mature, a very dramatic experience occurred which may have had something to do with my final decision.

It all happened in December 2005. I was invited to conduct a workshop on religious experience, formation of conscience, and discernment of spirits to be given to a group of junior professed Religious Sisters of Charity. I was invited by Sister Theresa, and I agreed to do this. The workshop was to be held in Kabwe about 140 km north of Lusaka.

I drove to sister's convent in Lusaka after lunch on 9 December, left my vehicle there, and drove to Kabwe with sister and three junior professed sisters in the backseat. We left at about three-thirty in the afternoon, and it was raining.

The drive to Kabwe was going well and we were probably slightly more than halfway there when suddenly sister exclaimed, "I'm losing control of the car!" We were skidding badly on the wet road, and I remember very little of what happened in the next few seconds.

We were on a passage of the road that covered a large culvert under the road which was marked on the surface of the road by a low cement wall. We crashed into that wall and then the car started moving down the side of the road. Fortunately it stopped before it went the full way into the ditch. All I can remember now is Sister Theresa coming to my side of the car opening the door and trying to get me out. I just kept repeating, "I can't breathe, I can't breathe". She got me out of the car and held me up. There was a good deal of blood on my body. Sister Theresa was praying, "Lord, don't let him die". With sister's help, I struggled to the edge of the road in great pain and still finding it very difficult to breathe. Sister Theresa was not very hurt. The three young sisters in the backseat were hurt, but not too seriously. A very kindly man with a single cab pickup stopped within the first 10 minutes of the accident. He took sister into the cab's passenger seat. He carried me into the pickup and laid me down. The other sisters were also assisted into the back of the pickup.

I must admit, that as I lay there in great pain and still finding it difficult to breathe, I honestly thought I was dying. I even prayed to the Lord that if it were his will he should take me. I felt I was ready to meet him, although, if I had the time to reflect on my past life, I might not have felt so prepared. All I know is that, at that moment, I was unafraid.

The driver took us to a nearby local hospital at Liteta. Like most rural hospitals in Africa, it was in rather bad shape. There was only one doctor there and he was a Nigerian. All he could say when he examined me was that I had broken several ribs. By this time I was in such great pain that I would not allow him or the nurses to move me from the gurney to a bed. Sr. Theresa used her cell phone to contact her religious superior in Lusaka as well as my own provincial. The kind man, who had taken us from the scene of the accident to the hospital, went back to the scene of the accident and collected all our personal belongings. I often think of the extraordinary generosity of this man whose name I do not even know. I felt he was like the good Samaritan in the gospel. I have prayed for him and I know the Lord will reward him for his great kindness.

It was probably about 7:30 PM when my provincial superior and his assistant arrived at the hospital. Before leaving Lusaka, they had arranged with a private hospital service to send two ambulances to the hospital. The ambulances arrived after 10 PM, and they carefully transferred me into one of the ambulances, and the two younger sisters who seemed to have the more serious injuries to the other ambulance. Sr. Theresa and the other younger sister went by car to Lusaka. We were taken to a private hospital in Lusaka which was very well equipped and they had a radiographer and doctor on hand to receive us. The x-rays showed that I had broken three ribs, a small bone in my right foot, and a vertebra in the lower part of the back. The bleeding on the head was superficial and there was no damage to the skull. After making me comfortable, they must have given me a sedative to put me to sleep.

The next morning, although still in some pain, I felt better. We were transferred to the Italian Orthopedic Hospital which was run by the Franciscan sisters, and had a very good reputation. For two days I shared a ward with one other man, but then was moved to a private room. At this point I knew that all would be well and I felt that I was in very good hands. The two sisters in the hospital, the nurses, and the doctors were all extremely helpful and did all that they could to make me comfortable. On that first morning that I was moved to the Italian hospital, I received a good number of visitors, including many Jesuits, but also many religious men and women who had heard about the accident. Within a day or so many of the lay people from the parishes where I had once said Mass also got to hear about it, and they started visiting me. The seminarians, who had not yet gone home for the Christmas holidays, were also regular visitors. I never felt alone. I was really a bit overwhelmed by the affection in which people held me. Even one of the nurses remarked one day that it appeared that I was very much loved. I was deeply moved by this, and I am very grateful for the affirmation that these people gave me.

I didn't intend to inform my family about the accident, as I knew that they would be very worried. However, within 24 hours of the accident my sister in Brooklyn had already heard of it. This was the product of our modern electronic age. Within hours of the accident the assistant to the provincial had sent out e-mails to all the Jesuits of the province informing them of the accident and asking them for their prayers for my recovery. One of the Jesuits who received this e-mail was a young Zambian, former student at CBU whom I had known as chaplain there, who was studying in Kinshasa. He, in turn, had been in contact with a former Jesuit, a Ghanaian and a good friend of mine, who needed someone in Kinshasa to help him obtain a transcript of his courses from the time that he was a Jesuit student there.

This Ghanaian friend is now living in New York. The Zambian in Kinshasa, reading about the accident on the e-mail, immediately e-mailed my Ghanaian friend in New York. Since he had come to know my family quite well, he phoned my sister. She immediately phoned the Jesuit novitiate to find out what had happened. With the help of a cell phone, I was able to speak with her the next day and reassure her that all was well. She then phoned me every day to find out what progress I was making.

The principal difficulty I had in the hospital was a severe pain in the thigh of the left leg. This apparently was caused by a pinching of the sciatic nerve caught in the fractured vertebra on the back. The pain was relentless, but the doctor did not wish to do any surgery to free the nerve, as he was quite sure that it would free itself in time. It took about two weeks before this happened, and those two weeks were very difficult. I remember praying on Christmas eve as I lay there alone in pain asking the Lord as a Christmas gift to give me a few hours of sleep.

In fact the prayer was answered and I did get a bit of sleep that night.

I had many visitors on Christmas day which distracted me from the pain. About a day or so later, the pain was suddenly gone. When the doctor was assured that I could take a few steps with the aid of a walking frame he allowed me to return to the nursing home next to the novitiate.

On the feast of the holy innocents, 28 December, I moved to a room in Chula House, our Jesuit nursing facility next door to the novitiate. I was delighted to be there as I would now have visitors from the novitiate who were members of my community. Father Klaus, the director of the nursing home, took very good care of me. He insisted that a novice should sleep in the same room with me so that if I needed assistance during the night he would be there for me. The novices took turns carrying out this duty until I finally moved back to my own room in the novitiate on 6 January. During all this time, I felt completely helpless and was very much dependent on others. But everyone assisted me with such care that I never felt embarrassed or ashamed to be so helpless.

The recuperation took many months before I was completely able to move about as I once did. I graduated from the walking frame to a cane, and eventually was able to walk without any physical aid.

It took me quite a while before I was able to celebrate Mass. But the recovery went well and as I sit here writing this journal, I am as strong as I was before the accident. There is only one physical remnant of that accident. The macula of my right eye was damaged by the trauma, and I cannot read well with that eye. However the peripheral vision is quite good and I have excellent vision with the left eye.

I learned many things from this accident. First of all, I appreciated more than ever the love and affection of the African people who saw me through this difficult time. Sr. Teresa, who was driving at the time of the accident, came very frequently to see me and was very supportive at every stage of my recovery. Secondly, I realized that it is not always easy to offer up one's sufferings in union with those of the Lord. It is easy to preach this, but I learned from my own experience that it was not easy to live it. I tried my best, and I always tried not to complain when visitors came, but always showed a smiling face, for I was truly grateful to be alive and to be surrounded by friends. But, finally, I learned that life can end at any moment. The accident could have been my death. I think that this self-consciously raised once again the question of returning to my home province so that I could do some work there before my life came to an end.

As it became clear to me that I should return to the province, I intimated to the provincial as well as to my spiritual director that I felt it was time for me to leave Africa. By the end of 2006, I had already begun to make my plans to leave. I decided I would remain in Africa until I had celebrated the 40th anniversary of my first arrival on that continent. Since I arrived on the continent on 11 September 1967, I proposed that I leave sometime after that date.

Father Pete Titland was appointed as the new novice master at the end of 2006. He would be celebrating his golden jubilee as a Jesuit on September 8, 2007. As Rector of the novitiate, I thought it would be appropriate that we have a joint celebration on 8 September. The community would be celebrating Pete's 50 years as a Jesuit and my 40 years in Africa.

Before that date, my calendar became very crowded as these would be my last months in Zambia. On the 12th of January 2007, I travelled by bus to the Copperbelt to attend the priestly ordination of one of my friends who completed the seminary in 2003. He had asked me to preach at his first Mass, and so wanted me to share the experience of his ordination. He was ordained on Saturday, the 13th, and celebrated his first Mass the next day. After the Mass I was back on a bus to Lusaka so that I would be back at home for the beginning of the provincial's official visitation of the house. It was during that visit in my personal report to him that I repeated what I had told him the year before: that I felt it was time for me to leave this province. He was very understanding and appreciative of what I had done there in the past 17 years.

Among other things that filled my final months, I celebrated the wedding of one of my former students. I was teaching courses to the novices, giving retreats to priests, religious and lay people. I ran two workshops of religious experience. This very busy and satisfying life showed how much I could still do in Africa. I was aware of this, and it made my decision to return to the United States all the more difficult. Yet I continued in my conviction that this was the right decision. After all, I had reflected on this for several years, and had spent a month in prayer discerning what God's will was for me. I was at peace, but I knew I would miss these people and this life very much.

One of the most touching final experiences was a retreat I directed at the seminary. It was a 5-day retreat to the third year theology class at the seminary. There were 33 on the retreat. At the end of the retreat, the seminary academic year closed with the ordination of 22 deacons from the class I had the retreat with. It was another happy occasion. Before the retreat, there was a farewell dinner to end the academic year. It is given each year to say farewell to the final year students. The occasion was also an opportunity for my own farewell. A representative of the students delivered a moving address and the seminary presented me with a beautiful gift. I will certainly miss the friends I had made at the seminary. My years there had brought me the friendship of many of the young priests in the country.

On the weekends of July, we Jesuits saw the ordination to the priesthood of one of our young Zambians and I personally witnessed the graduation of a group of 15 lay men and women who had completed their course as prayer guides. I had been involved in their formation and was very happy to see them graduate at a very colourful ceremony.

The month of July ended with a wonderful celebration of the feast of St. Ignatius on the 31st. It marked the 57th anniversary of my life as a Jesuit, almost all of which have been spent in Africa to my great satisfaction.

In the middle of August, I was entertaining a young Zambian friend, who is now a teacher, and was one whom I had known since he was in primary school and whose story I told earlier in this book. He came a long distance just to say farewell. I was very happy to have this time with him and felt very satisfied to see how a poor boy from a shanty compound had grown into a mature man who is now a successful teacher in a secondary school.

At the end of August, I made the short flight from Lusaka to Harare in Zimbabwe to say farewell to the Jesuit scholastics who are doing their studies there at Arrupe College. I was met at the airport by four of the scholastics. I knew that I would be missing them very much, and was glad that I made the decision to come to Zimbabwe to see them. The joy of spending time with all the scholastics was somewhat dampened by the sad condition of the country. The shops were all empty, electricity supplies were very erratic (the college has its own generator) and even the water supply could not be relied on. On arriving and leaving the new modern airport with all the latest facilities, I was shocked to see so few people actually coming to the country. Most of those who were leaving were going overland into Botswana, South Africa or Zambia.

Zimbabwe was once a rich and beautiful country, but at the time of my visit was being destroyed by the present political regime. Still I was encouraged by the ability of the good people to cope with all these problems and still somehow find it possible to smile.

During those final weeks, I had several farewell dinner invitations. The climax of all this was my own community's celebration on 8th September. We had a beautiful evening community Mass followed by a cookout. We had invited various friends to celebrate Fr. Pete Titland's (the new novice master) 50th anniversary as a Jesuit, and my 40 years in Africa. It was a wonderful farewell with beautiful tributes and many gifts to express appreciation. The next morning I celebrated a farewell Mass at a Catholic boys' secondary school where I had said Mass many times over the past 7 years. It was another memorable occasion with more speeches and more gifts. The next day, Monday, I celebrated my final Mass at the monastery of the Poor Clares, a cloistered contemplative order of nuns for whom I had celebrated Mass many times, and, on one occasion, preached their annual retreat. They also presented me with a gift.

Finally, the day arrived when I had to leave, Thursday, 13th September. I had to be at the airport at 1:30 p.m. I had a final lunch together with my community, and then most of the novices, some workers, friends, and some senior members of the community came to the airport to see me off. It was a very emotional moment with many tears. I knew it would be difficult for me to separate myself from such a loving group of people who had meant so much to me over the years.

I had planned a slow return to the United States. I wanted to revisit the places in Africa where I once lived and worked. So I flew first to Lagos, Nigeria. I arrived there on the early morning of the 14th and was met by a driver from the Jesuit community. I was taken to the house where I made my first home in Africa 40 years ago. The room I once lived in is now a small house chapel, and I was given one of the guest rooms.

I was quite amazed at how Lagos had grown. When I lived there, the population was only one million, now it is anywhere between 9 and 12 million. Sadly, the infrastructure did not keep up with the population and power failures are very frequent. Many people have private generators.

The Jesuit presence has grown as dramatically as the population. In 1967 there were only 6 of us there scattered around the country, each doing their own thing. Today, Nigeria and Ghana are part of the Northwest Africa Province with over 100 members, most of whom are Africans. They are running two big secondary schools, 4 parishes with many sub-parishes, a retreat house, and a novitiate to train our young men. The work they are doing is very impressive. When I visited the novitiate, I was treated as one of the founding fathers of the province, and had the chance to share my reflections with the young novices.

I also made a ten day visit to Ghana from Nigeria and had a very happy reunion with many old friends. The time passed very quickly, and I then returned to Nigeria for my final days in Africa. I flew from Lagos to London on the 8th of October, and spent a week there visiting friends, especially African Jesuits who are studying in England. On the 16th I made the last leg of my journey and arrived in New York on that same afternoon. I was picked up by my nephew who took me straight to my sister's house where I met many of the family. That evening, I moved into a Jesuit residence.

I have written in detail about my final days in Africa, not only because they are recent and more easily remembered but because they indicate how busy and happy I was in Africa. By leaving the continent, I was giving up all these various activities, which I not only enjoyed but also encountered through them so many wonderful young Africans who gave me so much hope for the continent. I realize that I could have continued doing the sort of things I have described. And this could have gone on for some more years, but the time would come when other younger people would come on the scene and replace me.

As I look back on these 40 years of my life, which represent most of my years as a priest, I can only be grateful to God for the extraordinary opportunity He gave me for discovering myself, for learning about what I truly believed from a people whose faith is so much deeper than mine, and for unalterably changing the way I see the world and other people.

EPILOGUE

As I look back over these years in Africa, I would like to summarise the values of the cultures I found there that are in contrast to what I have come to see here in the United States, the country of my birth and early education. I emphasise that it was the place of my early education. I am firmly convinced that my most valuable education was not the formal transfer of knowledge that occurred in classrooms and libraries, but the life situation education that I received in my years in Africa. What I express here is taken from the previous pages of this book.

I recently read a book by Richard Dowden, entitled "Africa. Altered States, Ordinary Miracles" published by Public Affairs, New York, NY in 2009. I was encouraged to read there some of the very thoughts I am expressing here. I would like to use these quotes to frame my concluding thoughts. The first quotation from this book is:

> **"Apart from Rwanda in 1994 I have never encountered hopelessness in Africa. Amidst the direst catastrophes—war and death, famine or just slow decline—Africans don't do hopelessness." p. 284**

Throughout my 40 years experience on the African mission, I have seen this thought confirmed over and over again. The most common images of Africa in the media are those of people dying of starvation, or brutally killed in civil conflicts, or emaciated bodies infected with HIV and dying of AIDS. These images are not created by the imaginations of the journalists, they are real, and I have seen them all in my own experience. But what touches me so much about Africa and its people is the spirit with which they can face such disasters, and the incredible ability to hope for something better in the future. It is a rare situation that can cause an

African to lose hope. And the reason for this hope, I think, is founded on two things: their experience of community and their faith in God.

The Bantu people have a proverb that says: I am because we are. A person takes their identity from the community. An individual may come or go, but the community remains. The loss of an individual can be a painful experience and a personal tragedy. It is also a community tragedy in that the community has been diminished; but the community will go on and will always live in the hope that new life will enter to enrich the community again.

The extended family is a great source of hope and strength in difficult times. If there is a death in the family, the children will not usually be orphaned. Immediately, someone will look after them. One of their aunts or uncles will take over the role of mother or father. Every child has several mothers and fathers, since they will always consider their aunts and uncles as such.

Again, poverty will not necessarily be an obstacle to education. Not only would an uncle undertake the responsibility of educating a niece or nephew, but even an older brother or sister would step in and help. And it is not just a matter of paying bills, the child will be living with the relative who takes on all the tasks of a parent.

I have known many Africans who have been brought up and educated by an older brother or sister, by an aunt or uncle. This concept of the extended family gives great stability to a person. If today this is breaking down under the financial pressures of a global economy, it is because the western influence has penetrated the traditional culture through television and cinema.

Another remarkable expression of the importance of the family or community is in the choice of a career. A child would always sit with his or her family to discuss the plans for their future. Normally, a family respects the wishes of the child. However, I had an experience where an intelligent and gifted young man changed his choice because of a need in the family.

You may recall the story of Anthony who had been crippled during a university rugby match. When Anthony was able to resume his studies after months in the hospital with a fractured neck, his younger brother was about to enter the university. His first choice had been to go to the university in Lusaka. But since his injured brother was at the Copperbelt University and would need someone to assist him, he changed his course and university to accommodate the needs of his elder brother. This sort of attitude is not at all uncommon. It is quite a contrast to the emphasis on the individual in my own culture. I feel more at home in the African culture. There is not only more security for the individual, but there is also a greater sense of being valued and loved.

Another way in which the sense of community reveals itself is in the attitude of the younger generation toward their elders. I was always impressed by the love, care and solicitude of the younger African Jesuits towards their much older Jesuit companions. I experienced this myself at the time of the accident in which I was seriously injured.

It is such a contrast to my own culture where young people generally avoid the company of older people, and so we have the institutions of nursing homes, whereas in Africa, the old people would be taken into the home of a family member and looked after with great affection.

A sick and dying Jesuit in Africa would never die alone. I witnessed many occasions when such Jesuits were accompanied 24 hours a day. Someone would be assigned to stay with them in shifts, even if they were unconscious. There is something very beautiful in this. Once again, it is the value given to community that is also the guarantee of the value of the individual. I believe this emphasis on community is behind the hope of the African.

There is a second quotation that is very meaningful to me and verified by my own experience. The context of the quotation is a group of three white journalists, travelling in a car with a team of election observers in Nigeria to go to a town where there was a recent election which was allegedly fixed. The people in the town are angry because they feel they have been cheated. There is an angry crowd at a roadblock at the entrance to the town. Yet, the people in the car are unhurt once the crowd sees the white journalists. Then the author writes:

"I wonder if a couple of black people would be as safe if they drove into an angry white crowd in Europe or America. There is still humanity in Nigeria." P. 483

One of the most amazing things about the African people is this extraordinary respect they have for the people of Europe and America. Considering the history of these people in Africa and the terrible sufferings inflicted on its people through colonization, exploitation, and the slave trade, it astounds me that they had any respect for the likes of me. It is not as if they are unaware of the injuries they had suffered at the hands of the white race. They are keenly aware of them, and they can recite to you many instances of life before independence. Despite these memories, they still show a remarkable respect for the descendents of those who did them so much harm. In all of my years on the continent of Africa I rarely, if ever, experienced any racial bigotry, and, perhaps, was insulted once or twice in 40 years. By contrast, I always worry and am anxious whenever an African friend of mine comes to the United States to study or visit. I fear they may experience insult or prejudice because of their race. The humanity of the African, referred to in the above quotation, has lifted my spirits on many occasions.

I never had any fear in walking through any neighborhood, rich or poor. There is a quality in their humanity that I find hard to describe because it is so extraordinary. The big smile in the face of terrible suffering would cheer any heart. I recall walking along the road on a rather cold morning in the Zambian winter, my arms folded tightly in front of me, with my eyes firmly fixed on the ground, when I heard a bright and cheery, "Good morning!" I looked up to find a smiling face, and felt the warmth of that greeting. In my own country I do not feel comfortable just meeting a stranger on the street. We have lost our sense of our common humanity and so treat each other almost as aliens.

A final quotation I would like to use from Dowden's book that encapsulates much of my experience is:

> **"If you arrive unannounced they will feed you without question, not entirely in the hope that you will do something for them one day. Africa is rich in manners. Every meeting begins with a long greeting. And when you go they will give you a gift. This is a family that could be anywhere in tropical Africa. What has Africa to offer the rest of the world? Patience, hope, civility—and music!"** p. 285

Hospitality and politeness are in the genes of the African people. What most impresses visitors to the continent for the first time is the warmth and exuberance of the welcome they will receive wherever they visit. There is a ritual in every African culture for welcoming a guest. But the ritual never gets in the way of the warmth of the welcome.

No matter what time you arrive, your hosts will always offer you something to eat or drink, even if it means going without something themselves. Of course, your hosts will inquire not only about your own health, but about your whole family. And when you are leaving, your hosts will not just say goodbye at the door, they will accompany you part of the way on your journey home. Even if you come with a private car, they will not go in the house until you are out of sight.

For me, all these human values are reflecting something even more. As a man of faith, I believe this great humanity is reflecting to me the God-Incarnate, Jesus Christ, I learned a great deal of what it is to be human by my life in Africa, but I also learned what my own faith meant.

One of my most treasured possessions is a wooden crucifix carved in Zaire in Central Africa. The image of Jesus is clearly that of a young African, clean shaven with kinky hair. You might wonder what the point of such a carving is. After all, Jesus was not an African.

Neither was he a European, yet most of our own crucifixes portray him as such. The truth is we don't know what he looked like, and this is probably just as well. Since he came for all people of all cultures and all times, it is up to each one to see him in the circumstances of their own age and culture. So we portray him as American, African, Asian, etc. And this artistic effort reflects the deeper theological truth I have just expressed.

As I try to bring these reflections to an end, I want to recall two of many experiences in which I truly found Jesus as an African. The carving of Jesus as an African on the cross was a symbolic representation of what I have come to know in reality in my 40 years of living in Africa.

In the gospel we read of the prostitutes, tax collectors, sinners of all sorts, and those rejected socially because of disease, such as lepers, the blind, the lame, and we read of how they came to Jesus. They must have felt that there was an enormous distance between them and Jesus. They were unclean, sinners, social outcasts, and here was Jesus, a prophet, holy, a man of God. What could there be in common between them. Yet he received them with great love and compassion. I saw this Jesus many times in Africa. Some years ago I was visiting a small village in Ghana. It had none of the conveniences we have come to take for granted. There was no running water, no electricity or plumbing.

I was to stay there for five days to visit the family of a seminarian. I was keenly aware of all that separated me from them. They were all black, I was white, a member of that race who had once enslaved their ancestors. I could not speak their language, and I wasn't familiar with their customs. Yet they embraced me with a love and acceptance that I would hardly expect from my own family. Here was Jesus, in these people, once again making the outsider feel accepted, wanted, loved.

We also read in the gospel of Jesus' great zeal for his Father's kingdom. In the gospel he sends out the twelve to help with the harvest which is very great though the labourers are few. He himself moved from village to village, preaching to the people. I saw this Jesus again in Africa. The Catholic Church in much of Africa is only a little more than 100 years old, yet in that relatively short time, it has grown enormously.

Three years ago, we celebrated the centenary of the church in Lusaka. In 1905 a single Jesuit priest settled under a tree in a forest area where no one had ever heard of the Catholic Church. One hundred years later, the archdiocese of Lusaka has about 65 parishes, and a Catholic population of over 800,000.

How did the Church spread so fast? Because of the zeal of the ordinary people, individual farmers and traders who were so filled with the love of God and the desire for his kingdom that they single-handedly brought the Church to many villages when there were nowhere near enough priests. Here was Jesus once again restless to be about his Father's business.

Jesus was one who sat at table with saints and sinners. He knew how to relax and share a very human moment with others. Each time I celebrated Mass in Africa, I experienced the same joy that he must have felt, and that the people certainly feel with him.

As I look back over all these years, one thing is very clear to me. I originally went to Africa with the intention of doing something for the people. But I as I return to the United States, I feel like a stranger in a foreign land. I am trying to once again come to know the country of my birth.

That will take time, just it did when I first went to Africa. However, I find in myself a deep sense of gratitude to the people of Africa. I don't know what I may have done for them, but I am quite certain of what they have done for me. They have made me a better person. For that, I am eternally grateful.

With the legion of Mary at the Yaba College of
Technology in Lagos, Nigeria around 1968

The Baptism of Raphael Fadeyi, standing to my
left, together with wife and friends at the Pacelli
School for the Blind, Lagos, Nigeria.

At a market place in Abidjan, Ivory Coast, during
a visit there from Ghana around 1984.

With major seminarians at St. Peter's Regional
Seminary, Cape Coast, Ghana, 1987

My house at St. Augustine's College, Cape Coast, 1978

My father and parish priest in Chikuni,
Zambia, during the visit of my parents.

At a farewell Mass at the Copperbelt
University, Kitwe, Zambia, 2000.

With my sister, niece and grandnephew at the
Copperbelt Secondary Teachers' College, 1998.

Edwards Brothers Malloy
Thorofare, NJ USA
October 1, 2014